FENG SHUI
& YOUR HEALTH
A Guide to High Vitality

FENG SHUI
& YOUR HEALTH
A Guide to High Vitality

Dr. Jes T. Y. Lim

平安国际出版社
HEIAN INTERNATIONAL, INC.

First published in German in 1997 by Joy Verlag GmbH
© Illustrations Joy Verlag GmbH

The English edition was first published in 1999
by Times Books International
an imprint of Times Media Private Limited, Singapore
a member of the Times Publishing Group

The first American edition was published in 1999
Second edition 2001
by Heian International, Inc.
1815 West 205th Street, Ste. #301
Torrance CA 90501
Website: www.heian.com
E-mail: heianemail@heian.com

Printed in Singapore

ISBN 0-89346-915-7

DEDICATION

This book is dedicated to all the wise sages – Taoist masters and scholars – who made great sacrifices, even losing their lives, to create and perpetuate feng shui consciousness, while practising it with conviction for the benefit of mankind over the last 6,000 years.

I also dedicate this book to those who have had the courage to practise feng shui even when sneered and laughed at, especially in the European countries, where feng shui in the beginning was branded as silly superstitions and the practice of black magic.

Illustration: Talisman for harmony by Julie Lim

CONTENTS

FOREWORD

It is a great privilege to write the foreword to this interesting book about the ancient imperial practice of feng shui.

The author Dr. Jes T. Y. Lim has combined his practical experience of years of natural medicine and research in this feng shui classic, focusing on the modern health movement.

Dr. Lim has travelled the world. Today he is sharing his very comprehensive knowledge about feng shui and natural medicine all over the world.

Feng Shui & Your Health shows in a pragmatic way the importance of the fine tuning in feng shui.

The author has an excellent reputation in the world of holistic medicine.

May the Great Tao bless the readers and Dr. Jes Lim with good health.

Lord Pandit Prof. Anton Jayasuriya
Chairman Medicina Alternativa Institute, UNO
Colombo, Sri Lanka

© Gerd Heidorn

ACKNOWLEDGEMENTS

With my deepest gratitude I wish to first thank Master Lee Fa-Sher who stimulated my interest in feng shui by giving me a complicated 38-ring Chinese feng shui compass (lo'pan) and educated me on its wisdom.

I wish to convey my thanks to all the teachers, masters and students around the world who gave up their valuable time to share their knowledge and further enlighten me on this mystifying subject.

To all the authors and writers of articles and books mentioned in the bibliography and references at the back of this book I thank you for having the courage to share your knowledge and opinions to give new meaning to feng shui. Your information has made my work and lectures in feng shui much easier in the European countries.

I would also like to convey my special gratitude to my father, who introduced me to feng shui when I was a little boy. He died of cancer due to insufficient knowledge of geopathic stress. But his death has given me exceptional strength to make sacrifices and to devote my later life to the study of Western geomancy combined with Chinese feng shui and natural medicine. My goal is the development of techniques to bridge health and feng shui together as a more holistic healing discipline. Now I am able to present to readers around the world practical feng shui knowledge with the inclusion of Western geomancy for healthy living.

My special thanks go to Nola Ann Lean for proof reading this English edition. Very special thanks also go to my wife Julie who drew the harmony talisman at the beginning of this book in addition to the calligraphy for each chapter. They provide the book with the 'Chinese flavour'.

Let us generously share our knowledge to promote better health, happiness and abundance to ultimately achieve world peace.

Love and abundance to all,

Professor Dr. Jes T. Y. Lim
Haikou, Hainan Island, China

INTRODUCTION

The tremendous economic success of the Asian 'dragon states' – Hong Kong, Taiwan, Singapore, Malaysia, Thailand and Indonesia – in the last quarter of the 20th century has prompted a key question in the developed countries in the West: 'Why have the 50 million overseas Chinese been so successful economically?' An often mentioned response is that the Chinese practise feng shui as part of their culture to enhance success and prosperity. With experience, you can detect in most Chinese restaurants around the world some form of feng shui remedy, an example being a gold fish aquarium.

In ancient China, feng shui practice was confined to the imperial court. During the 30 years from 1950–1980, the communist government of China restricted the practice of feng shui among the common people. I was however greatly surprised to see many holiday resorts, especially those reserved for senior party officials, designed according to strict feng shui principles. Nowadays feng shui is widely but often erroneously practised in China.

During the last few years feng shui has become more accepted in Europe, Australasia and North America. To cope with the strong demand for 'instant' courses, many teachers are teaching different forms of feng shui that often contradict one another and cause much confusion for Western students.

I have found that generally feng shui practice around the world can be summarised as follows:

- 80% are based on logic and common sense and can be proven
- 20% are based on superstition and wrong beliefs

This book has thus been written with three objectives in mind:

1) I want to share the results of my research carried out in more than 30 countries. Facts, superstitions and wrong beliefs will be clearly explained.

2) I will link feng shui with human health to prove that feng shui is a key factor in human longevity. Therefore I will constantly refer to the link between feng shui and health. This close connection between possible health problems and bad feng shui should not create fear. On the contrary, if you can understand a particular bad situation you can make changes.

3) You will obtain an overview of common feng shui problems as well as common solutions and remedies for your house and flat. This way you can train your perception to avoid negative situations or to use remedies. This knowledge will also be very helpful when you select a new flat or a house. But remember that there are always many ways to solve a problem. As a book cannot provide all possible solutions, it is therefore advisable to have an individual feng shui consultation.

This book is the first in a series of 12 planned books and can be used as a workbook. For several years I have been running courses in feng shui leading to a diploma in international feng shui practice. A degree course in feng shui and geobiology is now available in German and English. These courses will eventually be taught in universities around the world.

I welcome constructive comments from masters and teachers of feng shui on how we can further improve and prove feng shui for wider global applications. In this way, we can all help to create a greater acceptance of this discipline and promote a healthier and more successful environment for all to live in.

Chapter 1

WHAT IS FENG SHUI ?

The expression 'feng shui' comes from the Cantonese dialect of the Chinese language – feng means 'wind' and shui means 'water'. These two characters are pronounced in different ways, according to the respective Chinese dialects.

The term feng shui is commonly used by the 50 million overseas Chinese who originated mainly from southern China and who have perpetuated this ancient science and art wherever they went throughout the world.

But feng shui has a broader meaning. Feng covers wind, air, gas, clouds, energy fields and rays, radiation, storms and typhoons. Included in feng interpretation are features that direct or affect the smooth flow of wind, examples being hills, mountains, rocks, buildings and man-made structures. Shui includes lakes, ponds, rivers, streams, waterfalls, all running water, pools of water, swamp, rain, roads, streets, ice, snow as well as plants and other living things nourished by them.

I have read many feng shui books, and all of them differ in their interpretation of feng shui. I have also consulted many feng shui masters in China, Taiwan, Hong Kong, Singapore, Malaysia and the United States. Some say feng shui is the practice of natural science. Others say feng shui is 'correct placement'. But we all agree feng shui is about creating a more conducive, healthy and harmonious environment for living and working to enhance good health and prosperity and to provide abundance for the family.

However, I wish to expand the scope of feng shui as I perceive, feel and see this complex subject, based on my own work and research.

The Eight Levels of Knowledge

Feng shui can be broadly divided into eight levels of knowledge which should be considered in a consultation. The levels can be applied to an existing building or to one being planned.

1) **The effect of essential cosmic qi** and oxygen to enhance vitality and good health (two of the most important factors in feng shui);

2) **The yin and yang polarity principle** for harmony and balance;

3) **The five elemental universal principles** for mental, emotional and physical balance and harmony;

Wind

Water

4) **Macrospheric feng shui** – The study of astrology and cosmology and how the planets affect us. We can apply astrological and cosmological techniques by using the ancient Chinese feng shui compass (lo'pan) to determine the most conducive position to open the door of a house or where the best place is to sleep, work or perform other important human activities in a house. This also includes the application of the Lo-Shu, the flying star system or the nine star ki system (Japan).

5) **Microspheric feng shui** – This is the study of the landscape, rivers, lakes, oceans, hill and mountain formations, and building structures within 1 to 6 km from a building site;

6) **Immediate microspheric feng shui** – This is the study of the environment within 1 km (0.6 miles) of a building site. Includes the landscape, the flow of rivers, streams and other running waters, lakes, seas/oceans; hill/mountain formations and rock surfaces/formations; trees and plants; wind direction; the shape and form of buildings; the sounds and smells; the type of earth in the surrounding land; electrical power lines, radar systems, television transmitters; road and street arrangements and all features around a building site.

7) **Building site and structural feng shui.** The land energy – qi (positive energy) and the shia qi (negative energy) – of the site should be checked. On the site, check the type and condition of the earth, check for shia qi on the

land if, for example, the land has been used as a burial ground or ritual site. The land should be checked for toxic chemicals in the soil and for geopathic stress on the building site that may be caused by underground running water, fault lines or other harmful electromagnetic rays from the ground. This is also to ensure that the building design is symmetrical and in harmony with the earth and land formation.

8) **Immediate Environment Within House/Flat** – This is the most important part of feng shui. Check the cosmic qi level in every room, especially the bedrooms, and the whole house to make sure that cosmic qi presence is above 80% (out of a total of 80–100% in the open environment). Avoid negative attacking features, for example, sharp corners pointing at your body. Check the immediate surroundings where you sleep, work and do your activities. Select an ideal location for your bed, place to work or for activities. Check for: harmful geopathic stress lines and earth rays immediately underground; disturbing electromagnetic fields or rays within 1 m (3.3 ft) from your body; sharp corners of a table or other furniture, pillars, overhead beams, lighting systems, mirrors, plants and other features that may affect a person negatively.

Why is our immediate environment so important? We live in a modern society of the 21st century. We have little control over the environment outside our house. We cannot tell our neighbour not to build a road or a structure. And almost every household has some electrical equipment – perhaps a microwave oven, television set, computer or clock radio. Electrical wires are everywhere around our house, and we often sleep within centimetres of power switches and sockets that cause electromagnetic disturbances. We may have underfloor heating systems creating turbulence or sewage pipes for the toilet and kitchen next to our bed causing stress to our body. Our atmosphere is also infiltrated with harmful electro-smog and microwave radiation, for example, from mobile telephone systems. All these unnatural and harmful rays penetrate our body aura (energy field) when we are in our room or house. They are like a large net covering our house, blocking and distorting the benevolent natural rays from the cosmos.

The unnatural environment we live in has created extremely stressful conditions for our body, affecting our emotional behaviour, our psyche, our brain patterns and our health. Our ancestors who lived on this earth a thousand years ago would not have survived in our modern-day toxic living conditions.

It is, therefore, very important for us to protect ourselves in our immediate environment – creating the surroundings that are most conducive for harmonious living and working by applying the most effective feng shui techniques and remedies. We need to apply the best methods to protect ourselves from the harmful rays and negative energy fields around us.

The scope of feng shui practised in China for thousands of years must be expanded to include the modern living hazards of today. Feng shui practice can therefore be stated as the study of astrology, cosmology, natural science, geographical, environmental and harmonic sciences, and the blending of these sciences in addition to the ideal placement of furniture and fixtures in a room or building. Feng shui also helps increase cosmic qi and oxygen to lower stress. It does this by creating an environment similar to nature to boost our immune system for better health.

In short, we can therefore say that feng shui is the practice of selecting and designing the most conducive and healthy environment to live and work to enhance good health and longevity. With high vitality, we can perform better and have more abundance.

These are the reasons why the Chinese practise feng shui. They have always connected it with prosperity, abundance and wealth. To practice feng shui more accurately, a student must study all the eight levels of knowledge outlined above to obtain a complete picture of all the macro and micro aspects of feng shui. This is the only way to make feng shui practice a more credible science.

Cosmic Qi and Body Qi

Throughout the ages, many cultures have given cosmic qi different names. The Chinese call it ch'i or qi, the Indians call it prana and the Japanese call it ki. It is the life force energy that gives life to all living things. Qi can be likened to electrical currents moving at a certain frequency throughout our body, connecting all our body cells, just as electrical wires in our house connect the various electrical gadgets. This qi comes into our body when we breathe in qi and oxygen from the air. When insufficient qi is present in a body, a person does not have sufficient 'electrical charges' to give the necessary vitality to keep body cells and organs healthy.

The Chinese have practised acupuncture for more than 5,000 years. One of the main functions of the needle in acupuncture is to stimulate a faster flow of qi in certain parts of the body to clear energy blockages. It is also used to stimulate the flow of qi from one area or organ to another to balance the yin and yang qi. For example, a person with a paralysed left leg will be given acupuncture on the right side of the scalp to stimulate and clear the blocked qi. When qi starts to flow smoothly to the extremities of the left leg, the nerves, tendons and muscles are fed with more nutrients and oxygen and the leg can regenerate and function normally again.

What is Cosmic Qi?

Cosmic qi is the result of minute particles formed from the interaction of the sun's rays and the cosmic rays from the planets. Cosmic qi is found throughout the earth's atmosphere and many metres down into the ground.

We have found that cosmic qi is abundant around plants and near moving water and forested areas. Qi can be measured by special divination techniques such as kinesiology and the pendulum. Normally, the saturation of cosmic qi in the open environment is between 80–100%. Cosmic qi can be as high as 200–300% around blooming multicoloured flowers that have roots.

Freshly-cut flowers also attract about 150%–200% cosmic qi during the first three days. My findings show qi is attracted to real flowers by the flowers' radiant electromagnetic fields and by the flowers' symbols. It is very energising and relaxing to have a bouquet of flowers on the working table.

Even artificial, look-alike multicoloured flowers attract between 100–150% cosmic qi because of their shapes and symbols.

Cosmic qi also concentrates near running or bubbling water, especially waterfalls. The friction of water creates electromagnetic rays that attract qi. Research near Niagara Falls in Canada and other waterfalls in Europe show that the negative ionisation of the air near the white water is more than 300%, many times higher than normal air in open space. That is why we feel refreshed and highly energised near waterfalls and places where there is running water.

Folklore tells of ancient sages in India and Taoist masters in China having their best inspiration when they worked or meditated near waterfalls in their gardens or in the mountains. The ancients in China had created both actual waterfalls and drawings of waterfalls as effective feng shui remedies to improve and generate more qi. Today, we still use these remedies with good results. Old prominent European buildings and palaces have water fountains constructed in front, indicating they were designed by highly intuitive architects to generate more qi for the royal families living there. Wherever cosmic qi is abundant, the oxygen level is also exceptionally high. Following the laws of nature, the male

Qi
(Female/yin)

Oxygen
(Male/yang)

Diag. 1.1: Oxygen always follows cosmic qi very closely. This union becomes 'cosmic life'.

species is always attracted to the female species. For this reason, oxygen which is male or yang pursues cosmic qi which is female or yin.

Cosmic qi vibrates a natural frequency that draws it to all living things, including human beings. So we can conclude that whenever or wherever there is cosmic qi, oxygen will be there, and there will be life and living creatures.

When cosmic qi and oxygen molecules are bound together, they become 'cosmic life' – the lowest form of living intelligence on earth. Cosmic life is attracted to the magnetic rays of humans and other living creatures. So wherever humans or animals walk over an area – for instance, when we walk through a door – cosmic life follows. That is why the direction of the main door of a house and the facing directions of the rooms are so important in feng shui practice.

Here is an example to show the importance of qi. At the foothills of Mount Everest, many Breatherians have lived over 100 years by taking their main nutrients from the 'cosmic life' and other beneficial substances in the air. These Breatherians only supplement these nutrients by eating fruits once or twice a week. They practise special qigong (the fine art of breathing qi) breathing techniques to put their body into a state of relaxation to facilitate breathing in the nutrients from the air.

The Effects of Wind and Water on Humans and Animals

Wind Energy

For more than 6,000 years, Taoist masters have known that strong winds, whether cold or hot, have significant negative effects on our health and behaviour. Mild winds or a light breeze, on the other hand, are energising and refreshing and are good for our health.

All humans and animals have an aura that is the electromagnetic fields expanded from the body. The aura usually consists of the seven colours of the rainbow. It cannot be seen with the naked eye and is normally regarded as our spiritual body or sensor which gives us early warning when we are affected by harmful fields of energies which we cannot see, such as radiation or electromagnetic fields. When a strong wind blows towards us, our aura begins to flutter and move violently like the branches of a tree.

When we are consistently blown by strong winds, we feel uncomfortable and sometimes become dizzy and begin to lose our balance. Those who live on top of hills or near a beach with strong currents tend to have more balance problems and often have more wrinkles on their face and body, a sign of ageing of the skin.

We, therefore, feel more comfortable and relaxed when there is calm in our immediate environment as our aura is not disturbed.

Similarly, when the wind is calm or blowing gently and smoothly, birds fly down from their nests to feed. This is also the time when worms and insects come out of hiding to feed and begin their activities. If, suddenly, the wind begins to change and blows fiercely, which can be observed in the violent movements of tree branches, all birds disappear and return to their nests to seek protection from the winds.

Living in a house, we may not be able to feel the strong winds outside because glass windows and walls shelter us from the strong winds. However, the fierce wind's subtle energy can usually penetrate up to 2 m (6.5 ft) inside our house or flat through the glass doors, windows and walls. We discovered that if we stand or sit inside our house or flat within 2 m of a glass wall when strong winds are blowing outside, we are affected by the strong wind and become weak. This can be tested by using applied kinesiology techniques (see Chapter 10). Even though we cannot physically experience or feel the strong physical winds, the subtle second level of energy created by the strong winds is able to penetrate the glass and disturb our aura and cause balance problems.

A house that is constantly buffeted by strong wind is therefore not a healthy house to live in. We can use wind barriers like concrete walls or a bamboo or wooden trellis, or plant bushy trees, to divert or soften the effects of the wind. But then we are not living in a harmonious environment conducive to our health and wellbeing. We are still affected by the hot or cold energy of the winds.

Water Energy

Running or moving water from a lake, river or stream causes friction, which generates electromagnetic fields that attract good cosmic qi and oxygen. It is a good feeling to be near moving water, and we can design the main door of our house to face the water to receive the maximum qi benefits. Care, however, should be taken not to face the direct strong flow of a fast moving river because the strong water energy propelled by the water currents is overpowering and can be harmful to human health. Moving water attracts cosmic qi and is an essential element in feng shui practice. Chinese liken water to wealth and luck.

Water barriers like rocks and dams are often built to slow down fast moving rivers so that the maximum benefits from the qi energy can be reaped. Smooth and slow flowing water that is most beneficial to humans should not flow faster than 1 m (3.3 ft) every 6 to 8 seconds.

When we are in an open environment, near a waterfall, fountain or running stream, we are happy and fully energised. But when we are in an enclosed environment like the inside of a building, not all of us feel comfortable near an indoor waterfall, fountain or even a fish aquarium. Why?

We discovered that a person born in the year of the fire element according to the Chinese calendar feels most uncomfortable when standing within 2 m (6.5 ft) of some substantial water energy such as that created by a fountain, waterfall or aquarium inside a house. This is because the fire element is overpowered by the water element's energy (see Chapter 8 The Five Elemental Universal Energies).

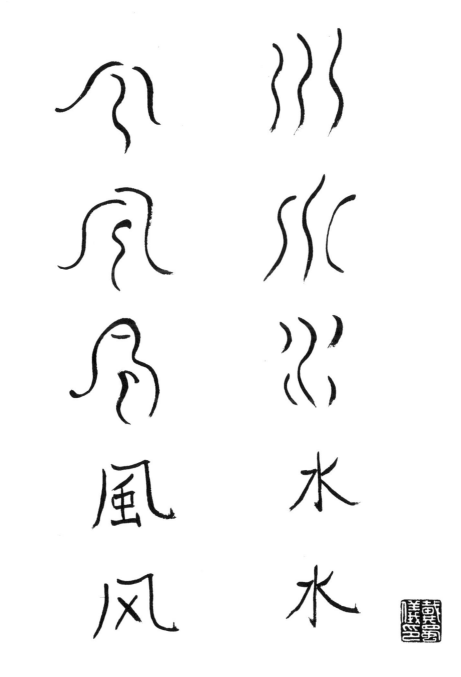

Diag. 1.2: The evolution of the written feng shui characters. Left: Characters for 'wind'.
Right: Characters for 'water'.

Chapter 2

A BRIEF HISTORY OF FENG SHUI

When we look at the history of the development of feng shui in China, we can gain a better understanding of why the Chinese throughout the world are so deeply rooted in their belief and practice of feng shui. During certain dynasties, the common people were not allowed to practice feng shui. During the first 30 years of communist rule, feng shui was also banned.

Many Chinese cultural practices are similar to those practised by the Jews and the people of the Middle East. Some people believe that a significant portion of the Chinese population today migrated from the Middle East thousands of years ago, especially after the Great Flood recorded in biblical history as the story of Noah's Ark.

Substantial volumes of Chinese historical records were destroyed by warring factions and succeeding dynasties. The last such wasteful destruction took place in 1966–1976 during the Red Guards' Cultural Revolution which saw the destruction of millions of volumes of valuable historical records.

In ancient times, there were few written texts exclusively devoted to feng shui. Feng shui information appeared in poetry, folk stories and medical texts. Available historical records noted that King Fu Hsi who founded the Hsia dynasty in 2205 B.C. was a master of divination arts and saw a horse and an old tortoise rising from the Ho River with special markings on their backs. The markings were transcribed onto bamboo and became known as the Ho-t'u (the drawing from the River Ho) and the Lo-Shu (River Lo Classic). From the Ho-t'u, the Earlier Heaven pa'kua (Eight Trigrams) evolved (see Diag. 2.1). The Earlier Heaven pa'kua facilitated the explanation of an ideal order of nature and its evolution in ancient times when weather conditions were predictable.

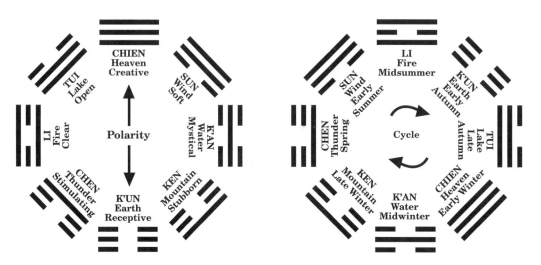

Diag. 2.1: The pa'kua of the Earlier Heaven.

Diag. 2.2: The pa'kua of the Later Heaven.

The Later Heaven pa'kua described the phenomenal changes in weather and conditions in nature according to the four seasons.

King Wen, the founder of the Chou dynasty (1122–25 B.C.), further developed the Ho-t'u and the Lo-Shu to become very powerful divination tools. He expanded the Lo-Shu pa'kua from eight to 64 hexagrams known today as the I-Ching (also commonly known as the Book of Change) that is used for divination purposes.

The grandson of King Wen, Emperor Shing, combined the Chinese compass with the I-Ching to form the earliest Chinese feng shui compass called the lo-ching.

Diag. 2.3: The ancient tortoise that emerged from the River Lo with special markings – the Lo-Shu numbers.

Diag. 2.4: Ancient Lo-Shu in Chinese numerology.

Diag. 2.5: Ancient Lo-Shu in Arabic numerology.

Feng Shui – An Imperial Palace Practice

During the time of Confucius (551–479 B.C.), feng shui texts recorded that officials of the imperial court had detailed and elaborate plans to direct the location of palaces, which the then emperor would occupy during the four seasons of the year in accordance with astrological calculations appropriate to him.

The yin and yang principle was conceived by Taoist masters in the practice of shamanism more than 5,000 years ago.

During the Han dynasty (206 B.C. – 219 A.D.), Tzu Kuei-Ku further developed the yin and yang practice that was subsequently included in feng shui.

At the time of the Han dynasty, feng shui reached its peak and became a recognised professional practice. It was then called 'kang yu', a form of divination based on an understanding of the changing conditions of the heaven and earth. Kang yu was created by Ching Hu and improved on by Yang K'un Sun during the Han dynasty. Kang yu then had 17 rings and 24 compass directions incorporating astrology, very similar to the modern lo'pan (Chinese feng shui compass).

The famous Chu-Kuo Liang of the Three Kingdoms (A.D. 220–265) developed the 'Chi-man tun-chia' system, which combined the pa'kua with the Nine Palaces (Lo-Shu chart for the movement of the nine flying stars), for divining auspicious and inauspicious places for rooms and buildings for the imperial court.

Kuo-p'u of the Chin dynasty (A.D. 265–420) consolidated the status of feng shui practice, which was now recognised by the imperial court as an accepted Taoist practice. He was well known for his special knowledge on choosing auspicious burial sites. He wrote two books on selecting burial sites: 'Ch'uang-shu' (Evaluation of landscape to select auspicious sites) and 'Ch'inglung Ching' (Discussions on the Green Dragon Mountains). Many modern-day feng shui consultants consider him the master of feng shui practice.

The Two Schools of Feng Shui

Two schools of feng shui were established, namely the compass school and the form or landscape school. With the formal establishment of these two schools, feng shui was made available to the common people for the first time. Previously, only the imperial court and senior officials were allowed to practice feng shui, and violation could mean imprisonment or death.

The landscape school was started in Kwangsi province by imperial court feng shui master Yang Yun-sung (A.D. 840–900) during the reign of Emperor Hi-Tsung (A.D. 874–888). Yang wrote the famous books 'Manual of the Moving Dragon' and 'The Methods of the Twelve Staves'.

The compass or lo-kang (lo'pan) school was headed by Wang Chih who, with several of his trusted students, consolidated various systems then practised into a practical working system in A.D. 960 during the Sung dynasty.

The compass school had its beginnings in the Fukien province. From this 'special' beginning, overseas Chinese from this province have perhaps the most millionaires and billionaires among the Chinese community today.

Written Records

Modern historians usually quote from the 57 books that were written on feng shui in the 'History of the Sung "Sung Shi"' during the Sung dynasty (A.D. 960–1129). Nevertheless, feng shui was also mentioned in many folklore texts. During the Ming dynasty (A.D. 1368–1611), the lo'pan was enlarged into 36 rings. A well-known Ming feng shui classic titled 'Tiu-Shi Yin Tzu Shin-Chih' ('Important Points in Geography and Land Formations') is also a good reference source on feng shui.

The Ching dynasty (a foreign government from the north) ruled China from 1644–1911. During this time, the practice of feng shui grew throughout China. A well-known book called the 'Lo-ching T'ao Chieh' (Complete Understanding of the Feng Shui Compass) was compiled. This book provided comprehensive explanations on the 36 rings of the lo'pan, which is used by some feng shui consultants and masters in Hong Kong, Taiwan and Southeast Asia today. Many old Sung and Chin dynasties feng shui classics are listed in the Bibliography.

Feng Shui Today

Many feng shui teachers and masters teaching feng shui over the last 300 years were not familiar with divination techniques that would have enabled them to check whether what they learned from their teachers/masters was universally or locationally applicable.

Many feng shui masters used old Chinese feng shui texts and manuscripts without truly understanding why the authors made certain statements. Many old feng shui manuscripts were written for specific locations in China where the authors lived for most of their lives and experienced their limited world. Due to transportation difficulties, many of the authors only travelled in a small part of a large Chinese province and therefore only understood their local conditions well.

But feng shui manuscripts for a localised area cannot be applied in their original meaning everywhere around the world without some modification. Therefore, we have to be extra careful when we apply feng shui outside of China (see also Chapter 6 – Feng Shui Myths).

The great demand for feng shui knowledge over the last 20 years due to the booming Southeast Asian economies has resulted in the establishment of many feng shui schools teaching techniques that are taken from ancient texts in their original form. Many schools which do not have the knowledge of divination to check whether the information they use is accurate, are teaching the subject in different ways, causing a great deal of confusion among today's students, especially the Western ones.

Thanks to the great demand, hundreds of feng shui books have sprung up in the bookshops. Unfortunately, the truly knowledgeable and great masters have little time to write books as the demand for their services is so great.

Most books are written by journalists and students with limited knowledge, who are either unable to be more explicit in explaining special feng shui features or misunderstood or misquoted statements made by masters. For example, feng shui problems are often all classified as 'shia qi' (negative energy) to avoid more explicit explanations. That is why students of feng shui find it so confusing and difficult to understand and learn practical feng shui.

A well-informed feng shui teacher should be able to explain either logically or scientifically feng shui applications and remedies. They should also be able to explain the what, why, how, when and where of feng shui.

I recommend, therefore, that feng shui students use applied kinesiology (which is explained in this book) and pendulum techniques to check the accuracy of what they learn. These techniques are a great help to facilitate the faster learning of accurate feng shui.

Listed below are the main disciplines of feng shui as practised by different schools:

The 12 Disciplines of Feng Shui

1) Cosmic qi characteristics, oxygen and air quality

2) Yin and yang principles

3) The five elemental universal energies

4) Landscape feng shui or the Four Animal Formation

5) The Eight Life Situations (Life Aspirations) Trigrams

6) The Earlier Heaven Trigram – Work with spiritual realm

7) The I-Ching Later Heaven Eight Basic Trigrams (East-West System) – location based

8) The Lo-Shu Flying Stars System – time factor (astrology and cosmology)

9) Geobiology and Geomancy – radiations from the earth, cosmos and environmental studies

10) Water and Mountain Dragon Classics – water flows, water quality and mountain formations

11) Graves and Burial Classics – mainly in the selection of good burial sites

12) Spiritual feng shui – the most advanced level

In North America and Europe, most feng shui consultants only apply the first six disciplines, which is inadequate. Ideally, at least the first 10 disciplines should be applied in a feng shui consultation. This book covers the application of the first five disciplines. The remaining disciplines will be explained in my further books on advanced feng shui.

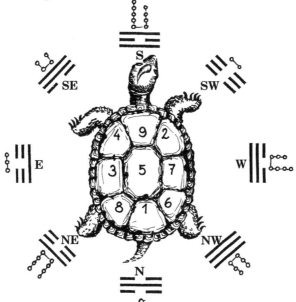

Diag. 2.6 Ancient Lo-Shu numbers on the tortoise with the compass directions and Eight Trigrams (East-West System).

Western Geomancy

The geomancy which is widely practised in Europe is similar to and complements feng shui practice. Western geomancy is a form of divination using the pendulum or the dowsing stick to detect harmful earth rays like geopathic stress lines, Hartmann lines, Curry lines and disturbing magnetic fields. Harmful rays from the earth and the cosmos cause most of the human and animal degenerative and terminal diseases. Thus, locating and avoiding negative earth rays is very important. We can apply the best feng shui practice, but when a person sleeps or sits over harmful earth rays, even the best feng shui remedies become less effective.

Geomancy originated in the ancient Arab states several thousand years ago. Arab traders brought their geomancy skills to Europe where it may have influenced the architecture of the ancient Greeks and Romans 2,000 to 3,000 years ago. Greek and Roman architecture have many forms and structures which comply with good geomancy and feng shui practice. During the first century B.C., the Roman architect Vitruvius practised a form of feng shui and applied a Roman system of divination. His work is described in 'The Ten Books on Architecture'.

The Venetian fortress of Palma Nuora in Italy was built in 1593 in a circular form with projections similar to the Chinese Eight Trigrams, showing good harmony for living, together with practical defence purposes.

In America, John Stilgoe, in his book 'Common Landscape of America – 1580–1845', described how early settlers in the Ohio Valley located their farmhouses in harmony with the land and in alignment with 'auspicious cosmic breath paths'.

I have founded the Qi-Mag International Feng Shui and Geobiology Institute which carries out in-depth research on feng shui. Its objective is to disseminate practical and accurate information on feng shui including the basics of European geomancy. Currently, courses are available in 15 countries in Europe, North America and Southeast Asia. Addresses can be found at the back of this book.

Chapter 3

THE EVOLUTION OF THE HUMAN LIVING SPACE

When humans were living in the open, all trees, rivers and everything else around them were part of their environment. The trees gave them shelter and protected them from the sun, rain and their enemies. Their skin and the hair on their body also protected them from the sun and the cold. Later, they found better protection by living in caves.

These caves provided better protection against their enemies and wild animals. Caves were thus man's first protective homes.

Diag. 3.1: Early humans living under overhanging rock for shelter.

Diag. 3.2: Humans seeking shelter under a tree and a fallen tree.

Diag. 3.3: Humans constructing a temporary shelter with branches and grass on the side of a hill.

Diag. 3.4: Humans constructing their first hut using branches, leaves and grass.

Diag. 3.5: Humans using the first sharp tools and stones to carve and dig into caves to obtain better shelter from the cold and more protection from fierce animals.

Diag. 3.6: A mud house with a door and two windows to look out from, looking very much like a human face.

The House Represents the Human Body

Over thousands of years, humans have lived in caves and homes made from different locally available materials and with different protective designs, for example, a sharp roof apex (see also chapter 12). Thus, a strong consciousness has developed where the design of the house represents the human occupants and their behaviour.

The walls of a house can be likened to the human skin, and the rooms to the organs. The structure of a house corresponds to the body and limbs. For example, the windows are meant for humans to look out of the house and thus represent their eyes.

Modern humans have isolated themselves from nature by spending more time in their homes. Now the structures of their homes have become part of their environment. The internal arrangements of the rooms – the furniture and the furnishings – symbolise the main occupants' behaviour, likes and dislikes. Any structures or symbols inside their home that are negative to them affects them mentally, emotionally and physically.

For this reason, any pillar-shaped object immediately outside a home (for example, a tree trunk or a lamp-post outside the front door) is an obstruction and attacks the 'mouth' of all the occupants of the home.

A tree trunk outside the window of a room is a direct attack on the 'eyes' of that room's occupants and an indirect attack against the occupants of the whole house. In such situations, we found that the occupants tended to have a higher incidence of eye problems.

Only trees with exposed straight vertical trunks that can be seen directly in front of the door or windows affect us negatively. A tree outside a wall that we cannot see from inside of the home does not affect us.

Many experiments have been carried out to prove the close link between the house and the human body. One easy and inexpensive method to demonstrate this connection is to scratch the wall of a house while its occupants are inside. By using a biofeedback machine or applied kinesiology techniques, we found that the immune system of all the occupants in the house became weak. The occupants become weak because the wall that represents their skin is hurt by the scratching.

Diag. 3.7: The original basic human house. It has a good likeness to a human face with hair, eyes, nose and mouth.

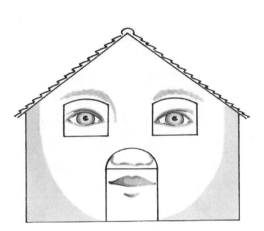

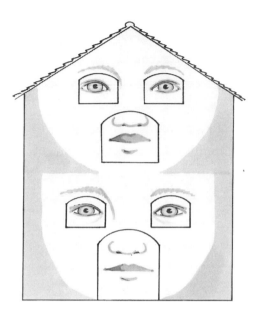

Diag. 3.8: A primitive modern house with a human face superimposed over the front to show the likeness.

Diag. 3.9: A two-storey building with two levels used by two different families is represented by two human faces. Each floor is represented by a human body and its respective consciousness.

Land for the House

Humans seeking even better protection decided to erect fences to block strangers and enemies from coming onto their land. In olden days, high walls were built around a town or city to protect its occupants. The 10,000 km (6,000 miles) of the Great Wall of China is a famous example of such protection. This need for better protection on one's land, village, town or city had now created another level of consciousness. The land around an occupant's house became part of his or her consciousness.

Any unsightly or negative structures, like a dying or dead tree, on the occupants' land outside a house can cause depression and health and work performance problems to the occupants. A tree planted on certain sections of the land can affect the occupants positively or negatively. According to some feng shui schools, a large healthy tree can provide strong support to the wealth and prosperity of the occupants, if it is planted in the correct spot on the southeast side of the house. Similarly, a negatively designed, tall, prominent building in the centre of a town or city also affects the residents of that place (see also chapters 15 and 16).

Shape of the Town

The design and layout of a village or town where we live also affects our wellbeing and mental balance. Ever wonder why some towns and cities are more vibrant and successful or, conversely, have more problems than others? In feng shui, we often have an explanation. A badly-shaped town only creates problems for its town folks.

Occupants living in the town in Diag. 3.10 tend to be confused and lack goals. This town is expanding in several directions in a disorderly way and pulling energy from the centre. A town should develop and expand from the centre and spread out evenly. Good town planning is very important in feng shui practice.

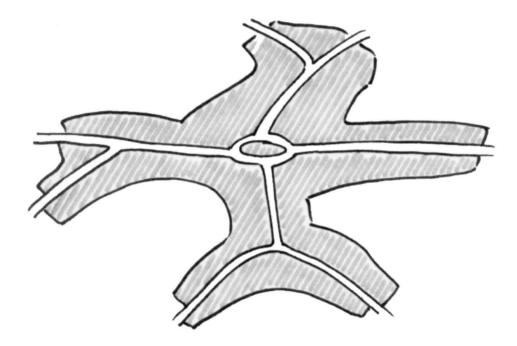

Diag. 3.10: Town with uneven shape.

Immediate Environmental Factors

Humans were also used to living in caves with harmonious rounded and curved structures. Anything sharp, like arrows, sharp metal and sharp rocks used to kill and cut animals, are potentially dangerous and disharmonious to us. Even in modern-day living, sharp objects are still consciously and subconsciously considered as threats. For instance, the sharp corners of a cupboard or the sharp corner of a wall directly facing us are regarded as an attack on us and our psyche and affects our immune system. We can use applied kinesiology techniques (see Chapter 10) to test and prove this point.

Now we know our home represents us and our behaviour, likes and dislikes. Often, we can predict the health and behaviour of a house's occupants just by looking at their house and the way they arrange their furniture and fittings and how they live.

We can also accurately predict the type of health problems expected to occur and whether the occupants will live a longer or shorter life span, by studying the design and internal arrangements of a building and its outside environment. We can also predict financial or relationship problems and the earliest time these problems could surface.

In feng shui practice, we must make sure that all negative features, both internal and external to the house, are eliminated or avoided. Harmonious, non-aggressively designed furniture, fittings and room arrangements give us complete harmony in our home. They are important basic factors for a healthy and fulfilling life.

Chapter 4

FENG SHUI IN DAILY LIFE

Our body needs a harmonious, smooth flow of qi to facilitate the nourishment of our cells with blood and nutrients and to support smooth metabolism and cell rejuvenation.

When the qi flow to an area of the body or an organ is sluggish, pain is felt which indicates some blockage of energy flow. When a person is suffering from a degenerative disease like arthritis, the problem can only be solved temporarily, even with acupuncture or medication, because the person is suffering from a general lack of smooth qi flow in the body. This is causing blockages at the joints, providing an environment conducive to viral attack on the joints' cartilage – the cause of arthritic pains.

Often, arthritic patients recover much faster by just breathing more cosmic qi and oxygen into the body by consistent abdominal breathing or qigong. Many hospitals in China are applying qigong to treat many diseases.

According to my findings, most health problems have their origin in the bedroom or house or in the person's working place. The bedroom and house of arthritic and cancer patients are always found to have bad feng shui and are therefore low in cosmic qi. This is why arthritis and cancer are so difficult to treat with mainstream medicine.

Feng shui remedies, together with acupuncture or the taking of natural herbal remedies, usually facilitate a longer term cure for arthritis sufferers or, for those suffering from other degenerative diseases, an improvement in their condition. Those who were continuously infected by candida and other fungal infections recovered after the feng shui of their houses were improved.

Energy in the House

European, North American and temperate zones' homes with a sharp, steep, 'A' shaped roof generally have cosmic qi of about 50% or less (see also Chapter 16). The weather in these countries tends to be cool most of the time and windows are often closed, slowing down the in-flow and circulation of fresh air and qi (see Diag. 4.1 and 4.2). This affects the occupants' vitality.

Diag. 4.1: In an open area we are exposed to 100% of the cosmic qi and fresh air.

*Diag. 4.2: When we live or work in a house with enclosed walls, up to 70–80%
of cosmic qi and fresh air are blocked from coming in. In feng shui, we can use certain
techniques and remedies to simulate open-air environmental conditions to enhance
the flow of qi and good quality air into a house.*

A general lack of cosmic qi in the home often results in reduced blood circulation and aggravated heart problems. This partially explains why Europeans and North Americans have the highest incidence of heart problems as compared with Southeast Asians. In the warmer climate of Southeast Asia, windows are open throughout the day most of the year, allowing more benevolent qi and fresh air to come into the house. With more qi and oxygen, Asians are more active and vibrant in everyday life.

I found that many people with long life spans of over 90 years live in places with high energy and excellent feng shui. There are also no geopathic stresses or earth ray disturbances in their bedroom.

Feng Shui, Relationships and the Family

Feng shui seeks to enhance harmony and good health for married couples and partners, and also to strengthen family relationships.

In my earlier work as a marriage and family relationship counsellor, I found that when a house had bad feng shui of below 40%, disharmony usually occurred between couples and between family members. Relationships with partners and children deteriorated more and more the longer they stayed in their houses.

With low vitality, adults begin to draw on their reserve energy from their sex chakras (gonads), thereby draining their vital sex energy and making them more tired. The kidneys which control the sex hormones are considerably weakened and partners do not feel sexually attracted to each other any more. (According to traditional Chinese medicine, the vital reproductive energy is stored in the kidneys.) In a house with bad feng shui, it is common for a couple not to make love for months or even longer. A lack of body contact and love is a key factor in partner relationship problems.

Sexual activity is the most important factor to cement a good relationship. High stress factors associated with bad feng shui are usually why a couple's relationship deteriorates and ends up in divorce or separation.

In the case of children, low cosmic qi in a house with bad feng shui results in hyperactivity, agitation, aggressiveness and other unbecoming emotional behaviour. Lack of concentration is common and academic performance usually suffers.

Adults living in a low-energy house are more stressed, easily agitated, bad tempered and often depressed. They also have problems earning a good income.

Often, after feng shui remedies are carried out, sexual activity quickly returns to normal and the couple and family members usually improve their relationships.

The following is an example from my practice. In Copenhagen, Denmark, a couple had decided to divorce. I told them that the main cause of their poor relationship was the bad feng shui of their house. They were sceptical, but decided to give feng shui a try. Feng shui remedies were carried out, and three months later I received a letter from the couple thanking me and saying that they were happy being together again. Their children's academic performances which had deteriorated after moving into the new house, had also improved dramatically.

Feng Shui, Work Performance and Prosperity

The feng shui of our work place is also very important to our wellbeing and performance. We found that when work places had bad feng shui, workers tended to be very tired by midday or afternoon. They were also more stressed and made more mistakes. Workers tended to be less friendly and because their general performance was below average, the business as a whole was unsuccessful.

Lack of qi and oxygen put our whole body's energy centres and chakras (see Diag. 4.3) in a stressful state, thereby inhibiting our sacral energy from rising to our head to activate our crown chakras and enhance our intuition. That explains why people living and working in poor feng shui buildings are less balanced, less intuitive and less successful in life.

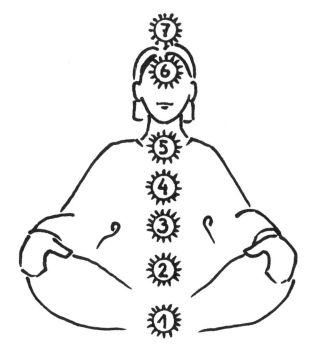

Diag. 4.3: The seven main human chakras – 1=root chakra, 2=sacral chakra, 3=solar plexus, 4= heart chakra, 5= throat chakra, 6= third eye, 7= crown chakra.

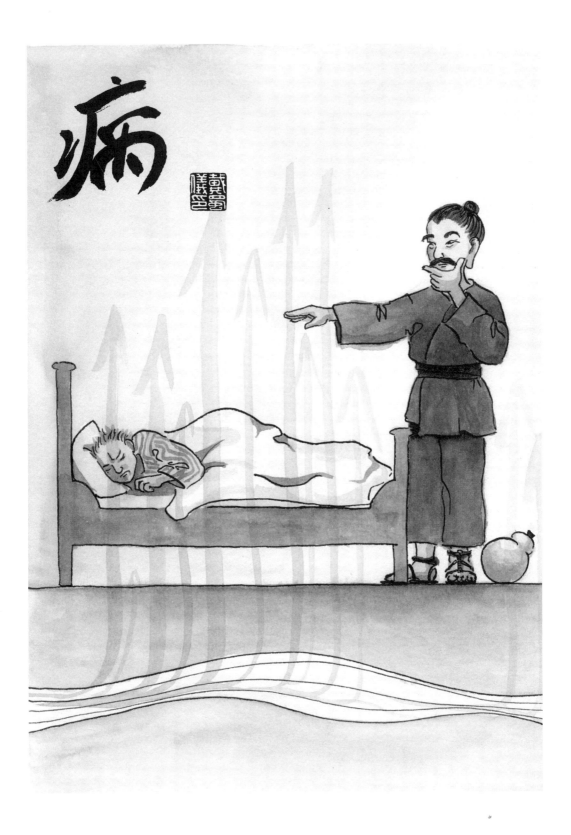

Chapter 5

THE CONNECTION BETWEEN BAD FENG SHUI AND DISEASES

In our search for the link between the feng shui of houses and degenerative and terminal health problems, we came up with some interesting statistics tabulated below:

Table 1 shows the average figures derived from divining the cosmic qi level in a bedroom or a building, mainly in temperate countries like Europe, North America, Australia and New Zealand. In tropical countries where there is more sunshine and better ventilation throughout the year, bacteria and fungus levels tend to be substantially lower.

On my scale, the normal amount of qi in the open air is 100%. Depending on the environment, the qi may be higher or lower than 100%. In the rainforest, cosmic qi rises to about 100–120%. In big cities with high pollution levels, cosmic qi may drop to below 60%. (Normally, cosmic qi in the open environment is between 80–100%. In wooded jungles, cosmic qi is around 100–120%. In polluted cities, cosmic qi can be well below 60% saturation.)

From the figures in Table 1, you can see that when the cosmic qi level in a room is lower, it provides a fertile breeding atmosphere for fungus and bacteria to grow. We discovered with great interest that when the cosmic qi level of a room or a house fell below 40%, which meant very bad feng shui, most of the occupants suffered from general fatigue and needed to sleep for more than seven hours a day. The more they slept, the more tired they became. We also observed that the occupants who had lived in these houses for more than three years tended to suffer from degenerative diseases affecting the heart, artery and joints and showed a general lack of vitality. Moreover, when a person slept over a crossing of geopathic stress lines (see Diag. 5.4 to 5.14) cancer appeared in over 80% of the cases.

Cosmic Qi in House/Flat	Fungus in the air		Bacteria in the air		Freshness of air
100		0		0	100
90	2 –	4		0	95
80	4 –	5		0	90
70	5 –	10		0	70
60	10 –	20	2 –	5	60
50	20 –	30	5 –	10	50
40	30 –	40	10 –	20	40
30	40 –	60	20 –	30	30
20	60 –	70	30 –	50	20
10	70 –	80	50 –	60	15
0 Grave	Over 80		Over 60		5

Table 1: Percentage of qi in the home.

You can see from the table that when cosmic qi falls below 40%, the fungus level reaches as high as 60% and the harmful bacteria level reaches 30% or more. People living and working in this type of environment are breathing in toxic fungus and bacteria into their lungs with every in breath.

This confirms the belief that cancer is linked to fungus infection. Medical scientists in developed countries have always found fungus and viruses in the blood of cancer patients – a phenomenon which they could not account for. More and more doctors now agree that cancers are connected with geopathic stress and electromagnetic radiation.

In my consultations, I also found that houses with less than 40% cosmic qi often have substantial geopathic stress, caused either by underground running water or by fault lines passing underneath a house. People living or working in these houses (often called 'sick buildings') and especially those sitting or sleeping over the stress lines often suffered from chronic fatigue syndrome.

Such people tended to eat more, especially sweet food, to try to boost their energy levels, often resulting in obesity.

Consider the following situation (see Diag. 5.1): We assume that a room's cosmic qi is about 35%. At the time of going to bed, a person may have high body vitality and energy closer to 80–100%. By the time this person gets out of bed 7–10 hours later, his or her body energy would have drained to the level of energy of the room. When a room has low energy, the occupants cannot recharge during sleep. With reduced vitality, they tend to have problems getting out of their bed. This is what we call the 'vampire effect'.

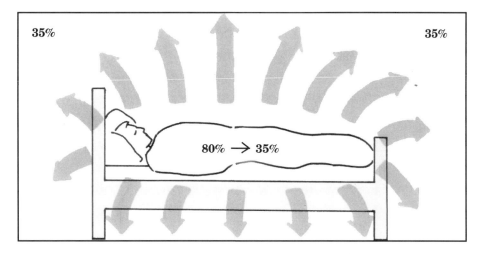

35%

35%

80% → 35%

Diag. 5.1: Vampire effect in rooms with low energy.

Feng Shui Complements Medical Treatment

As a feng shui consultant, I strongly believed doctors and health therapists should suggest to their patients that they include feng shui in their therapy. Many of my students who are practising doctors and therapists have combined feng shui remedies with natural therapies to give exceptionally good results.

After attending my feng shui seminar in Munich, a doctor advised one of his patients suffering from terminal cancer, who was told by other doctors she had three months to live, to move out of her house, pitch an igloo-shaped tent in her garden and sleep there so that she could take in more fresh air and more cosmic qi and oxygen to help her recover. In the summer of 1993, this lady slept in a dome-shaped tent in her garden. At the end of three months, she went back to the hospital for an X-ray and medical check-up and was told that her cancer was completely gone! In my opinion, this was no miracle. The main cause of her health problem was removed when she changed to a better place to sleep and her body was given a healthy environment conducive to healing. Sufficient cosmic qi and plenty of oxygen or rather good feng shui in the open air facilitated her cure together with medication.

I have found that over 80% of people coming to my consultations who were suffering from severe high blood pressure or severe heart problems, were sleeping or working over geopathic stress lines or living/working in a low feng shui house.

With good feng shui remedies, we found that in most cases, their blood pressure became lower and heart conditions improved considerably within six months.

The reasons are obvious: Once the body was no longer exposed to geopathic stress, cosmic qi and oxygen levels increased to a healthy level of 80–90%. Body cell stress and free radicals were reduced very substantially, allowing the body to heal itself. The living space/rooms saturated with cosmic qi and oxygen allowed the body's skin and lungs to absorb them in large quantities to rejuvenate body cells and soften hardened arteries and veins.

It is, therefore, vitally important to include feng shui remedies with medication in the treatment of heart patients to ensure a faster recovery from heart problems.

Danger from Geopathic Stress Lines

Underground running water flows along rock surfaces, causing friction. This friction causes radiation known as water line radiation. The radiation moves upwards above ground along the path of the running water, penetrating rocks, wood, steel and even solid concrete buildings. Sometimes, it rises up to 30 storeys high. Thanks to modern construction techniques and materials (such as steel supports or pipes), the radiation can spread even more widely and increase many times. A stress line is usually about 1 m (3.3 ft) wide, although I have sometimes found lines as wide as 2 to 3 m (6.5 to 10 ft) or even wider.

When a person sits or sleeps above the path of a geopathic stress line, the radiation penetrates and violently vibrates through his or her body (see Diag. 5.3). These disturbing frequencies which are considerably higher than the earth's normal frequency cause extreme stress to body cells. The body's immune system

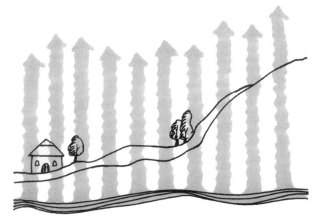

Diag. 5.2: Geopathic stress caused by underground water.

naturally perceives this as an attack and acts to protect the body. The heart beats faster to expand the body's aura (electrical field), causing extreme stress and weakness to the heart. A person quickly depletes their body vitality and becomes easily tired. Prolonged sleeping or sitting over a geopathic stress line causes chronic fatigue and degenerative diseases.

When two geopathic stress lines cross, they form a spiral of energy that rapidly surges upwards like a tornado and cause faster health deterioration. We discovered that with all cancer patients who slept or sat over geopathic cross lines. The area where the stress lines cross is the area in the body that becomes weak and diseased.

Diag. 5.4–5.14 show examples of the effects of geopathic stress lines caused by underground running water and the health problems which can possibly develop, depending on the constitution of individual persons.

Diag. 5.3: The aura is shaken by a geopathic stress line.

Possible health problems and diseases caused by geopathic stress

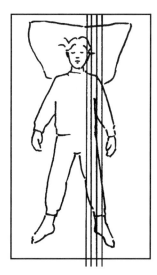

Diag. 5.4: Single waterline – Arthritis and problems in the left limbs.

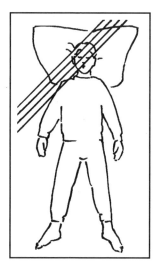

Diag. 5.5: Single water line – Depression and diseases in the head area.

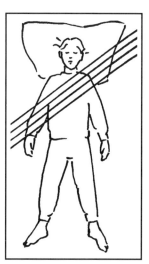

Diag. 5.6: Single waterline – Heart problems and breast diseases.

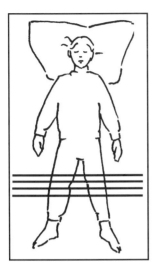

Diag. 5.7: Single waterline – Problems in the knees and lower leg area.

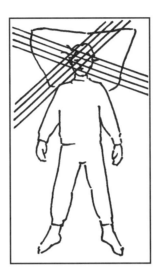

Diag. 5.8: Waterline crossing – Brain tumour, epilepsy and severe migraine.

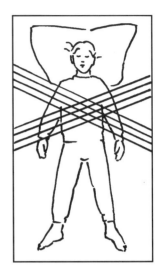

Diag. 5.9: Waterline crossing – Lung cancer, spleen cancer and severe digestive problems.

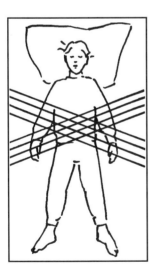

Diag. 5.10: Waterline crossing – Cancer of the stomach, kidney and large intestine.

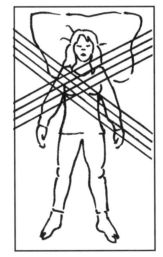

Diag. 5.11: Waterline crossing – Cancer of the right breast and numbness of the right shoulder.

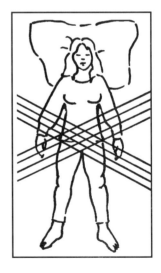

Diag. 5.12: Waterline crossing – Cancer of the uterus and intestine, and severe menstrual problems.

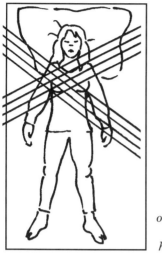

Diag. 5.13:
Cancer of the
upper body
organs, multiple
sclerosis and
heart problems.

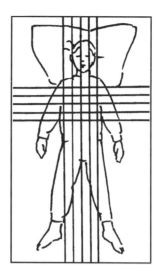

Diag. 5.14:
Waterline crossing
– Fatal cancer.

To measure the intensity of geopathic stress, I have set up a scale from 0 to 50%. Cancer could occur when a stress line creates stress of over 5%. When a stress factor of over 20% is found, a person may suffer from cancer within three to five years of sleeping over a water line crossing. However, about 5% of people can tolerate geopathic stress of below 10% very well – these people rarely suffer from cancer, but tend to have degenerative health problems instead when they sleep or sit over a geopathic stress line. In the Appendix are some common natural remedies to facilitate a faster recovery for people who sleep or sit over geopathic stress lines. We suggest you consult your doctor or therapist before you use these remedies.

Even though a person with a strong body constitution may not suffer from severe health problems when they sit over geopathic stress lines, we found that office workers are unable to perform their best and lose their concentration and intuition to make correct decisions.

Example: A medium-sized company in Switzerland suffered losses for six years after they moved into their new modern building. I discovered that in addition to some feng shui problems, six of the company's top executives, including the chief executive, were sitting over geopathic stress lines. Seven months after the remedies were carried out, the company's sales and profits began to rise substantially even though Switzerland was going through an economic recession at that time.

We can implement the best feng shui remedies or employ the best brains to work in a company, but if the senior executives are affected by geopathic stress lines, they can never perform to high expectations.

Similarly, you can create a perfectly designed feng shui house and introduce the best feng shui remedies, but they become less effective when a person is sitting or sleeping over a geopathic stress line. Therefore, all aspects of geomancy connected with earth energies and earth grids need to be considered as well.

Chapter 6

FENG SHUI MYTHS, SUPERSTITION AND REALITY IN CHINA

Many rules and practices adopted by ancient feng shui consultants in China were based on local beliefs and events which actually happened as a result of certain practices and experiences in specific locations according to certain formations of landscape, hills and water flow. But some of these practices and rules may not be applicable to areas outside China. Some feng shui practices that were relevant in ancient China are now obsolete in today's modern consciousness and hectic lifestyle.

In this chapter, I would like to put forward my views and research regarding a few of these common misconceptions.

Southeast – Prosperity and Wealth Area

In China, the southeast has been regarded as a prosperous and wealthy area for hundreds of years.

Delicious red lychee fruits, highly sought after by the northern imperial court and nobles, were grown in abundance in the south and southeast of China. Chinese sailors sailing south and southeast to the Philippines and the Indonesian archipelago came back with rich spices and South Sea pearls which were highly valued and sought after as jewellery by the imperial court and the wealthy court officials.

When Chinese civilisation moved closer to the coast along the Yellow River and Yangtze River, the estuaries of these two great rivers were situated on the southeast sides of ancient China and were considered to be prosperous areas. Many big cities like Shanghai (which has a population of 15 million today) developed along the southeast coast of northern China. Hong Kong, situated in the southeast of China, has by today's standards, become a model of immense prosperity.

During the last 1,000 years, the southeastern part of China covering Guangchou province and Canton has supplied an abundance of food and helped other parts of China to survive famines and food shortages.

The southeast, therefore, has become accepted as the 'wealth area' and has accordingly been incorporated into the Eight Trigrams feng shui practice. Some feng shui schools have determined that the wealth corner in a building lies in the southeast. Furthermore, the southeast area in the Eight Trigrams is attributed to the wood element, completion of growth and flowering, which also represents growth, progress and success.

The wealthy industrial areas in Germany, on the other hand, are in the northwest and west. In Austria, the more wealthy areas are in the west. In the United States, the rich areas are in the northeast, covering Michigan and New York state, with the world's financial centre – the famous Wall Street – in New York City.

Yet the northeast is called the 'Devil's Gate' by feng shui masters in China and Asia. This is because in China little has changed over thousands of years. We can safely say that the southeast is the 'wealth area' because this area has become part of the Chinese consciousness and really exists. If you are in China or Hong Kong, by all means use the southeast of the building to activate wealth and prosperity. But be careful how you apply this rule in other parts of the world.

Northeast – Devil's Gate

For hundreds of years, villages along the northeast coast of China facing Japan were plundered by Japanese pirates and the Manchurians. Genghis Khan also attacked China from the weak northeast, and the Mongols ruled China from A.D. 1271–1368. Similarly, the Yellow River in the northeast has flooded and overflowed its banks for hundreds of years, causing famine and the loss of many thousands of lives. Because history seems to have decreed the northeast of China a disaster area, imperial court feng shui experts decided to term the northeast as the 'Devil's Gate'. They recommend you avoid placing your door and master bedroom here, just in case disasters strike you and your family. However, this principle does not apply to all countries, as pointed out earlier.

Those of you who are not living in China can sleep in peace if your door or master bedroom is situated in the northeast!

Southwest – Devil's Backdoor

In the southwest of China lie the provinces of Xinjiang and Tibet. These areas are dry, harsh, windy, sandy and difficult areas in which to live. The lands are less fertile and mostly hilly. Thousands of years of erosion have created a bare landscape with little vegetation. In the past, Xinjiang, bordering Pakistan and the former southern USSR states of Tajikistan, Kyrgyzistan and Kazakhstan, was constantly attacked and raided by nomadic tribes. It was also an area that was difficult for China to govern because of the nomadic tribes living there. Xinjiang was called the last frontier, and members of the royal family and nobles who were considered undesirable were often exiled there.

Since the southwest is opposite the northeast, feng shui masters called the southwest the 'Devil's Backdoor'. People in China were advised not to place their main door, master bedroom and important rooms in this area, just in case the devils come in or out of the backdoor to cause misfortune.

But if you live outside China, I believe you have little to worry about.

North Facing Devil's Door and Negative West Door

Many feng shui consultants advise their clients not to position their front door towards the north. They generally recommend that the best place for a house's main door is facing south where prosperous and benevolent qi can come in.

In China, it is sensible to place your door in the south to face the warmer south winds to avoid health problems. This advice is good advice if you are living in northern China where the cold winds blowing from Siberia can cause severe health problems.

In tropical countries and in places in the southern hemisphere such as Australia, South Africa and South America, this north-facing rule does not apply. In these countries, it is, in fact, not advisable to place a main door facing south because cold winds from the Antarctica could cause severe health problems to the occupants, especially during the winter months.

Chinese living in the western part of China were also advised not to place their doors facing west, otherwise 'evil spirits' would come in and control their home.

Western China consists mainly of arid mountains and the Gobi Desert. Positioning your door in the west would let dust and sand into your home, causing lung and sinus problems. Similarly, those living in the eastern part of Australia, in arid areas, should avoid placing their doors in the west because of the dry, dusty Australian desert in the west.

All temples in China and some old churches in Europe, however, face west, the direction from where spirits and gods are believed to come. West is also regarded as a yin direction because the sun sets in the west.

The environment around your town is an important factor when determining where to place your main door. The main door of a house should face an open space, preferably with calm moving water in front and a green forest or hill at the back. More factors affecting door placement are explained in Chapter 17.

The Colour Black

Some historians believe that a major segment of the Chinese population left the Mesopotamia area after the Great Flood recorded in the Bible. They migrated along the southern border of Russia and settled for a while along the Black and Caspian Seas, where they called their kingdom the 'Middle Kingdom' – the centre of many civilisations.

The Chinese population living along the Black Sea began to prosper and grew fast. Other inland Chinese settlements were less successful. The waters of the Black Sea were dark and were regarded as 'black'. Water in deep wells and in Chinese rivers is also often dark and cloudy. So in the olden days, it was quite logical for the Chinese to think of the colour of water as black.

The Chings from Manchuria conquered China in the 17th century and ruled the country harshly for 267 years (1644–1911). Many Chinese leaders and nobles grieved that China was controlled by an illiterate and brutal foreign regime and began to wear black silk clothing as a sign of mourning. It was said that they would only change their clothes to blue again after the overthrow of the Ching dynasty. When a Ching emperor asked the nobles and leaders why they all wore black clothing, they told the emperor that it was a colour for leaders and therefore indicated respect for the emperor. The Ching emperor accepted the comments of the Chinese leaders and decreed that all Ching senior officials should change their official clothing to black. In China, political power and rank means authority, wealth and abundance. So from then on, black came to be associated with power, money and wealth.

In ancient China, water was associated with the successful cultivation of crops. The colour black and water were thus wrongly associated with prosperity and wealth.

Misunderstanding arose because black was regarded as the colour for water, and the symbol for wealth and power. Till today, black is accepted by many feng shui consultants in China and Hong Kong as the colour symbolising wealth and prosperity. However, I believe this is a serious misinterpretation that has caused many catastrophes in feng shui practice.

Even today, there are feng shui consultants who recommend that companies place an aquarium with black goldfish at the entrance area for more success and prosperity. But when people look at black fish, they become depressed and weak. This may adversely affect the staff and cause the companies to be less successful – or even lead to bankruptcy.

Black is a mystical colour connected with death and evil. Executioners in ancient times always wore black. And those who indulged in mystical practices – witches and magicians – often wore black.

The seven colours of the rainbow come from water and the sun rays that give life. When these seven colours are mixed, they become white; black is absent in the seven rainbow colours. All healthy humans have the rainbow colours in their aura. When the rainbow colours disappear, a person dies.

Experiments were carried out with healthy people who were asked to wear a black coat. After putting on the black coat, each of the persons recorded a drop in body energy and their immune system weakened. Using applied kinesiology, we discovered that all their body joints had become weak. We discovered that the black coat blocks the body's seven main chakras and the body cells from absorbing the seven colours of the rainbow. We also discovered that people who wear black clothing tend to be more depressed – they have a strong inner grief, often accompanied by a subconscious death wish, which may be caused by a sad event and/or deep unhappiness.

We also found out that when people are suffering or unhappy over a national issue they tend to wear black clothing. For example, when North Vietnam was being heavily bombed by American warplanes more and more North Vietnamese began to wear black clothes. Many innocent lives were lost when the American soldiers mistook black-clothed Vietnamese for the Vietcong.

During the late 1980s, when the progressive New Zealand government carried out dramatic welfare reforms and cut social benefits to balance their excessive budget deficit, New Zealanders found their 'God-given paradise' under threat and free spending habits came to a stop. To suddenly leap from a socialist state to a 'pay-for-all-services' capitalistic state was traumatic for most New Zealanders. Interestingly, many New Zealanders unconsciously wore black clothing, expressing their inner grief and unhappiness. One company became very successful from selling a lot of black and dark clothing.

Black is, therefore, a very dull colour that is connected with unhappiness and grief and should be avoided at all cost, unless worn during mourning. Grey is just one shade before black and is also a negative, unhappy colour.

Unpolluted and clear waters sparkle and radiate blue energy, the same colour as the clear blue sky. When the sky is covered with black clouds, we know that bad weather and storms are approaching.

When the bluish-coloured rain water which falls during spring and the yellow rays of the sun combine, the two colours give plants and trees their green colour. In areas with little water and plenty of sunlight, plants tend to be yellowish and light brown, taking on the excess energy of the sun. In areas where there is plenty of sunlight and water, as in the tropical regions, the leaves of plants and trees tend to be greener. If water is black, it cannot give birth to green coloured leaves and plants.

Black, therefore, CANNOT logically be regarded as the colour for water and for wealth, prosperity and abundance.

If you want to be successful, prosperous and happy, blue is your colour for water and you should wear multicoloured or light-coloured clothing often. Avoid black and grey for clothing and furniture – choose pastel or bright colours.

阴
阳

Chapter 7

THE PRINCIPLE OF YIN AND YANG

Feng shui was first evolved from the yin and yang principle. Everything on earth and in the universe exists in a pair with opposite polarity, with one having predominantly male characteristics and the other having predominantly female characteristics. Yet in each of the male (yang), there are elements of female (yin) and vice versa. Because of their dual characteristics, they can combine to form a unit or entity. A male and female cohabit to bear offsprings.

The yin and yang signs combine with the circle on the outside to 'give birth' to the Tai Chi symbol (see Diag. 7.1A–E). The circle represents the universe, the yang and the yin represent the phenomena and living creatures on earth. Everything in the universe can be attributed to the yin and yang:

The Yin and Yang Forces of Nature

Diag. 7.1A: Yin matter

Diag. 7.1B: Yang matter

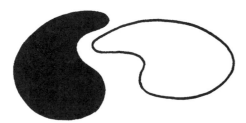

*Diag. 7.1C: Yin and yang matter
attracted to each other.*

Yang	Yin
white	black
light	dark
male	female
sun	moon
living	dead
activity/movement	static
pointed	rounded
shallow	deep
mountain	valley
forward	backward
hot	cold
stimulating	tranquillising
daylight	night
left side of house	right side of house
house – ground floor	house – top floor
front of house	back of house
activity room	relaxation room
workroom	bedroom

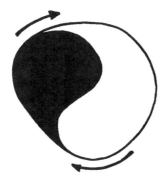

*Diag. 7.1D: Yang matter
embraces the yin matter and
spins round clockwise.*

*Diag. 7.1E: The modern Tai Chi
symbol is formed.*

Yin and Yang Factors in Health and Feng Shui

In the study and practice of feng shui, we must first understand our body's yin and yang responses to our outside environment. Our body cells and organs are healthy if their yin and yang polarity are in balance (see Diag. 7.2 (A)). If the yang is in excess (see Diag. 7.2 (B)) in an organ, the organ becomes unhealthy. The result may be a health problem caused by the excess yang energy generating too much internal heat. This phenomenon could be caused by eating too much yang food, hot and spicy or grilled, a hot wind or overexposure to the sun.

Similarly, an excess of yin (see Diag. 7.2 (C)) may be caused by too much strong cold air blowing or the weather suddenly becoming too cold and the body being unable to respond fast enough to balance the yin and yang factors.

We must shelter ourselves from excessive yin or yang in our living environment. For instance, if the winds blowing at your house every day are too strong and cold, feng shui remedies have to be applied to avoid or counter the negative effects to keep you and your family healthy.

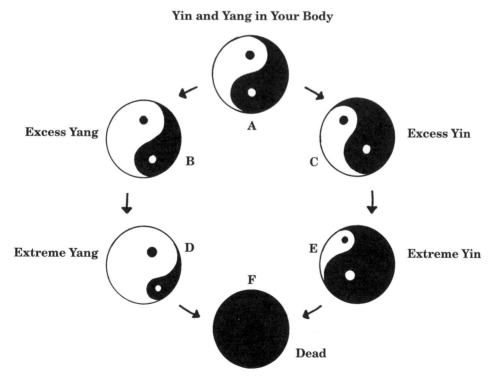

Yin and Yang in Your Body

Diag. 7.2: Yin and yang factors in the human body.

Four Animals Landscape Formation

In the practice of feng shui, we study the environment to select a good site and make use of the best local resources. When we build our house to live and work in, it should have the yin and yang factors in balance and harmony.

The yin and yang principle forms the basic foundation in the Four Animals Landscape Formation feng shui. A housing site or land with the complete Four Animals Formation is considered the best feng shui site. People living there tend to be more successful and prosperous. Traditional Chinese often look for similar sites to build their family home and to bury their close relatives to ensure that their future generations will prosper as well. My great-grandfather travelled several thousand kilometres in a small sailing boat from southern China in the 1870s to look for such a site in Borneo (now East Malaysia) for his family.

In the Four Animals Formation (Diag. 7.3–7.7), the Dragon is considered the most dominant yang animal, indicating where the powerful earth qi flows and generates. It can be represented by a high and long mountain/hill range (Diag. 7.4), tall trees (Diag. 7.5), or tall buildings (Diag. 7.6). A road with moving traffic is also acceptable but not as good (Diag. 7.7).

Pairing with the Dragon is the Tiger (yin), sitting opposite and waiting quietly for its 'prey'. The Tiger side is where the spent, stale and dirty air and energy

Diag. 7.3: The Formation of the Four Animals Landscape.

flow away (the Tiger represents negative energy in this case). In practical feng shui, the Tiger is represented by low and wide, spreading hills or low trees/buildings. A road with traffic moving away from the house, taking the stale energy with it, is also an acceptable feature for a good building site.

The Tortoise represents calmness, stability and a solid backing foundation that is yin in character. The Tortoise is represented by high, smooth hills, tall even-levelled buildings or tall trees of even height that block the good qi from escaping and redirect it back to the house.

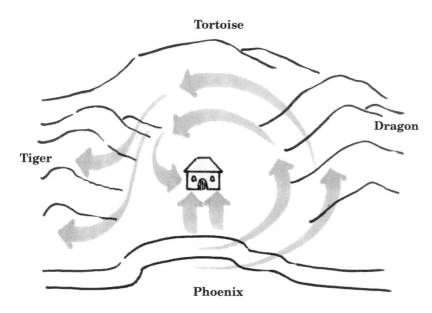

Diag. 7.4: Interpretation of the Four Animals Formation in an actual landscape.

The opposite of the Tortoise is the energetic Phoenix (bird, yang) flying high and moving all the time. The Phoenix flying high with a good bird's eye view is interpreted to mean open ground with plenty of space and qi, preferably with some moving water like a slow flowing and meandering stream or river, or a fountain in front of a building. There should be no obstacles in front – the building has to be clearly visible.

The animals are not always attributed to a particular compass direction. Their positions are determined by the entrance of the building. When you are standing in front of the entrance (with your back towards the building) and looking outside, the Dragon is on your left, the Tortoise is behind the house, the Tiger is on your right and the Phoenix is in front of you.

The formation of the Four Animals representing high vitality, wealth and prosperity in feng shui has the shape of a horseshoe, which is also considered a lucky symbol in European tradition.

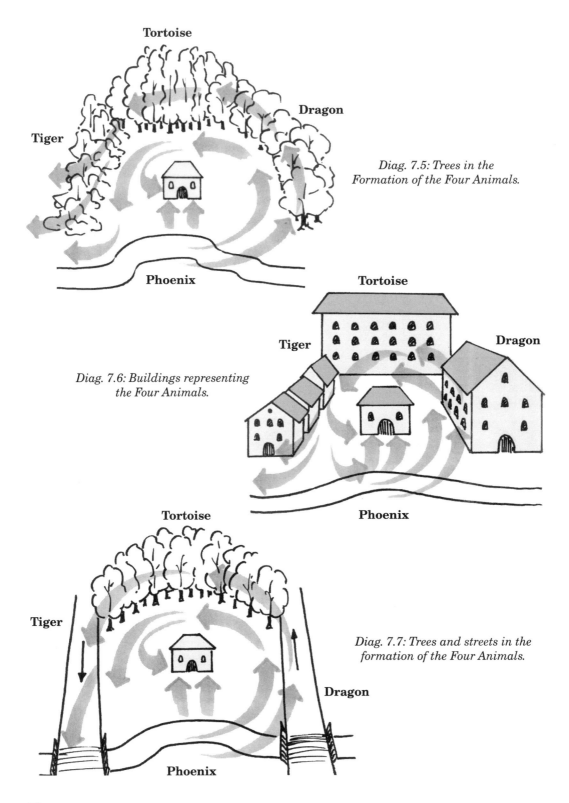

Diag. 7.5: Trees in the
Formation of the Four Animals.

Diag. 7.6: Buildings representing
the Four Animals.

Diag. 7.7: Trees and streets in the
formation of the Four Animals.

The Yin and Yang of House Design

Different parts of a house can also be classified into yin or yang (see Diag. 7.8).

The left side represents the Dragon (yang) male side. The right side represents the Tiger (yin) female side. If the entrance is on the Dragon side, the men in the house are more dominant. The same principle applies for women when the door is on the Tiger side. A door in the middle of the front is neutral (see also Chapter 17).

The different areas in a house can also be yin or yang. We can thus arrange rooms harmoniously for healthy living according to their qualities.

Here are some basic principles:

- The front of a house is for activities and is yang, while the back of a house is yin for quiet resting (Diag. 7.9).

- All yang activity areas such the living room, dining room, kitchen and children's playing area should be placed in the front. Bedrooms and the study should be placed at the back, while the toilet and store should be on the Tiger side or at the back of the house.

- A house with two storeys is classified into the yang area (activity area) for the ground floor and the yin area (resting area) for the first floor where the bedrooms are situated (see Diag. 7.10).

When the yin and yang qualities are incorporated into the design of a house, occupants tend to have more balance, harmony and better health.

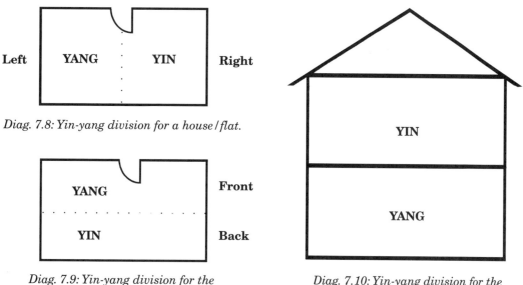

Diag. 7.8: Yin-yang division for a house / flat.

Diag. 7.9: Yin-yang division for the rooms of a house / flat.

Diag. 7.10: Yin-yang division for the different floors.

┌───────────────┐
│ *Chapter 8* │
└───────────────┘

THE FIVE ELEMENTAL UNIVERSAL ENERGIES

The Principle of the Five Elements has a history of about 3,000 years. Through patient observation and research, the Chinese found that everything on earth and in the universe can be assigned to one of the five elements. The Greeks, Egyptians and Indians also distinguish between the four elemental energies of fire, earth, air and water.

In feng shui, we study how the elements interact with each other and affect humans, and how they can be used as remedies.

All the five elemental symbols have their special energies, characteristics and behaviour.

For example, through experiments we found that a person who belongs to the fire element according to their year of birth immediately becomes weak in all their body joints when they sit or stand within 1 m (3.3 ft) of a water fountain (representing the water element) in a room. Some fire element persons are even more sensitive and cannot take the overpowering effects of a water fountain within 3 m (10 ft) of them in an enclosed room.

In feng shui, we therefore do not recommend water element remedies to a person who belongs to the fire element. (In this section, the elements referred to are the birth year elements according to the Chinese calendar and NOT the personal trigram elements.)

An earth element person feels similarly uncomfortable sitting next to a large green plant in a house or in an enclosed area.

According to the Principle of the Five Elements, this phenomenon occurs when the elements are in a 'destructive or controlling cycle' (see Diag. 8.2), that is, when water destroys fire and wood breaks up the earth.

However, out in the open, a fire element person is not adversely affected by a water fountain, waterfall or large pool of water because they then become part of the open environment, unlike when they are confined in a room or a house. Similarly, a fire element person is quite comfortable naked in a bathtub of water because they are in a water environment without their clothes.

The same principle applies to the earth element – in the open environment they are not affected by the wood element because the person and the trees and plants are part of the natural environment. Elemental conflict only occurs in enclosed areas.

The Productive Cycle

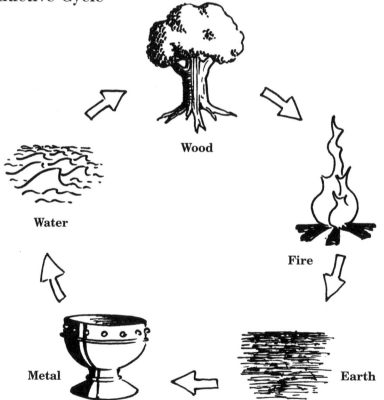

Wood

Water

Fire

Metal

Earth

Diag. 8.1: Wood produces fire, fire produces earth, metal is found in earth.
melted metal becomes liquid like water, water feeds wood.

The Destructive Cycle

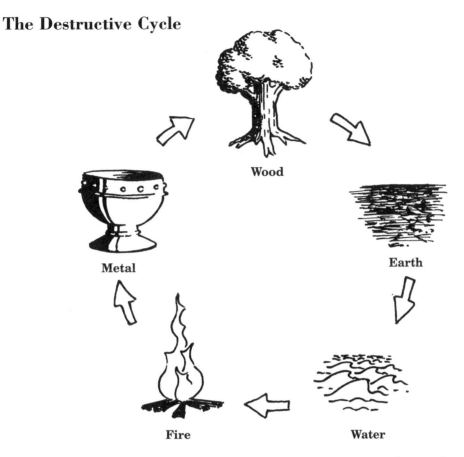

Diag. 8.2: Wood breaks up earth, earth sucks up water, water destroys fire, fire melts metal, metal cuts wood.

Difference Between the Elements in Chinese and Western Astrology

What is the difference between the Western astrological signs and the Chinese elemental symbols? A person may belong to a fire sign in Western astrology while in Chinese astrology based on the year of birth he may be, in complete conflict, a water element person. The main determining criterion is how quickly the elements influence a person's health and behaviour in their immediate environment.

Through experiments, I have found that the five Chinese elemental energies affect the human physical body significantly and immediately in their immediate environment. For example, if the person's Chinese birth year element is fire, they should avoid being very close to the water element in a room. But if the person belongs to the fire element according to Western astrology, the person will not be negatively affected by the water element.

The Western astrological elemental characteristics affect us from a great distance as a result of the planetary movements. The effects are slow and gradual. As earth beings, the five Chinese elemental energies have priority over the Western astrological signs as they affect us immediately in our immediate environment.

However, both are just as important because they determine our body constitution and behaviour. To find your Chinese birth element, please refer to Chapter 17 Table 7.

The Birth Year Element and the Trigram Element in Chinese Astrology

In feng shui practice, a person has to consider several elements – the birth year element, the birth trigram element, and so on. The trigram element is determined according to the system of the Eight Trigrams. In this book, we can only mention the following points:

The birth year element represents the physical body and the aura. Both are in direct interaction with the immediate environment. The personal trigram element can be compared with the elements of Western astrology. It affects us more slowly than the birth year element.

Often, there is the question of whether the personal trigram element should be considered when selecting colours to implement feng shui practices and remedies. According to our kinesiology test results, the personal trigram element is less important in this case. Still, ideally, the chosen colours should be in harmony with the birth year and the personal trigram elements. More details on trigram elements will be given in one of my subsequent books.

The Wood Element

The wood element symbolises an expansion of energy outward in all directions like a tree sprouting shoots and roots and growing rapidly during the wet spring season (see Diag. 8.3A). It also represents growth and rapid development and is green in colour. Anything that is green in colour belongs to the wood element. A wood person is energetic, performs lots of moving activities, seeks growth and is progressive in outlook.

The wood element needs substantial water energy (blue colour) and sun rays (yellow) to facilitate its rapid growth and expansion. From the combination of blue (water) and yellow (sun rays), we derive the green in wood. This is part of the birth cycle of the Principle of the Five Elements – wood develops from water. The wood's enemy is the hard, stubborn and contracting metal element energy.

Wood's expanding energy breaks up the earth energy and slowly destroys it. Therefore, the wood element is the earth element's enemy. Wood's green colour enhances the heart chakras (fire) connected with blood circulation and the immune system. Wood element shapes are long, cylindrical and narrow.

Diag. 8.3A: The colour of wood is green. Movement of wood – expansion and growth in all directions.

Diag. 8.3C: A healthy tree – the roots with their expanding wood energy break up the earth and deplete earth's energy.

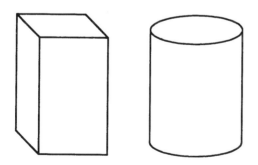

Diag. 8.3B: Shapes of the wood element.

The Fire Element

The fire element supported by wood in the productive or birth cycle creates intense heat during burning which moves energy upwards (Diag. 8.4A). All objects or material with red, purple, violet, pink or maroon colour, or with sharp shapes or shapes that cause an upward movement of energy, such as a pyramid or sharp-pointed objects, belong to the fire element.

The fire element person flares up easily and is generally impulsive. However, his good traits include energetic, outgoing leadership qualities and passion in the things he does. Red activates the base energy chakras (Diag. 4.3) connected with the reproductive and sex organs.

Fire element shapes are sharp and pointed and energy moves upwards.

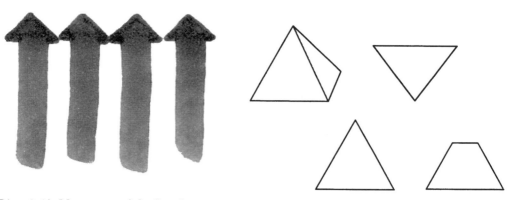

Diag. 8.4A: Movements of the fire element – pushing upward and forward. Fire element colours – red, violet, purple, pink, and maroon

Diag. 8.4B: Shapes of the fire element.

Fire is vulnerable to water which has a downward, condensing and cooling energy. A large amount of water destroys fire. But some water and plenty of fire creates steam and is a source of powerful energy. The old trains and ships were powered by steam. So it is not always negative when fire and water energies meet.

The Earth Element

When fire reaches its peak and dies away, it produces ashes which become earth.

The earth element energy which is created by fire, moves horizontally to and fro, retracting and absorbing (Diag. 8.5A). We can observe this phenomena by looking at the landscape around us. With the influence of underground earth movements, flat land becomes hills, mountains and valleys. Earth easily absorbs and sucks in water energy, but is vulnerable to wood energy which moves rapidly inwards and outwards like the roots of a tree and destroys its form (Diag. 8.3C).

The earth element is represented by flat and completely round objects (Diag. 8.5B and 8.5C) and has the colours brown, yellow, orange and beige. Earth elemental objects include ceramic and earthen vases and brick, stone, soil, and clay derivatives.

An earth person is generally more grounded and moves with caution.

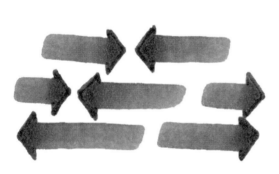

Diag. 8.5A: Earth element movements – horizontal, expanding and contracting. The earth colours are brown, yellow, orange and beige.

Diag. 8.5B: The round shape representing planet earth is often regarded as the earth symbol.

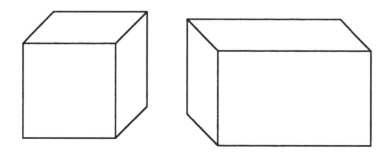

Diag. 8.5C: Earth element shapes are square, rectangular and flat, with flat surfaces.

The Metal Element

The constant movements and reactions in the earth facilitate the formation of metal underground. Metal energy tends to solidify, contract and move inwards (Diag. 8.6A).

Metal is the most solid of the five elemental energies. It represents hardness, inward-looking stubbornness and rigidity in form and reactions. A person who belongs to the metal element often has similar characteristics. Positive traits are discipline, strength and stability. Fire energy is its greatest enemy. Heat from fire energy soon dissolves and melts metal into liquid water energy.

Diag. 8.6A: Metal element movements –
inwards (the opposite of wood).
Metal colours – gold, silver and white.

Diag. 8.6B: Shapes of the metal element.

Metal's inward, contracting and hard energy squeezes, suffocates and cuts down the expanding wood (tree) element.

All curved and semi-round shapes that contained energy belong to the metal element. The colour for metal is gold and silver. White is also often used to represent metal because white is close to silver. White contains all the seven main spectrum colours that are also the rainbow colours and is therefore a neutral colour.

The Water Element

The water elemental energy is the most important energy in feng shui practice and is synonymous with wealth and prosperity. Water has historical importance to Chinese farming peasants. With plenty of water, rice can be cultivated and fish can breed – both essential to the Chinese diet. In ancient times, plentiful food was synonymous with abundance and wealth. Moving water energy attracts cosmic qi and oxygen which are the key factor in feng shui practice. Water energy is represented by waterfalls, fountains, aquariums, swimming pools, paintings and pictures of waterfalls, lakes and ponds as well as photos and paintings depicting the wavy water symbol.

Water energy moves downwards and sideways and fills all the holes and empty spaces (Diag. 8.7A). This movement is opposite to its enemy, the rising fire energy (8.7C). That is why the water energy's greatest enemy is the earth energy, which can suck in and deplete its energy. Water, on the other hand, weakens metal through corrosion.

Water energy is represented by wavy and stepped shapes. The colour for water is blue. Although black is often used to represent water, it is a gross mistake (see Chapter 6). Black is depressive and is a symbol of mourning, authority and death. Many Chinese restaurants around the world mistakenly use black for furniture and walls, hoping to boost prosperity and success. But the liberal use of black furnishings is one of the reasons companies go bankrupt. The blue of water strengthens the throat chakra connected with authority – the respiratory organs and the thyroid and parathyroid glands. These three organs regulate body weight. Blue, which is antibacterial, is also good for relieving body pains. If only a small amount of water is present and it descends into substantial fire energy, we have a great expansion of steam which is a positive energy that can be harnessed for use as a power supply. In this case, a little water versus a big fire is positive in the Principle of the Five Elements. Conversely, a huge water energy would surely destroy a small fire energy.

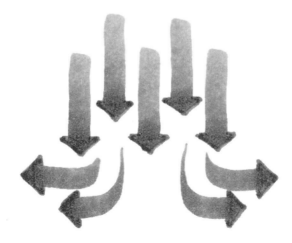

Diag. 8.7A: Water element movement – downwards and sideways. Colour is blue.

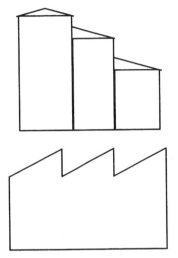

Diag. 8.7B: Water element shapes.

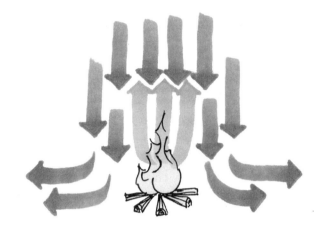

Diag. 8.7C: Powerful and cool downward movements of water destroy the upward thrust of hot fire energy.

Application of the Principle of the Five Elements

Now that you are familiar with the Principle of the Five Elements, you can apply it when selecting colours for your rooms.

First check your birth year element in Table 7 of Chapter 17. When choosing colours, make sure you are surrounded by colours that are in harmony with or that strengthen your birth year element and preferably also your personal trigram element.

Here is how you should apply the colours of the productive cycle. The colour preceding another colour in the productive cycle (for example, water before wood) is like a mother (water) producing and nourishing the succeeding element (wood).

Examples of colours in the strengthening productive cycle: Wood creates fire (red-green), fire produces earth (red-brown), in earth you can find metal (brown-gold), metal supports water (gold-blue) and water nourishes wood (blue-green).

White, in this case, is neutral and can be combined with all other colours. However, some feng shui consultants like to use white which is similar to silver (an ancient Chinese money token) to represent metal.

Avoid matching together the colours in the destructive cycle. For example, you should not put red (fire) and blue (water) next to each other. Similarly, if your birth element is fire you should not paint your room blue. On the other hand, you may use the same colour as your birth element to strengthen it (water-blue).

A person belonging to the earth element, for example, has the following possibilities: They can select the colours of their element such as beige or yellow. Alternatively, they would be strengthened by the fire element which produces earth in the productive cycle. Thus pink or light red may also be used for walls, carpets and furniture.

Positive Colours for the Elements

Wood element – green, blue
Fire element   – red, pink, purple, violet, maroon, green
Earth element – brown, beige, yellow, orange, red
Metal element – gold, silver, brown, beige, yellow, orange
Water element – blue, gold, silver

Colour Conflicts

We should avoid colours that are in conflict with our birth year element according to the destructive cycle.

Blue, for example, is calming and is a good colour for hyperactive children. But care should be exercised to ensure that the child occupying a blue coloured room is not a fire element person. Otherwise, the child could become nervous and aggressive due to the elemental conflict.

When colours are used which are in conflict with each other, they should not be placed immediately next to each other. You may select another supporting and harmonising colour from the productive cycle and place it between the conflicting colours to reduce the conflict and avoid a drain of energy.

If you have a carpet in a colour not in harmony with your birth year element, you can put another small carpet in a colour which strengthens you, under the chair or bed to protect yourself from the conflict.

For example, a metal element person will not feel good with a big red carpet in the room (fire melts metal). They can use a small beige carpet as a remedy (earth nourishes metal and is not in conflict with fire).

Negative Colours for the Elements

Wood element – gold, silver
Fire element   – blue
Earth element – green
Metal element – red, purple, violet, pink, maroon
Water element – brown, beige, yellow, orange

Chapter 9

FENG SHUI MEASUREMENTS AND NUMEROLOGY

Developments in nature like plants and animals evolved through a specific harmonic matrix within nature's harmonic measurements.

Plants exist in accordance with a certain matrix, that is, a certain leaf shape and a certain number of petals in each flower. Interestingly, the number of petals in each flower corresponds to the numbers 3, 5, 8, 13, 21, 34, 55 and 89. This progression of numbers is obtained by adding the first two numbers and subsequent last two numbers together according to their evolution:

$$1 + 2 = 3 \qquad 8 + 13 = 21$$
$$2 + 3 = 5 \qquad 13 + 21 = 34$$
$$3 + 5 = 8 \qquad 21 + 34 = 55$$
$$5 + 8 = 13 \qquad 34 + 55 = 89$$

A marigold flower has 13 petals while daisies have 34, 55 or 89, depending on the species.

These numbers and measurements of nature are known as 'feng shui harmonic measurements'. Some people strongly believe that they represent the ideal human harmonic DNA matrix measurements.

Feng Shui Ruler Applications

The use of feng shui measurements was first mentioned during the Sung dynasty (A.D. 960–1128). The imperial carpenter used these measurements to build furniture, windows and doors for the imperial palace.

The special markings on the feng shui ruler specified the auspicious and inauspicious dimensions for two types of dwellings – yang dwellings (homes for the living) and yin dwellings (homes for the dead, that is, coffins and grave sites). On a feng shui ruler or measuring tape, the top markings are for yang dwellings.

What is presented here are the markings and dimensions for use in yang dwellings.

For yang dwellings, there are eight sections in the feng shui measuring ruler. Four of these are generally auspicious; the other four are inauspicious.

The ruler measures the equivalent of 16 15/16 in or 42.96 cm, which is then divided into eight sections (adding the numbers in 42.96 together, we obtain 4+2+9+6=21=3, meaning 'alive and continuous living' in accordance with the living matrix, the symbol of life in all living cells, including humans). The sections are divided further into four subsections, each measuring 0.525 inch or 1.34 cm. They also have specific meanings (see the table on main sections and subsections and their meanings). 42.96 is actually the factor of the girth of the planet earth. This factor affects all living beings on earth.

The positive sections are: the first called 'chai' (wealth), the fourth section 'yi' (noble), the fifth section 'kuan' (official power) and the eighth section 'pen' (capital).

The inauspicious measurements are in the second, third, sixth and seventh sections and are called 'ping' (sickness), 'li' (separation), 'chieh' (catastrophe) and 'hai' (harm and injury) respectively.

Note that measurements in the metric system are more accurate than the imperial system for measuring long lengths.

After the eighth section, the whole length of the eight sections repeats again. For measuring long lengths, place the ruler along the length and then take the remaining section where the measurement ends. You can measure more easily and precisely using a special 5 m (16.5 ft) feng shui measuring tape. You may also make your own ruler from cardboard or paper, or mark the sections on an ordinary measuring tape.

The Chinese Feng Shui Divination Ruler

A summary of the meanings of the Chinese feng shui divination ruler is listed below:

Section 1
0 – 5.37 cm (0 – 2 2/16 in)

CHAI – Wealth
Subsections
a) Fortune comes
b) Plenty of resources
c) Six harmony and luck
d) Abundant prosperity

Section 2
5.38 – 10.74 cm (2 2/16 – 4 4/16 in)

PING – Sickness
Subsections
a) Loss of fortune
b) Bad encounter with public service
c) Severe enforcement of laws imprisonment
d) Orphan, widow or widower

Section 3
10.75 – 16.11 cm (4 4/16 – 6 6/16 in)

LI – Separation
Subsections
a) Denial of wealth
b) Money lost
c) Cheated of wealth
c) Loss of everything

Section 4
16.12 – 21.48 cm (6 6/16 – 8 8/16 in)

YI – Nobleness and Integrity
Subsections
a) Gain descendants
b) Profitable income
c) Talented offspring
d) Very lucky and prosperous

Section 5
21.49 – 26.85 cm (8 8/16 – 10 10/16 in)

KUAN – Official Power
Subsections
a) Plenty of food
b) Side income and lottery
c) Improved income
d) Rich and noble

Section 6
26.86 – 32.22 cm (10 10/16 – 12 11/16 in)

CHIEH – Catastrophe
Subsections
a) Death and departure
b) Loss of descendants
c) Forced to leave ancestral home or loss of job
d) Loss of money

Section 7
32.23 – 37.59 cm (12 11/16 – 14 13/16 in)

HAI – Harm and Injury
Subsections
a) Disasters and calamities
b) Possible death
c) Attracts sickness
d) Litigation and quarrels

Section 8
37.60 – 42.96 cm (14 13/16 – 16 15/16 in)

PEN – Source or Capital
Subsections
a) Wealth comes
b) Plenty of promotions in job
c) Arrival of plenty of wealth
d) Everything turns into plenty

Human Visual Perception

Ever wonder why you like a particular picture or a person? Their dimensions or matrix have a lot to do with this first impression.

When we look at a person or an object, we focus our sight first on the outline of the person or object.

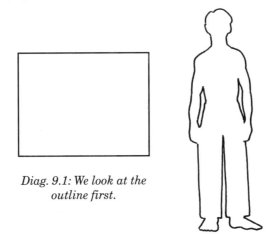

Diag. 9.1: We look at the outline first.

Next, we focus our sight on the most prominent features of the person or object.

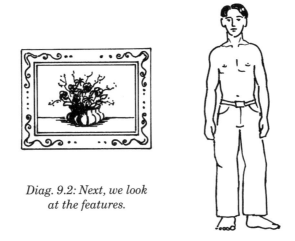

Diag. 9.2: Next, we look at the features.

If you find your body height measurement to be negative, you can neutralise it by wearing high heels, a hat or 'high hair' to get into the next positive measurement. Give it a try and see whether you feel better with this new size and are able to find a new partner more easily.

In feng shui, however, we check mainly the measurements of doors, windows, beds and other furniture.

Measurements of Windows, Furniture and Doors

The dimensions of forms or objects we see affect us immediately, either positively or negatively. These forms or objects are symbols that are continuously in our line of sight when we sit, say, in front of a window looking at the window panels. The dimensions of the window panels affect us. Sitting in front of a window with inauspicious measurements makes our immune system weak. As we sit, work or eat at a table, we are weakened by the negative dimensions of the table. Working at an inauspicious table causes problems in concentration. You are then more prone to making mistakes. Eating at a dining table with inauspicious dimensions may cause you to have digestion problems.

Windows

Take three measurements of the window – frame, glass and the inside measurement when the window is open.

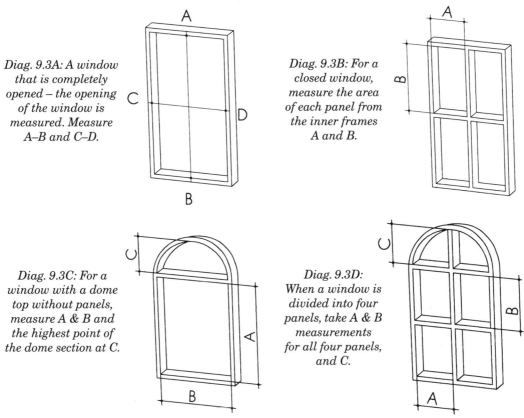

Diag. 9.3A: A window that is completely opened – the opening of the window is measured. Measure A–B and C–D.

Diag. 9.3B: For a closed window, measure the area of each panel from the inner frames A and B.

Diag. 9.3C: For a window with a dome top without panels, measure A & B and the highest point of the dome section at C.

Diag. 9.3D: When a window is divided into four panels, take A & B measurements for all four panels, and C.

Remedies for Inauspicious Window Measurements

Example: the width of the window in Diag. 9.3E is 49 cm and comes under 'ping' (sickness) in the main section and under the 'loss of wealth' subsection. Its height is 115 cm which comes under the main section 'chieh' (catastrophe) and subsection 'loss of descendants'.

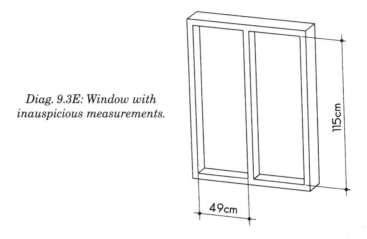

Diag. 9.3E: Window with inauspicious measurements.

When you encounter an inauspicious feng shui measurement for a window, you do not have to change all your house windows. Remember the saying, the best solutions are the simplest solutions and the easiest to arrange.

By placing a 1-cm coloured strip along the width of the window to reduce the measurement to 48 cm, the new measurement of 48 cm comes under main section 'chai' (wealth) and subsection 'fortune comes'. Similarly, we can reduce the height by 3 cm by putting one-and-a-half cm coloured strips at the top and bottom of the window. Now the main section comes under 'kuan' (power and wealth) and subsection is 'rich and noble'.

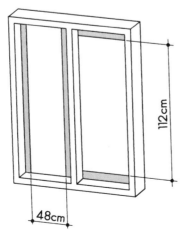

Diag. 9.3F: Remedy for inauspicious window measurements – change measurements using strips.

Tables

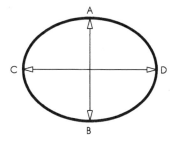

Diag. 9.4A: All round tables or objects – measure diameter (A–B).

Diag. 9.4B: Oval tables – measure the longest (C–D) and widest (A–B) points.

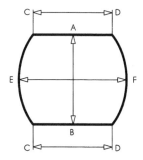

Diag. 9.4C: Table with rounded sides. Measure A–B, C–D and E–F.

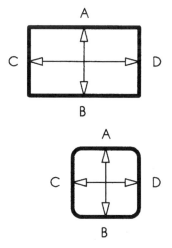

Diag. 9.4D: Square and rectangular tables. Measure length (C–D) and width (A–B).

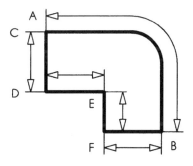

Diag. 9.4E: Table with rounded corners. Measure A–B, C–D, D–E, E–F and F–B.

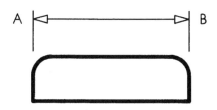

Diag. 9.4F: Tabletop with curved edges on one side. Measure the widest distance A–B.

Coloured strips

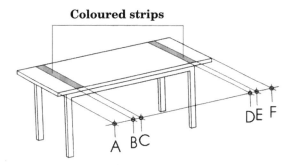

Diag. 9.4G: When a table has an inauspicious width or length, it can be remedied by putting a strip of coloured tape of a different colour to break up the inauspicious measurement. In this case, two strips are put on either side of the table. Now the new lengths of the table are measured as A–B, C–D and E–F instead of just the complete length. Ensure that A–B, C–D and E–F are auspicious measurements.

Some Auspicious Table Measurements:

Length	Width	Height
88 cm	65 cm	69 cm
112 cm	69 cm	81 cm
132 cm	82 cm	
155 cm	89 cm	
193 cm	89 cm	
198 cm	89 cm	
215 cm	107 cm	

Note: The height of a table is usually not so important. Any of the lengths can combine with any of the heights and widths.

Doors

Our doors are our mouth. The dimensions of a door represent a symbol for qi to enter a house. When the measurements of a door are inauspicious according to nature's auspicious matrix or geometry, the door symbol vibrates a negative energy, attacking those who pass through it.

My wife and I have performed experiments on the effects of door measurements in more than 30 countries. We found that not only Chinese but also people of all other nationalities were equally affected by the feng shui measurements.

When the dimensions of a door did not conform with good feng shui measurements, a person's body became weak. As they entered the door, their whole body's electrical circuits, triggered by the response of their immune system, became weak. It was as if their body was under attack by some invisible forces.

A door with inauspicious measurements can cause the immune system of a person walking through it to become weak for 30 minutes to several hours. I found that where there were sudden mood changes as people entered their own house, the changes were due to inauspicious measurements at the doorway in most cases.

I once gave a feng shui consultation for a company which carried out almost all my recommended feng shui remedies, and the business continued to prosper. But the company had a great deal of problems with staff harmony.

The company had five doors frequently used by most staff. All had inauspicious measurements, especially the heights which were in the disharmony measurement called 'disharmony forcing to leave village'. This can be interpreted to mean disharmony in the company, which was actually the case. One of my original recommendations was that all the door measurements should be changed, but it was overlooked for one and a half years. Eventually, all the door measurements were changed into auspicious measurements, especially the height to 192 cm under 'tar cheh', meaning 'very lucky and prosperous', and the staff's rivalry disappeared.

How to Determine Door Dimensions

The feng shui dimensions of a door are the inside measurements of the opening or the hole. Usually the measurements of the opening are smaller than the actual door itself. For a double door, if only one wing is opened, the opening wing measurements are the most important. Ideally, all measurements should be positive.

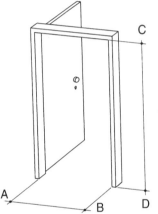

Diag. 9.5A: Measure A–B and C–D.

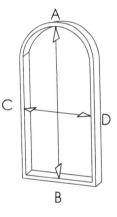

Diag. 9.5B: First measure A–B, then C–D.

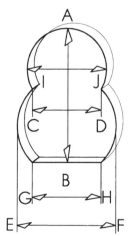

Diag. 9.5C: Measure A–B, I–J, C–D, E–F and G–H.

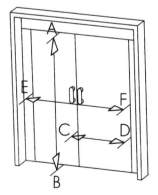

Diag. 9.5D: For a door that opens from both sides, measure each side (for example, A–B and C–D) and then measure both doors E–F together.

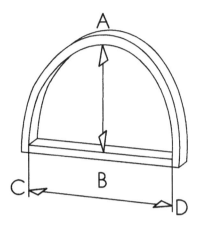

Height	Width
192 cm	63 cm
198 cm	69 cm
210 cm	82 cm
218 cm	89 cm
236 cm	107 cm
	112 cm
	132 cm
	150 cm
	172 cm
	175 cm

Diag. 9.5E: Measure A–B and C–D. Curved door measurements are made on the highest curved point A–B and the base C–D.

Beds

Having the correct measurement for a bed is very important because we spend about a third of our lives in bed. If your bed's measurements are inauspicious, it can affect your sleep negatively. Many people around the world do not sleep well or have bad dreams. Often, the main cause is the inauspicious feng shui measurements of their beds. Many beds in Europe and America have measurements similar to that of a coffin. Imagine a person sleeping in a coffin – the human psyche is under tremendous stress!

It is also common in the West to use 2 m (6.5 ft) as the length of a bed. The 2 m measurement is 'losing descendants or no children'. Sleeping on a 2 m bed is one major reason why many couples lack fertility.

The most important bed measurements are that for the length of the area where a mattress is inserted (A–B in Diag. 9.6) and the width (E–F) of the bed. We can also check on the total measurements of the bed, including the outer measurement (C–D). The height of the bed is the least important.

The best bed measurements are listed in Table 2. You may also choose any other auspicious measurement for length, width and height.

If you have a bed with inauspicious measurements, you can put panels of wood inside the bed frame to reduce the inner frame measurements to positive measurements.

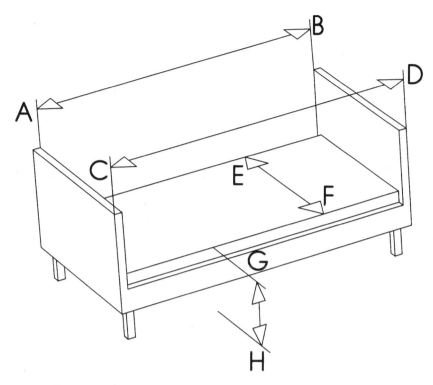

Diag. 9.6: If possible, all bed measurements should be positive.

Measurement in cm	Single Bed		Double Bed		Child's Bed	
Inner Length	198		198		103	– 112
of Bedframe (A–B)	210	– 219	210	– 219	125	– 132
Total Length	210	– 219	210	– 219	107	– 112
of Bed (C–D)	232	– 236	232	– 236	128	– 134
Width of Bed (E–F)	82	– 90	167	– 176	60	– 69
	103	– 112	189	– 198	80	– 90
Height of Bed	38	– 48	38	– 48	22	– 25
With Mattress (G–H)	60	– 69	60	– 69	38	– 48

Table 2: Most favourable bed measurements.

Ideal European Measurements (Golden Cuts)

The Chinese feng shui measurements were derived from complex mathematical calculations based on the matrix of harmony in nature. They are, however, different from the Western law of perception of the 'good shapes' or 'golden cuts'.

Many European students have asked me whether there is a connection between the European and Chinese measurements. They carried out experiments using applied kinesiology and found that there is no connection and that the European measurements are not necessarily auspicious.

Let us take the A4-size paper as an example. It has bad measurements and represents a bad symbol. Its length (29.7 cm) means 'loss of descendants' in feng shui. But fortunately, the width of 21 cm is 'tah cheh', meaning 'very lucky and prosperous'. However, this auspicious width cannot neutralise the very negative length. If the length is changed to 26.5 cm, it comes under the main section 'rich and noble' and the subsection 'great prosperity and abundance'. This would make the A4-size paper used in the developed countries more auspicious. Perhaps it is time we changed the dimensions of A4 to make it more harmonious.

Numerology in Daily Life

The Chinese are affected by numbers, both by the written form, whether they are written in Chinese numerals or the common Arabic numerals, and by the pronunciation of each number, based on a Chinese dialect. Examples are listed here:

Chinese number	Arabic number	Chinese number and pronunciation	Implied Meaning
一	1	Yii (Mandarin) Yat (Cantonese)	Raining Daily
二	2	Er (Mandarin) Yee (Cantonese)	Ear Easy
三	3	Sheng (Mandarin) Sang (Cantonese)	Alive Alive
四	4	Sher (Mandarin) Sei (Cantonese)	Death Death
五	5	Wu (Mandarin) Ngg (Cantonese)	Nothingness Completion
六	6	Lieu (Mandarin) Luk (Cantonese)	Moving around Rolling on or green
七	7	Cheh (Mandarin) Shat (Cantonese)	To go ahead Sure
八	8	Faat (Mandarin) Pat (Cantonese)	Prosper Prosper
九	9	Jeu (Mandarin) Kau (Cantonese)	Long or Longevity Long or Longevity
十	10	Ssher (Mandarin) Sap (Cantonese)	Rock or strong Sure

Table 3: Chinese numbers and implied meanings.

When the numbers have similar meanings or inference in Mandarin (spoken by 1.3 billion Chinese) and in Cantonese (spoken by about 400 million Chinese), the effects become more pronounced – for example, 3, 4, 6, 7, 8, 9 or 10.

Some Special Meanings for Numerals

1 is a spiritual number meaning 'with god' or 'with oneself'. It is a lonely number which is sometimes associated with authoritarian rule.

2 is a pair of 1s – a positive number. The Chinese like everything in a pair. It is a symbol of unity and mutual trust. It is a good number that also infers 'easy'.

3 with three strokes or three persons can mean father, mother and child, symbolising posterity. 3 is a positive number meaning 'alive' and 'continuation'.

4 is a negative number. The Chinese numeral is a rectangle enclosing two things or persons. This means a couple without children, thus implying death to their posterity.

My wife and I have done experiments with people of more than 30 nationalities. We found that when we asked them to say 4 in their native language, their body's electromagnetic fields shrank immediately, and all their body joints became weak as a result of the response of their immune system.

Some combinations of numbers with 4 are also negative for Asians:

24	–	easy to die
64	–	six deaths or continuing death
74	–	sure to die
84	–	prosper and then die
94	–	longer-term death
744	–	sure to die and die

To minimise and neutralise the negative effects of 4 and other combinations of numbers with 4, put a circle round the whole number. A red circle is even more effective – it represents the fire surrounding and burning the negative energy of 4. For example, ④ ⑷⑷⑷

In my consultations, I have also found that in business, when 4 appears at the beginning and or at the end of a telephone number (for example, 465324 or 432614), a business can lose customers. Experiments carried out in New Zealand, Singapore, Australia and Germany have confirmed that when two telephone numbers were listed – 42 13 74 on top and 60 18 15 below – customers used the second, more positive telephone number without 4 more frequently. Telephone numbers beginning with 4 or ending with 4 are avoided by many intuitive people. In an area with telephone numbers commencing with 44, business volume tends to suffer over the longer term.

When a telephone number commences with 4, its negative effect can be lessened by an 8 at the end – for example, 43 65 78.

Those born on the 4th should not be unduly worried because we must include the complete birth date, that is, time of birth, day, month and year, when making calculations on a person's life.

5 represents the five elemental universal energies which everything in this universe must belong to. It can also represent a void in the Eight Trigram feng shui practice. Some feng shui schools do not like 5 because they regard 5 as a void which is associated with bad spirits. It is actually a neutral number which represents all aspects of things we can all use without any negative effects.

6 in Cantonese infers 'rolling on' or 'green'. Someone rolling on, like a rolling stone, gathers no moss and thus no wealth. Some superstitious Chinese do not like 6, which when pronounced as 'green', infers that a partner is wearing a 'green hat', that is, being unfaithful. The number 6, however, is also positive as it is widely regarded as a spiritual number.

7 for the Chinese has the meaning 'very sure'. It can be good or bad depending on which number follows. 74 is 'sure dead', but 78 is 'sure prosperous'. 789 is 'sure prosperous forever'. 7 is a number favoured by Christians as a holy number. God created everything and then rested on the 7th day.

8 is the symbol of infinity. It is also a symbol found in the cells of all living creatures and plants. You can trace along the whole 8 and never get out. For 5,000 years, Taoists have assigned 8 as the symbol for harmony and wealth. It is also the coming Aquarian Age's symbol of harmony, unity, peace, prosperity and fun. It is a very positive number. The Aquarian Age starts in the year 2008 when females will take over the power on earth and replace the 'men's society'. This process has already begun, and we are now seeing more and more women in key positions as prime ministers and leaders in parliament and holding top positions in large corporations.

When a house has design problems, the Qi-Mag International Feng Shui and Geobiology Institute suggests using a double eight (88) as a remedy to overcome problems in balance and harmony. This handy symbol really works. Everybody can try it by placing the 88 symbol (preferably in the colour of your birth year element – for example, in red, green or blue) on the wall inside of your door entrance or in the foyer, so that you can see it when you enter your house.

The best measurements for the double 8 are 21 cm for the width of each circle and 42 cm for the height of an 8, as shown in Diag. 9.7. You may also use 8 in other sizes and dimensions and function well, but the best is the auspicious measurement of 21 cm x 42 cm.

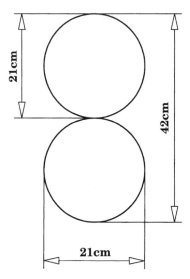

Diag. 9.7: Auspicious measurements for the 8.

Los Angeles's San Gabriel Valley, where many Chinese live, is one of the most prosperous areas in the United States. Many Chinese and Asians living and working in this valley attribute their wealth and success to the auspicious 818 telephone area code. In Chinese, 818 sounds like 'prosper and prosper'. Many Asian families moved to this area because of this 818 area code.

In 1996, the Pacific Bell Company announced that they would be changing the area code to 616. Most residents were angered by the announcement. 616 sounds like 'rolling on and on', gathering nothing in the end and lacking in prosperity. Just like a rolling stone that gathers no moss or wealth. Many residents and even the city council started legal proceedings against the telephone company.

9 is the perpetuity or longevity number. 99999 is infinity. The Chinese like 9 because it infers longevity.

10 represents completion. 10 is a pair of 5s or five pairs of 2s. It is an auspicious number.

11 When we add 1+1 we get 2. 11 thus represents harmony and a good relationship.

12 is 1+2=3, meaning 'alive', and is an auspicious number for both the Chinese and the Western world. Jesus Christ selected 12 disciples so that his teachings could be perpetuated and kept alive forever.

13 is 1+3=4, an unlucky number for many. It can be neutralised like the 4 by putting a red circle around it. But those with birth dates on the 13th are generally very spiritual and highly intuitive people.

古今

術

卜卦

Chapter 10

DIVINATION TECHNIQUES TO MEASURE FENG SHUI

European geomancy experts use the pendulum, dowsing stick and divination rod as divination techniques to check for underground water, harmful earth rays and harmful earth grids like Hartmann lines and Curry lines. The pendulum as a divination technique was invented by the ancient Arabs to find water in the desert and has a history of at least 5,000 years.

The pendulum and the dowsing stick can be used to carry out all types of divination in our daily life. These divination techniques can also be used to check feng shui problems and to assess the appropriateness and extent of remedies to be carried out. However, these techniques take slightly longer to learn and the right procedure has to be followed to ensure their accuracy.

In this book, a simple technique called applied kinesiology will be described in detail for readers to apply.

Applied kinesiology was first discovered in the 1960s by Dr. George Goodheart (USA) and Dr. John Diamond (Australia). It is also known as the muscle biofeedback test.

It works based on the response of the human immune system and energy meridians. Many of my readers will be familiar with the 'body electrical circuits', well known in the practice of acupuncture, where qi flows. A person responds to different negative and positive conditions and emotions in their environment. The common testing medium is a set of body muscles. This can be explained as follows:

When a person is confronted by positive environmental conditions and the respective emotions, the immune system is strong and the energy can move smoothly in the body's meridians. In these favourable conditions, all the electrical circuits in the body are 'connected', resulting in all the body's muscles and joints working in unison – this makes them very strong. We can carry out a muscle test on any part of an outstretched arm or leg, and it will remain strong even under extreme pressure when a positive thought or situation exists.

In the reverse negative conditions, when a person is confronted with something negative, the immune system immediately becomes weak. At the same time, all the meridians, especially the central energy meridian at the front and the governing meridian at the back of the body, become weak in their pulsations. The result is that the whole body's muscles, tendons and joints lose their strength. A muscle test on, say, the forearm using the deltoid muscle on the shoulder joint, gives a weak response when applying a downward pressure.

The police lie detector machine works on a similar principle. When a person tells a lie their immune system becomes weak, causing a change in the electric circuits which are then recorded on the graph of the machine.

This response to environmental conditions is the human survival mechanism. During the primitive stage of evolution, when humans saw a large and fierce animal, fear overcame them and their whole body's electrical circuits slowed down. The weakening of the muscles and tendons meant that they could not run and so they had to hide for their own safety. If their muscles and tendons had remained strong, they would have tried to run and would have been caught and eaten by the fierce animals.

If we understand this principle, we can use applied kinesiology to check how we are affected in our daily lives and then find the answers to resolve the issues.

Applied kinesiology is a scientifically accepted neurobiological method that is also used by many medical physicians, healing practitioners and therapists in the West. They use applied kinesiology to check which remedy is most suitable for a treatment. With this tailor-made method, side effects from 'trying out' several drugs can be avoided. Dentists, for example, use applied kinesiology to test whether a person is affected by amalgam or mercury toxicity. It is also used to test which dental filling composite is most suitable for individuals to avoid any side effects.

Nutritionists use kinesiology to test a person's nutritional deficiencies to offer the most balanced and appropriate nutrients.

In feng shui practice, we apply kinesiology to check on the extent of the problems and confirm recommendations made to a client. We can also check:

• the energy and oxygen level in a room or workplace

• the level of toxicity and pollutants and what allergens are present in a room

- if the position of a bed or a place of work is affected by geopathic stress or other harmful rays

- the best orientation for a house for a family

- the correct type of remedies and the size and location for each remedy

- whether it is in harmony for a family to continue to live in a particular house

- when is a good time and date to move into a house or when to commence construction work on a house

- whether a house is haunted by spirits

- whether a town or city is in harmony with a person or a family, and so on.

Applied kinesiology provides endless possibilities to find answers to difficult questions in feng shui and other issues in daily life. To ensure accuracy, the right procedure must be applied. Like everything else in life, the more we use this technique, the more familiar we become with it, and the more we are guided by our intuition to apply it correctly.

How to Use Applied Kinesiology

Applied kinesiology can be used by any person, irrespective of age or educational background, or even whether the person believes in it or not. It still works. Five factors are important to ensure its accuracy:

1) The person doing the testing (tester) and the person being tested must be neutral, with no preconceived idea or judgement that could influence the result. If, for example, they strongly believe that the result should be negative, then the result will be negative. Both tester and the person being tested can mentally influence the result.

2) The person being tested must not be dehydrated. Drinking a glass of water would ensure that the body's electrical circuits can function properly and are ready for the test.

3) The person being tested must be emotionally balanced and not standing over a geopathic stress line caused by underground water or be within 1.5 m (5 ft) of electrical equipment or electrical sockets or switches that radiate harmful electromagnetic rays.

4) The person being tested must be ready and willing to cooperate in the test.

5) The procedure to do the test must be correct.

The Procedure for the Muscle Test

1) Remove all metal and jewellery like watches, rings and necklaces from the body of the tested person to avoid causing electromagnetic disturbances.

2) The tested person drinks a glass of cool or lukewarm water and must be relaxed and calm.

3) The tested person breathes normally and puts their tongue behind their upper teeth, resting on the upper palate, to connect the lower body and upper body's circuits.

4) The tested person and tester must be in a positive mood and should be mentally neutral without any negative thoughts or preconceived ideas about the result or outcome.

5) The tested person should be standing and in comfortable clothes. The place should be well lit, but not glaring.

6) The tested person simultaneously uses the fingers of the left hand to rub horizontally above and below their lips, and the fingers of the right hand to rub the navel area (alarm points of the central and the governing meridian) in a circular movement at least six times.

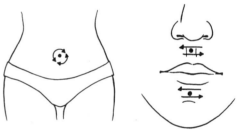

Diag. 10.1A: Points rubbed before the kinesiology test.

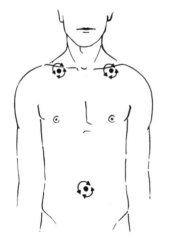

Diag. 10.1B: Navel and kidney points.

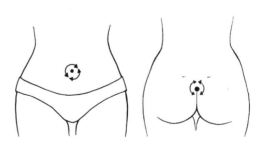

Diag. 10.1C: Navel and tail bone areas.

Next, rub the navel area and the kidney points just below the collar bone.

Then, use the fingers of both hands to simultaneously rub the navel and the tail bone in least six circular movements to connect the lower body circuits.

Massage each area with the right and then with the left hand. Change and massage again.

7) The tested person breathes slowly and deeply down to the feet at least six times to connect all body circuits and to ground the body.

8) The tested person stretches out the left arm parallel to the shoulder joint. It is also possible to test the right hand. If tester is shorter than the tested person, the hand can be adjusted lower.

9) If the right arm is tested, the tester puts their right palm on the tested person's left shoulder, and left palm on the tested person's right forearm, just above the wrist, as indicated in Diag. 10.2.

Diag. 10.2: Starting position for testing.

10) The tester gives the tested person a warning, 'Hold', to indicate that they are ready to carry out the test. The tested person immediately responds by holding their arm and hand firm in the same position when pressure is applied by the tester. If the tested person's arm can be easily pressed downwards, we have a 'negative' reaction meaning 'no'.

If the arm muscle tests strong, this means 'positive' response or 'yes'.

11) First, test whether the tested person is in balance by checking their positive and negative response.

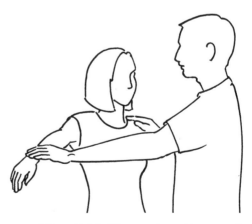

Diag. 10.3A: The arm is easily pressed downwards – 'negative' or weak response.

12) The tester thinks of something positive about the tested person (for example, you are a nice, happy person). Immediately he says 'Hold', counts two counts (to give sufficient time for the tested person to respond) and then applies light pressure on their palm on tested person's arm. The arm should be firm and strong. If the tested person's arm becomes weak on applying pressure, then the person is not in balance or not ready for the test. Or they may be standing over an area affected by an underground geopathic stress line

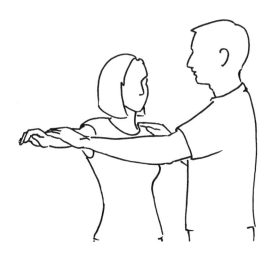

Diag. 10.3B: The arm can hardly be pressed downwards – the person tests strong.

caused by underground running water, a volcanic fault line or other negative environmental factors. Move the person to another location and do the test again. If they still become weak then repeat steps 4 to 12 again.

13) The tester thinks of something negative about the tested person. Again they say 'Hold' to give warning, count two counts and apply light pressure with their palm on the tested person's arm. The arm should become weak when pressure is applied.

14) When the tested person's positive response is strong and negative response is weak, this means that they are balanced and ready for a set of applied kinesiology muscle tests.

15) For applied kinesiology practice, you can only ask a straightforward question which requires a 'yes' or 'no' answer, just like the function of our binary mind.

Practical Example

Let us test whether a person is in harmony with the orientation of their main door.

The tester either verbally or mentally (mentally is preferred because the tested person may like the direction that the door of their house faces) asks whether the tested person is in harmony with the position of the main door. The tester says 'Hold', counts two counts and applies pressure on the left hand of the person being tested. If their arm remains strong and firm, then the answer is YES. If their arm suddenly becomes weak, then the main door is not in harmony with the person.

The questions you ask can only be answered by 'yes' or 'no' and can determine:
a)   remedies to carry out, if any
b)   the best place or compass direction to open the door.

When a house is occupied by a couple, it is best to confirm the result with both partners to ensure all-round accuracy that suits both of them. Alternatively, you can test only one partner and ask, for example, the following question: Is South the best direction for you and your partner? Check each compass direction until you confirm the best direction.

However, it is always best to ask the question mentally as the tested person may consciously or unconsciously influence the result with their own preferences.

The technique of applied kinesiology is simple to learn and to apply. It makes the practice of feng shui much easier and the professional practice of feng shui much more accurate and quantifiable. Instead of just accepting that your house's feng shui is now 'good' following a feng shui consultation, you should ask the consultant, 'How good?'

For example, you can ask, 'What was the percentage of cosmic qi for my house before and now?' The answer could be, 'Before it was 40%, but now after carrying out all the suggested remedies, it is 80%.'

::: Chapter 11 :::

ENVIRONMENTAL FACTORS – POSITIVE AND NEGATIVE ASPECTS

Every time humans come up with a new technology or an ultramodern building design, the side effects of these technologies or designs on humans, animals and the environment are seldom taken into consideration.

For example, the many transmission and relay stations for mobile phones are causing mental imbalance and health problems to their communities where they are located. The microwave and radiowave rays that are being constantly generated are affecting the psychic and mental wellbeing of humans and animals. These technological hazards are very important factors to consider in feng shui practice. After all, what is the point of designing a perfect feng shui house when your immediate environment is not conducive to healthy and harmonious living? The practice of feng shui enables us to detect (and provide remedies) or avoid home sites with these negative facilities.

In this chapter, I will describe 19 types of environmental energies that we often encounter in our environment. These factors are listed and explained to create an awareness of their effects.

A question that is often asked is, 'Which of these energies are more important in feng shui practice?' The answer is, those that are immediately life threatening, followed by health hazards affecting our emotional, mental and physical wellbeing.

When an environment is not conducive to us, we just cannot perform well under such stressful conditions and therefore cannot be successful.

Each of the listed energies has either a positive or negative effect on a person, depending on its unique quality and frequency.

Remember that all energy in this universe can be positive or negative! It always depends on how the energy is used. Negative energy can be harnessed for positive application. For example, the negative energy of a torrential waterfall can be harnessed to move a turbine and produce electrical power.

The Most Common Environmental Factors

When carrying out a feng shui investigation we normally consider the environmental factors and weigh their effects on us. Below are the most common environmental factors to observe.

1) Sound
2) Smell
3) Earth rays and cosmic rays
4) Wind
5) Water
6) Dust and environmental toxins
7) Shapes and symbols
8) Yin and yang principle
9) Astrological and cosmological influences
10) Five elemental energies
11) Colours
12) Lights
13) Radioactive rays
14) Radio and microwave rays
15) Electromagnetic rays
16) Shia qi and shah qi
17) Plants and trees
18) Overpowering room energy
19) Computer & TV screen waves

1) Sound

Positive Types – Sounds of soft running water, birds and insects singing in soft rhythmic tones and soft harmonic music like classical music are relaxing and soothing to hear and enhance the body healing process.

Positive sounds are used for healing purposes, including the treatment of cancer, by many health therapists. Soft, soothing harmonic music can put a person into an alpha state to facilitate the body's self-healing process and also enhance intuition for making good decisions.

Negative Types – Loud, sharp-pitched music, on the other hand, affects the hearing, the kidneys and the heart, causing health and balance problems and a shorter life span. Pop stars tend to suffer more from depression. Other examples of negative sounds are sharp noises made by certain types of insects, the ringing of a telephone, the sound of building construction equipment, the sound of vibrators, heavy traffic noise, screams of children, noise from passing trains and aeroplanes, and explosions.

We found that people working or living near loud, noisy factories had a higher incidence of irritation, fear, depression and heart, hearing and kidney problems.

In feng shui practice, we avoid areas where negative sounds are generated; many countries today have noise pollution standards. Often, almost inaudible soft music can be used to counter negative, noisy sounds (see Diag. 11.1).

Loud   **Soft, gentle music**

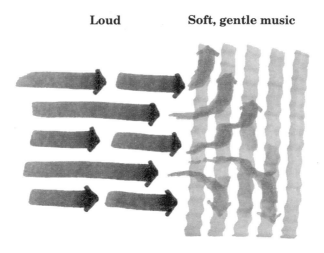

Diag. 11.1: Soft music frequencies counter loud noises.

2) Smell

Positive Types – Sweet smelling flowers, natural perfume, the sweet smell of spring breezes, the aroma of good food and the rich smell of naturally ripened fruits.

The perfume of flowers and plants is uplifting and energising. The smell of good food, for example, from a nearby bakery or restaurant, stimulates the appetite.

Negative Types – The smell of sewage water, sulphur or ammonia, car fumes, animal manure, rotten meat and garbage.

Bad smells from rotten materials and sewage are created by bacteria and germs that are harmful to our health. When we encounter offensive smells, our breathing tend to become shallower, thereby restricting the inhalation of fresh air, qi and oxygen. This reduces the vitality of the heart, lungs, blood circulation and sinuses, causing a general lack of vitality.

In feng shui practice, we locate home sites where there is plenty of fresh air and where the air is not subject to any bad or unpleasant smells. Care is taken to avoid living near a sewage recycling centre or near factories that produce bad smells. The aroma of oil burning in water or an oil lamp is a good remedy to counter a persistent bad smell.

3) Earth Rays and Cosmic Rays

Positive Types – Most old churches were built on land with very high earth energy. Generally, this type of land has 100–200% qi.

This high earth energy may be generated by natural underground quartz and amethyst and is generally very positive.

The holy city of Lourdes in southern France, for example, has earth energy of 150–200%. I estimate that the energy of the spring water which comes out near the statue of Mary is over 300%. The spring water is known worldwide to have excellent healing powers. Japanese researchers have found that this water contains a very high concentration of germanium which facilitates oxygen assimilation in the body.

Geopathic earth rays generated by underground water with a stress factor of less than 2% are invigorating and enhance the human body's electrical energy.

Negative Types – Many types of energies and rays are generated from the ground, depending on the types of minerals and materials under the earth. The most dangerous rays are caused by underground running water. These rays are harmful to health if their stress factor exceeds 3%. Such stress lines are usually around 1–1.5 m (3.3–5 ft) wide. Geopathic stress is the main cause of cancer, chronic health problems and degenerative diseases.

Although some lines are positive, most are very negative. They cause health problems and disturb a sound sleep. The rays from Curry and Hartmann lines are less dangerous because their crossing points cover small areas that can be easily avoided.

Some earth rays are very negative when their energy is generated by rotten, swampy vegetation. Some underground minerals, like uranium which generates radioactive rays, are harmful to human health. Land with uranium deposits is not suitable for human settlement. In feng shui, we identify where negative earth rays like geopathic stress are and either avoid or neutralise them so that the house occupants are not affected. We also identify the types of rays, for example, Hartmann or Curry lines, and warn occupants of their presence in relation to where they sleep or work. The best feng shui remedies or even a well-designed house are pointless if the occupants are sleeping or sitting over these highly dangerous rays.

4) Wind

Positive Types – A softly blowing cool breeze is invigorating and uplifting because it brings fresh air, qi and oxygen. This type of wind can be identified when the leaves of plants and trees move about one cm (0.4 in) to and fro. It cleanses our aura (body electromagnetic field), and yet does not cause anxiety or any disturbance to our aura.

Negative Types – Very cold, hot or strong winds are negative. Strong winds are when the leaves and branches of trees move at least 6 cm (2.5 in) violently to and fro. Very strong cold and hot winds can cause colds, influenza and lung-related health problems. A strong wind usually causes balance problems and anxiety. It also causes wrinkles and eye problems. Strong winds are common along coasts that have high waves suitable for surfing.

In feng shui practice, we avoid sites that are constantly affected by negative strong, cold or hot winds, or design houses with special protective features like a trellis, wind breakers or high walls to protect house occupants.

5) Water

Positive Types – Slow-moving water flowing not faster than 1 m (3.3 ft) every 6–8 seconds against rocks is very invigorating and energising. When water moves against rocks, it causes friction that then generates electromagnetic rays that attract cosmic qi and oxygen. Smooth waterfalls, fish aquariums and water fountains are also very positive. Bubbling white water causing a lot of friction is fresh and highly negatively ionised. It contains exceptionally high levels of qi which attracts oxygen. The main factor in feng shui is the qi that is attracted by moving water. Water is likened to wealth and abundance in Chinese culture because moving water attracts qi and oxygen. Water also provides irrigation for growing food in China.

Negative Types – Fast-rushing water near the front of a house; living near a large waterfall; a house facing a fast-moving river. These types of strong water produce too much yin energy and qi. As a result, the strong qi becomes overwhelming and suffocating. Stagnant, non-moving water also breeds bacteria and germs that are harmful to health.

6) Dust and Environmental Toxins

Negative Effects – Dust and environmental toxins do not have any positive effects for people. Often, dust in the air, which cannot be seen by the naked eye, is carried many kilometres away, causing health problems, especially to the lungs, sinuses and throat.

Pesticides, household detergents and fumes from vehicles are all toxic to humans. Research has shown that people who live within 100 m (330 ft) of busy highways and trunk roads tend to have a higher incidence of Alzheimer's disease. The higher levels of lead and aluminium in their brains are caused mainly by fumes from vehicles.

In feng shui, we advise people to avoid living near dust-generating factories, busy highways or main trunk roads. As a guideline, residents should stay at least 300–500 m (1,000–1,650 ft) away from main roads and highways. Care should be taken to ensure that residential areas are at least 5 km (3 miles) away from factories or industries that produce dust and toxic chemicals.

7) Shapes and Symbols

Positive Types – The rounded corners of walls, the round shape of furniture and the roofs of houses are positive forms. Humans and animals, through evolution, are more in harmony with round objects, which are perceived as not life-threatening and not attacking our psychic or physical body.

Positive symbols include the figures 8 and 88; the symbols of love, the Aum symbol and the heart shape without a sharp point; the symbols of prosperity for all races and ages, the Ankh and the horseshoe shape; symbols of longevity, flowers, a smiling person, a happy smiling baby or child, as well as the many prosperity and love symbols of different cultures.

The egg shape as a symbol of fertility and virility, although not often used today, is also a positive symbol.

The circle representing the universe, harmony and protection is a powerful positive symbol. The circle should never be broken. If it is broken, it is like the universe being destroyed. Similarly, the half circle is also positive if the line in the semicircle is not broken.

Negative Types – All sharp shapes and symbols in our immediate environment are considered to be attacking and harmful to humans. Shapes like the sharp gable of a house, a pyramid-shaped roof or pyramid, the sharp corners of walls (inside and outside of a flat or house), and the sharp corners of cupboards, tables, decorations and furniture are all negative shapes.

116

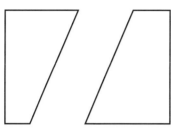
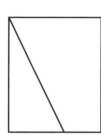
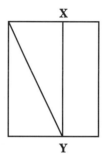

Diag. 11.2A: Negative symbol.   Diag. 11.2B: Negative symbol.   *Diag. 11.2C: Remedy for Diag. 11.2B – Place a strip from X to Y to make the window look more balanced.*

Ways to Neutralise Sharp Corners

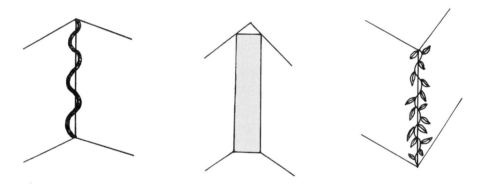

Diag. 11.3: Sharp corners can be neutralised by ribbons, pieces of wood, artificial plants or by placing a cupboard in the corner.

8) Yin and Yang Principle

The design of a house should conform to the yin and yang principle, otherwise its occupants could suffer from balance problems resulting in health difficulties. For more details, please refer to Chapter 7.

9) Astrological and Cosmological Influences

This refers to the Eight Trigrams East-West system, the flying stars system and the Lo-Shu magic numbers, which will be covered in my planned book about trigrams feng shui. There are areas in a house that are either more or less harmonious to individuals. By applying the Eight Trigram system and the flying stars system, we can identify the problem areas in a house and determine auspicious locations for individuals.

10) Five Elemental Universal Energies

Please refer to Chapter 8 of this book for more detailed explanations.

11) Colour

Colours are closely connected with the five elemental energies and affect us in our daily lives.

Positive Types –

- Red (fire element) stands for joy, happiness and vitality. However, some people may not like red because it is too stimulating or aggressive.

- Green (wood element) is for growth, rejuvenation and expansion.

- Blue (water element) is for calming, healing and improving vitality.

- Pink (fire element) is for love, happiness and lifting one's mood.

- Purple and violet (fire element) are for spiritual advancement and activating the crown chakra.

- Yellow (earth element) uplifts mental capability.

- Beige, light brown and brown (earth element) are for grounding and balance.

- White, which contains all the seven colours of the rainbow or colour energies of life, is uplifting and gives clear vision and purity.

Negative Types – Black, which is the absence of the seven colours of the rainbow or the absence of life, is a negative colour best to be avoided. Grey is one step before black and is also not a good colour. Too much purple or violet, especially if a room is painted with these colours, is destructive and causes mental, psychic and balance problems due to the overstimulation of the crown chakra. When animal cages are painted violet and purple, the animals become diseased. Their health improves when the cages are painted blue.

In feng shui, we seek to balance the colours and colour schemes in a room or house according to the five elemental principles so that clashes and conflicts with an individual's elements are minimised or better still, avoided.

For example, a person who is a fire element person according to their year of birth, cannot live or work comfortably in a room that is painted completely blue, which represents the conflicting water element. The fire element person is, instead, supported by the colour green. Please see Chapter 8 for more details on colours.

12) Lights

Positive Types – Full spectrum light contains the seven colours of the rainbow, so natural daylight is best. In a room, light similar to normal daylight is best for the eyes, heart and arteries.

Lights should not flicker. Most fluorescent lights do and are not suitable for work and study requiring deep concentration. We recommend the traditional, spherical clear light bulbs or full spectrum lights for home and office use.

Negative Types – Flickering fluorescent lights that emit microwave radiation from both ends of the tube are harmful to eyesight and health. Too bright a light or glaring lights hurt the eyes, drying up the human aura as they use up valuable oxygen in a room.

Light that is too dim in a room also causes problems to eyesight and is depressive. Prolonged darkness or dim light in a room can cause a room to become too yin, thereby inducing spirits and ghosts to come in and generate 'shah qi' (see Factor No. 16). People living or working in a dark or very dimly-lit room tend to be more depressed, and records indicate a higher incidence of suicide and accidents.

Candlelight is only negative in that it is not bright enough and burning candles use up lots of oxygen in a room. They are often the main cause of a house fire.

In feng shui, we use good, harmonic lighting to stimulate and induce qi and oxygen to come into the rooms of a house. Dark or dim areas in a room should have lights to enhance yang energy and qi, which are in harmony with living humans. All good lighting should make us feel comfortable and balanced without any bad health effects. The colour scheme in a room, of course, helps to enhance the good effects of the types of lighting used.

13) Radioactive Rays

Radioactive rays come from different sources. The first source is a nuclear power plant, a nuclear facility or industries using nuclear energy. The second source is equipment like X-ray machines and other machinery using radioactive energy. The third source is underground deposits of uranium – for example, in Northern Australia.

It is advisable to live at least 10 km (6 miles) away from a nuclear facility. Although a person may not be directly affected by the radioactive rays, winds could carry the radiated particles many kilometres away and cause contamination to plants and food in the fields after rain or snowfalls.

Officials often claim that it is safe to live near a nuclear facility because they fear negative repercussions. But it has been found that people who live 1 to 2 km (0.6–1.2 miles) from a nuclear facility tend to suffer from more health problems, especially cancer, leukaemia and other blood disorders.

Similarly, the series of underground nuclear tests carried out by the French government in the Pacific in 1995–96 was claimed to be of low risk to humans. However, because nuclear contamination of the water and food chain affects pelagic fish like tuna which travel a great distance, the tests could also affect European, Japanese and American populations living thousands of kilometres away from the test areas. Radioactive rays, like all energies, come in two forms. The physical form can be detected by instruments, but the more subtle energy like the human aura is too subtle to be picked up and measured by measuring devices. Radioactive energy is subtle energy that is particularly dangerous to health. Those who are affected by radioactive rays or radiation should consult a homeopathic or natural therapeutic doctor. Some of the negative rays can be removed by taking special hot baths (see Appendix).

14) Radio and Microwave Rays

Radio and microwave rays from radio and TV transmitting stations and mobile phone relaying stations are a potential health hazard. Often, we found that people living within 1 km (0.6 miles) of such stations become weak when we apply a kinesiology test on them.

TV receiving dishes are a common sight on modern buildings around the world. We found that when a TV dish is situated on the roof of a two-storey house, people standing within a 5 m (16.5 ft) radius of the dish and standing 5 m below on the ground floor, have a weakened immune system. When they are more than 5 m from the TV dish, their immune system becomes strong again. Why? We believe the 'suction effect' of the TV dish, attracting multiple energy frequencies

Diag. 11.4: Signals and frequencies are attracted towards the TV dish, but its immense pulling effect also attracts other energies towards the dish.

from great distances, also attracts other energies outside of the dish. People within 5 m (16.5 ft) of a dish of 1 m (3.3 ft) diameter are bombarded by the large volume of energies outside of the TV dish (see Diag. 11.4).

A safe distance to observe or locate a TV dish with a diameter of about 1 m (3.3 ft) is 12 m (40 ft) from a house. It is best to install a TV dish in the garden as far away from a house as possible.

15) Electromagnetic Rays

The most dangerous electromagnetic rays are those generated by high tension interstate electrical power lines (see Diag. 11.5).

Diag. 11.5: A very negative high-tension power line close to a house.

Research has found that those living within 50 m (165 ft) of high tension interstate power lines have a higher incidence of severe health problems, especially chronic fatigue, cancer and blood disorders like leukaemia. This could be due to their body cell water crystals absorbing the electrical radiation from the power lines. This foreign electrical radiation in the cells causes energy blockages in the body. Those who live within 100 m (330 ft) of high-tension power lines have higher radiation in their body.

Our tests showed that people who stood within 100 m of high tension interstate electrical power lines became completely weak in all their body electromagnetic circuits; their body's joints were also completely weak. At a distance of 150 m (500 ft), their body's electromagnetic circuits became stronger again.

There is also another negative effect. The electromagnetic rays penetrate the air and interact with living organisms and matter, producing pollutants in the air which cause unhealthy living within an area of 200–300 m (650–1,000 ft) from high tension power lines. Residents living within 200–300 m of high tension power lines also tend to have a higher incidence of allergies, indicating poor air quality. Often, winds carry those toxic pollutants to a greater distance. A safer distance for homes and offices is more than 500 m (1,650 ft) from interstate power lines.

A town's electrical power transmitting station is even more dangerous to health because its electrical radiation is more intense and severe. A distance of at least 500–1,000 m (1,650–3,300 ft) should be allowed between an electrical power transmitting station and a residential area. Residents living in the 'danger zones' should move out to safer areas as soon as possible to avoid deteriorating health. The first indication that a person is affected by intense electrical and electromagnetic radiation is when they suffer from general fatigue. This fatigue disappears when they go on holiday or move to another location.

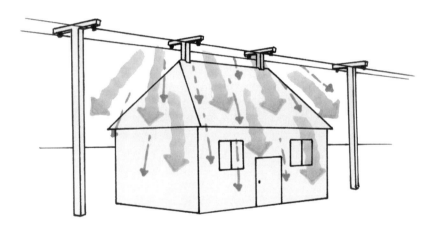

Diag. 11.6A: Electrical cables on roof of house. Electrical and electromagnetic radiation moves down 20 m (65 ft).

It is also a common practice in some parts of Europe to install electrical cables on roof tops, from house to house. These cables radiate electrical and electromagnetic radiation 20 m (65 ft) down into each house. This means the radiation penetrates the entire house, causing extreme stress, especially for those living in the attic or upper floor. Common complaints are depression, headaches, memory loss and fatigue. One remedy to block at least the subtle electrical and electromagnetic radiation from coming into a house is to place natural quartz crystals immediately below the roof line and facing the power lines.

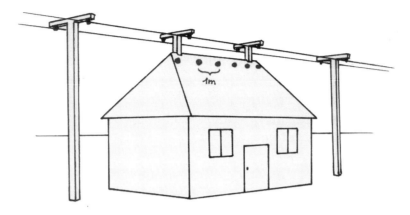

Diag. 11.6B: Remedy – Under the roof and immediately below the electrical cables, place natural quartz crystals three times the size of an adult thumb at 1 m (3.3 ft) intervals to block the subtle electrical radiation.

16) 'Shia Qi' and 'Shah Qi'

'Shia qi' is a Chinese feng shui phrase meaning 'negative attacking energy'. Many feng shui consultants use this phrase loosely to mean all types of negative energies affecting humans.

From my experience, shia qi is actually connected with the negative energies of the spiritual realms and with spirits. In the cemetery, shia qi is very high because of wandering spirits. 'Shah qi' or 'killing qi' is overwhelming 'shia qi' and occurs in ritual grounds or in places where bad spells have been cast to prevent people from coming into an area. When a house is haunted, we say the house has shah qi. Shah qi also occurs in places used for brutal killings or for the enactment of a ritual to cause harm to others.

Some towns have very high shah qi due to cruel and bloody wars. Many German cities such as Ulm, Regensburg and Berlin have very high shah qi because of their past history of suppression, torture and killings. However, we do not call an attacking corner shah qi because we can see it and we can easily put up remedies to neutralise its negative effects.

Negative Energy at Places of Worship

People with problems often go to religious places of worship (church, mosque, synagogue, temple, chapel, and so on), hoping to get spiritual help. Very often, these people have uncleansed auras which have spirits attached to their bodies. Spirits are often wandering outside places of worship. Places of worship are also used to hold last rites for the dead and spirits are attracted to these places as observers to welcome the souls of the dead persons into their realm.

We found that shia qi, and sometimes shah qi, within 50 m (165 ft) of places of worship can be as high as 90%. From 50 m to 100 m (165–330 ft), these negative energies are gradually reduced to 40–50%. From 100 m to 150 m (330–500 ft), these negative energies are further reduced to 20–30%. Normally, these negative energies become negligible after 200 m (650 ft).

In large places of worship where several hundreds to several thousand people go to worship, these negative energies are found to exist as far as 300 to 500 m (1,000–1,650 ft) away.

The compounds of places of worship, especially those with a long history, may have been used for hundreds or even thousands of years for burying the dead. It was customary to bury the dead within 200 m (650 ft) of a place of worship. The gravestones and grave markers have disappeared over hundreds of years, giving the impression that the land is free of any encumbrance. But the energies of the dead, whose bones were buried there, still exist.

Houses that are built over graves tend to have a higher incidence of family disharmony and more accidents and suicides caused by shah qi and shia qi.

Homes, therefore, should not be built within 300 m (1,000 ft) of a place of worship or a graveyard. The safe distance is around 500 m (1,650 ft).

When a house is found to have shia or shah qi, two symbols are recommended to urge spirits and ghosts to move away. According to my research, the highest symbols that spirits and ghosts respect are the Chinese pa'kua (Diag. 11.7) and Solomon's seal (Diag. 11.8). Both symbols can be worn on the body as pendants or they can be placed on a wall in the foyer or inside a room to block spirits and ghosts.

Diag. 11.7: The Chinese pa'kua of the Earlier Heavens with the yin-yang symbol in the centre turning counter-clockwise. It is the most powerful symbol that gives protection from spirits.

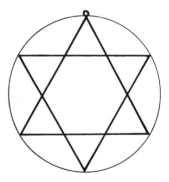

Diag. 11.8: Solomon's seal – A Jewish symbol with a strong protective effect.

Although these two symbols were originally discovered by the Chinese and the Jews respectively, they are actually universal symbols that can be used by people of all races and creeds.

17) Plants and Trees

Please see chapter 22 for more detailed explanations on plants and trees and their positive and negative effects on humans.

18) Overpowering and Suffocating Room Energy

When the main entrance of a house is directly opposite the door of a room, especially a small bedroom, most of the cosmic qi for the whole house is directed into one room (see Diag. 11.9). In this typical example of Western flat design, the room opposite the entrance receives most of the cosmic qi meant for the whole house. Too much cosmic qi becomes overpowering and suffocating, resulting in hyperactivity, agitation and insomnia, especially when the space is used for sleeping. The other negative aspect is that other rooms and areas are deprived of good qi.

Home buyers should watch out for this special 'main door-face-room door' layout and try to avoid buying a house with this negative feature.

The common remedy for Diag. 11.9 is to hang a small windchime made of solid tubing not more than 20 cm (8 inch) long (as shown in Diag. 11.9) very close to the ceiling and about 1–1.5 m (3.3–5 ft) from the doorway, to redirect the intense incoming qi into the other rooms.

Room energy that is too high can also be caused by excessive use of feng shui remedies such as waterfall pictures and flutes, which can increase the room energy to over 150%. On average, a room's cosmic qi should not be more than 110%.

Generally in the temperate countries, occupants are used to low cosmic qi due to the poor design of houses and buildings. If we increase the energy excessively in our rooms, we will have difficulty getting used to staying in low energy places elsewhere.

An example of the effect of too much qi energy in a room: A man practising feng shui in northern Germany increased the cosmic qi of his room to 200% to try to reduce his sleep from eight hours to five hours. As a result of the excessive energy, he couldn't sleep at all!

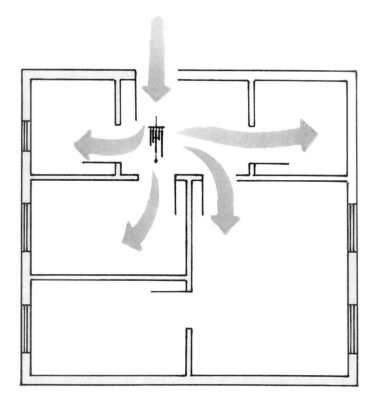

Diag. 11.9: A small windchime is installed in the entrance area to disperse incoming qi.

19) Electro-smog from Computer and TV Screens

Computer and TV screens generate a huge volume of electro-smog that hangs in a room's atmosphere. In temperate countries where all the windows of a house are often closed, electro-smog can stay in a room for several days. When inhaled in large quantities, electro-smog can cause allergies, lung problems and swellings on the face.

It is usually not advisable to have a computer or TV in a bedroom. If this arrangement cannot be avoided, then before a person goes to sleep, they should open all the windows for 10 to 20 minutes to allow fresh air to come in and clear away the electro-smog.

Electronic equipment also emit radiowaves, microwaves and other harmful rays that attack the human aura and cause a general weakness of the immune system. Researchers in Canada and Britain have concluded that pregnant women who worked long hours in front of a computer had a higher chance of giving birth to deformed babies. A remedy to protect against harmful computer and TV radiation is a natural quartz crystal three times the size of an adult's thumb, placed in front of the screen to deflect and disperse the negative attacking rays. A natural quartz crystal with a sharp point can also be used, but the sharp point must be pointing towards the screen.

Intense radiation also come out from the back of the TV and computer. A large natural quartz crystal should likewise be placed at the back of a computer or TV if it is facing another person within 3 m (10 feet).

It is not advisable for a person to sit opposite the back of a TV or a computer. Experiments were carried out with a switched-on TV with its back towards a 12 cm (5 in) concrete wall. On the other side of the wall in an adjacent room, a person without knowledge of the TV's presence sat within 30 cm (12 in) of the wall and became so agitated he was unable to sleep throughout the night. Even a wall up to 20 cm (8 in) thick is unable to block the powerful and penetrating electromagnetic, microwave and radiowave rays emitted from a TV or computer. Just imagine the harmful effects when a person is sitting unprotected, immediately in front of a computer or within 3 m (10 ft) of a TV that is switched on.

邪種類輪廓

Chapter 12

ATTACKING SHAPES AND STRUCTURES

Our house is like our body. Any negative symbols or shapes that are immediately present in the surrounding of our home constitute an attack on our house and thus our body. This directly affects us emotionally, mentally, physically and spiritually.

Negative symbols are sharp objects, sharp-pointed structures and long, straight poles or structures pointing upwards or facing your house. Through their long history of evolution, humans still have a conscious awareness of sharp or sharp-pointed objects or structures, reminding them when they have been used as weapons. We have inherited our ancestors' 'consciousness'. We begin to feel nervous in our psyche when sharp objects or structures are pointed directly at us. Even though we do not see, say, a sharp corner of a wall directly facing us, our subconscious is aware of its presence. We feel uncomfortable sitting or standing where we are. Instinct tells us that 'danger' is near and we have to move to another place to avoid the sharp attacking corner.

The following are a few common negative symbols that are found around our homes.

House Gable Attacking Neighbour's House

In Diag. 12.1, the sharp gable of building B is pointing directly at the main door of building A. In feng shui, it is interpreted to mean the total physical and spiritual energies of building B and all its occupants are attacking the 'mouth' of building A and the mouths of all its occupants. If building B is larger than building A or building B has more occupants than building A, then the attack is overwhelming.

Such an aggressive attack by building B causes extreme fear which severely affects the health of the occupants of building A. The occupants of building A will also tend to have heart and digestion problems, and a shorter life span. In an overwhelming situation, it is very likely that a key member of the family in building A could soon have a quick death (from a heart attack, brain haemorrhage or accident).

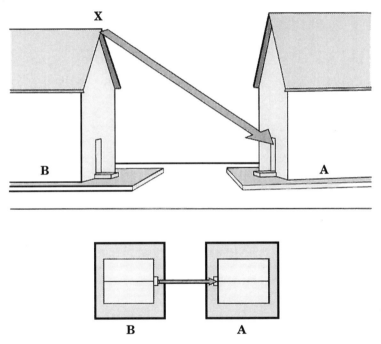

Diag. 12.1: Sharp gable attacking the door of building A.

The best remedy to resolve this situation is to ask the occupants of building B to cover up the sharp gable, thus neutralising their attack (see Diag. 12.2A–C).

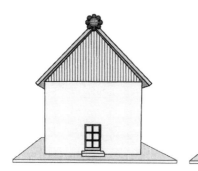

Diag. 12. 2A: A flower pattern (eight petals is an auspicious number) is placed over the gable.

Diag. 12.2B: A round circle is placed over the gable.

Diag. 12.2C: An animal shape is placed over the gable to neutralise its attacking energies. This practice is quite common among the farming communities in southern Germany, Austria and Indonesia.

When it is not possible to get the occupants of building B to cooperate to implement remedies as shown above, the remedy in Diag. 12.3 must be carried out. Otherwise, all the occupants of building A are advised to vacate within six months of moving into the house as the attacking negative energies are too overpowering.

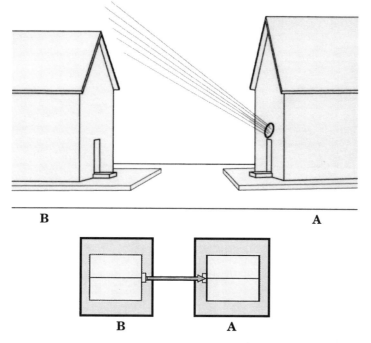

Diag. 12.3: Mirror remedy for gable attack.

In Diag. 12.3, the occupants of building A need to install a concave mirror (magnifying mirror) of at least 17–20 cm (6.7–8 in) diameter above their main door. It is important to point the mirror in the same direction as the attacking gable but facing slightly above the sharp gable. The diagonal and upwards reflection of the concave mirror deflects and renders the attacking energies harmless.

If the mirror's reflection was directly facing and attacking building B, this would represent a counterattack from A to B which should be avoided.

To remain effective, the concave mirror must be cleaned and polished weekly if it is placed outdoors. A better way is to place the mirror inside the house in front of the see-through glass panels above the main door so that less regular maintenance is required.

Many feng shui consultants suggest the use of the pa'kua mirror (Eight Trigrams mirror, see Chapter 23) to neutralise the attacking gable. The pa'kua mirror is only used to protect occupants from 'shah qi', or qi connected with ghosts and spirits. It does not work against a 'physical' roof gable.

In Diag. 12.4, the sharp roof gable of building B is attacking the front of building A. The front of a house represents the faces of its occupants. It is like the faces of the occupants of building A being attacked. Occupants (especially males) in building A may suffer from facial diseases or accidents affecting the face. You should implement remedies similar to Diag. 12.2A–C or the mirror remedy according to Diag. 12.3.

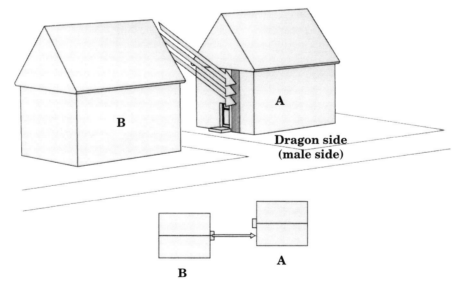

Diag. 12.4: Gable attack to the side of the door.

In Diag. 12.5A, the sharp gable of building B is attacking the left side of building A. The left side is the Dragon side or male side. Male occupants of building A will tend to have more health problems. The occupants of buildings A and B will tend to be less friendly and will often have many unnecessary arguments over small non-issues. When building B is a two-storey or taller building, then the remedies suggested in Diag. 12.2A–C or 12.5B are recommended.

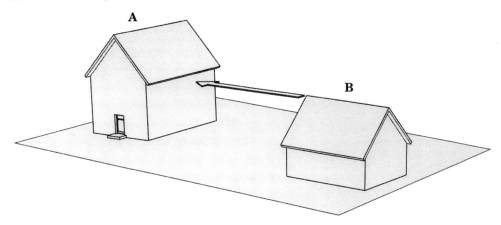

Diag. 12.5A: Building B's gable attacking the leg and thigh area of the male occupants of building A.

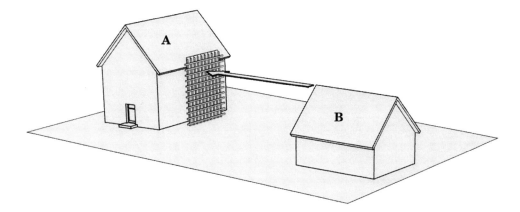

Diag. 12.5B: A high trellis made from bamboo or wood with creeper plants to block the attacking energies of building B's gable.

Sides of House Roof Attacking Neighbour

In Diag. 12.6A, the sharp side roof of building B is attacking the front door of building A. The sharp side roof is also like a sharp chopper cutting down building A. This negative attacking feature is half as dangerous as the attacking roof gable, and must be neutralised using remedies similar to those used to neutralise the sharp attacking roof gable. When placing a mirror, it must be directed slightly above the attacking building, and not directly at the house, otherwise it becomes a counter attack. The negative attacking corner shown above is about a quarter

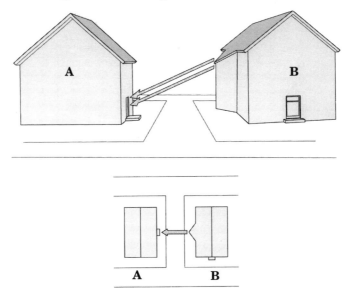

Diag. 12.6A: Building B's sharp side roof is attacking the main door of building A. The occupants of building A will tend to have more fear, and suffer from mouth problems.

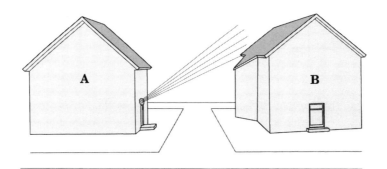

Diag. 12.6B: Remedy – Install a concave mirror facing the attacking arrow, but make sure the mirror points above the attacking arrow and not directly at the attacking sharp corner. It is not advisable to retaliate by counteracting any part of building B.

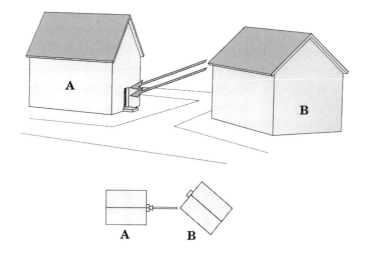

Diag. 12.7A: Building B's roof corner is attacking building A,
causing anxiety and discomfort to the occupants of building A.

as dangerous as a sharp roof gable. It generally affects the immune system of the occupants of building A and causes health problems to older people or those with a weak body constitution. If the sharp corner points at a window, the occupants of that particular room will tend to have more general health problems as well as problems connected with the eyes.

Remedies are a concave mirror (Diag. 12.3) or a trellis fence (Diag. 12.5B). When a window is attacked, a concave mirror can be used; a windchime or a natural quartz crystal three times the size of an adult thumb can also be hung in the middle of the window (see Diag. 12.7B and 12.7C) to divert the attacking energies.

These attacks do not only affect the occupants' health. In my experience, neighbours become much friendlier once the attacking corners of roofs and buildings are remedied.

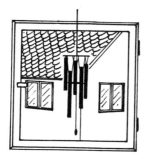

Diag. 12.7B: A windchime in the middle of the
window blocks the attacking corner of the roof.

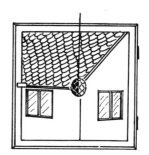

Diag. 12.7C: A natural quartz crystal
in the middle of the window also blocks the
corner of the roof.

Trees Attacking the Main Door

Trees growing around a house is a common sight. Trees give shade, cool the house and act as a barrier to block and slow down strong winds and storms. Trees also generate more fresh air that is important for healing humans and the environment.

Care, however, should be taken to ensure that trees are not planted in front of the main door or in front of windows or glass walls. A tree with an exposed trunk directly in front of a main door constitutes an attack on all the occupants' mouth area (see Diag. 12.8A).

Diag. 12.8A: Tree with a straight exposed trunk in front of the main door.

In Diag. 12.8A, the complete energy of the tree is attacking the house and the occupants, causing health problems, especially to the mouth area, eyes, liver and heart. However, if no exposed trunk is seen, with only the leaves and small branches visible from the main door, then it does not constitute an attack (see also Chapter 22). Although a large tree with branches spreading wider than the main door and within 10 m (33 ft) from it may not be attacking the main door, it is blocking good qi from entering the house. There should be no trees or bushy plants immediately in front of a house for a distance of at least 50–70 m (165–230 ft).

The door is not attacked if the straight trunk is shielded by bushy trees. But when leaves drop during autumn and winter, the trunk may be exposed and attack again.

When a tree with an exposed trunk is in front of a house, the intensity of the negative effects depends on three factors:

a) The bigger the tree trunk the more dangerous it is to the occupants of the house.

b) A straight trunk is more dangerous than a slanted branch. The more slanted a trunk or a tree branch the less 'dangerous' it is.

c)   The distance the tree is from the house is another factor. It is most negative and dangerous when the tree is within 10 m (33 ft). The danger is reduced as the distance between the main door and the tree is increased. This is because the blowing of the wind, the passing of vehicles and various outside environmental conditions help to distort the negative effects. On a calm quiet day, a tree trunk, even 70–100 m (230–330 ft) away, still constitutes a bad attack.

Remedies to neutralise the attacking energy of a tree with an exposed trunk are listed below:

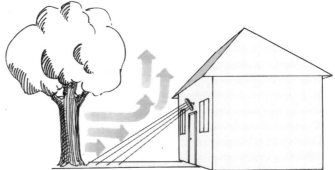

Diag. 12.8B: Concave mirror remedy.

In Diag. 12.8B, a concave mirror of 12–15 cm (5–6 in) diameter is installed on top of the main door, pointing down in front of the tree to distort the tree trunk's attacking energy. Preferably, the concave mirror should be placed inside the house so that it is not easily soiled by weather conditions, thus requiring less cleaning and maintenance. The mirror must be visible from the tree. A feng shui mirror has to be cleaned and clear to be most effective.

When an exposed tree trunk is 15–20 m (50–65 ft) from the main door, a trellis fence can be erected in front of the tree to block the attacking energy (see Diag. 12.8C).

Diag. 12.8C: Trellis fence gives protection from tree attack.

Attack by Posts and Straight Poles

It is quite common to see a lamp post, power line pole, bus stop, traffic sign pole and water hydrant directly in front of the main door of houses. These negative straight features in front of a main door constitute an attack into the mouth of the house and the mouths of its occupants.

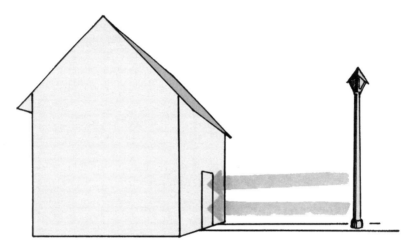

Diag. 12.9A: Attack by a lamp post.

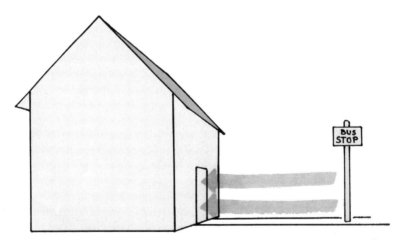

Diag. 12.9B: Attack by a bus stop.

The remedies to counter the negative effects are similar to that for an exposed tree trunk (see Diag. 12.8B and 12.8C).

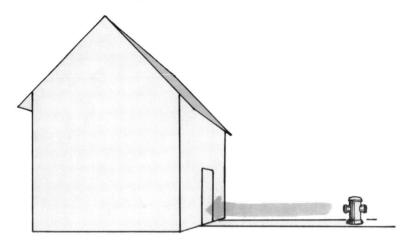

Diag. 12.9C: Attack by a hydrant.

Trees and Posts Attacking Windows and Glass Walls

The windows of a house are like a person's eyes. Any straight symbols, poles, exposed tree trunk or branches immediately outside and visible from the window (Diag. 12.10A–C) constitute an attack into the eyes of the occupants, especially the occupants of the room where the window is located, causing eye, liver and general health problems. For remedies, please refer to Diag. 12.11A–C.

In many modern buildings, glass walls are used instead of concrete for a better view and to allow more light and heat into a building. This design idea is excellent provided that no exposed tree trunk, lamp post, flag pole or any long structures are situated immediately outside the glass walls. Any visible long structure like an exposed tree trunk constitutes an attack into the body of the house and directly affects the occupants of that house negatively.

Illustrated below are various symbols attacking windows and glass walls and the recommended remedies:

Remedies

Diag. 12.10A: Straight tree trunk outside a window.

Diag. 12.10B: Bus stop post outside a window.

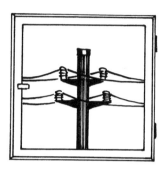

Diag. 12.10C: Power line pole outside a window.

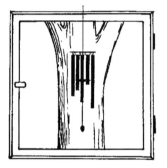

Diag. 12.11A: Hang a windchime in front of the trunk or in the middle of the window.

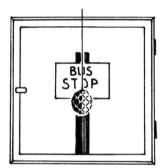

Diag. 12.11B: Hang a natural quartz crystal 3 cm (1.2 in) wide and four cm (1.6 in) long in front of the attacking post in the middle of the window.

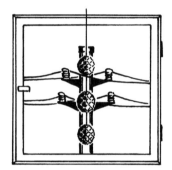

Diag. 12.11C: Power line pole outside a glass wall. Hang quartz crystals. (Note: Glass crystal and lead crystal do not have the desired effects.)

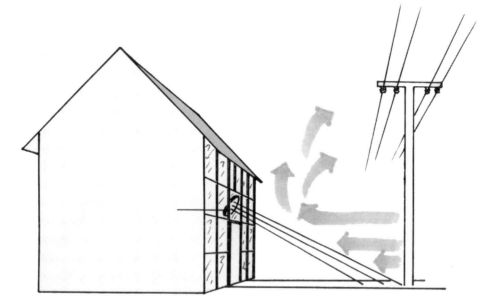

Diag. 12.11D: Install a 12–15 cm (5–6 in) concave mirror inside the house in front of the glass wall, pointing directly at the foot of the power line pole to distort the attacking energy.

There is a second way to neutralise the attacking power line pole (see Diag. 12.11D above).

Exposed tree trunks and long structures outside a house that are in front of a concrete wall are not negative and are not considered as harmful because the solid concrete walls are the outer protective walls of the house. Glass walls can be seen through and are more fragile than concrete walls. They break under any strong impact and are therefore not regarded as protective solid walls. Although indoor curtains may be drawn over glass walls, they do not give the desired protection.

選屋位

Chapter 13

SELECTION OF HOUSE SITES

There is a saying in China – 'The selection of a good house site is like meeting a good mentor'. A good house site enhances the harmonious development and growth of the family and endows them with great abundance.

A house site is where a family puts down its roots and lays the foundation for its success and the success of its future generations. A bad site erodes and tends to destroy what prosperity, posterity and good health a family has built up.

Some guidelines are listed here to assist readers in selecting a site. They are also useful for those who are living in houses with feng shui problems.

Qi from the Universe

Earth Qi

Diag. 13.1: 80–100% qi.

1) The best way is to have a feng shui consultant check whether the land and the area is in harmony with you and your family. Often a good site will not enhance health and prosperity if it is not in harmony with the senior family members. Disharmony with the land may cause health problems.

2) Check the quality of the earth underneath. The earth of a good site should be fertile and moist, showing that the earth qi is 'alive' to generate growth. Check whether the land has an earth qi of 80–100%. Cosmic qi from the universe is between 80–100%. For good 'grounding', we need an earth qi which is as high as the qi from the universe (see Diag. 13.1).

A site with an earth qi of below 70% (for example, a swampy area or an underground coalmine) is not suitable for human living. Harmful gas and negative energy will rise from the ground and cause unnecessary health problems. As the qi from the universe, which is yang in character, is 80–100%, the earth qi, which is yin in character, should be 80–100% for good balance and grounding.

3) Make sure the land shape and the landscape are harmonious (Chapter 14).

4) Check the land to avoid dangerous volcanic fault lines and major geopathic stress lines caused by underground water affecting bedrooms and working areas where people sit.

5) A good site should face calm, moving water – for example, a lake, a calm sea, a slow-running stream or river, a big pond or a man-made fountain.

6) There should be a smooth green hill or a gently sloping or rolling mountain at the back of a site to give good backing (see Diag. 13.2A–D).

7) A good land site should have the Four Animals Formation.

8) The land should be on higher ground but not on top of a mountain or hill exposed to continuous wind. It should not be prone to flooding.

9) Sites with rugged, sharp hills and high cliffs at the back within 3 to 5 km (2–3 miles) should be avoided (see Diag. 13.2E–F).

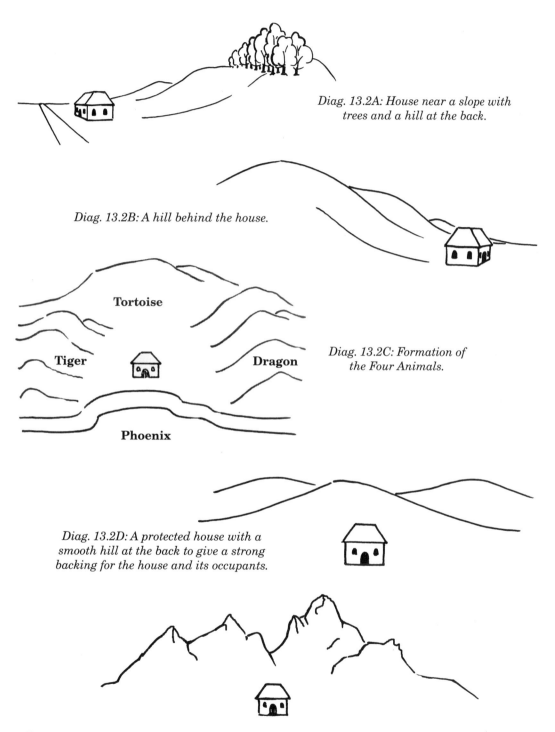

Diag. 13.2A: House near a slope with trees and a hill at the back.

Diag. 13.2B: A hill behind the house.

Tortoise

Tiger

Dragon

Phoenix

Diag. 13.2C: Formation of the Four Animals.

Diag. 13.2D: A protected house with a smooth hill at the back to give a strong backing for the house and its occupants.

Diag. 13.2E: An inauspicious site. The rugged, sharp and uneven hill formation causes lots of wind turbulence. Residents living within 5 km (3 miles) of this type of landscape will tend to have more depression, emotional problems and hormone imbalance.

Diag. 13.2F: A rugged cliff behind a house. Occupants live in fear of fallen rocks. Lots of wind turbulence is very drying, causing dry skin and lung and kidney problems.

10) A house on a hill spur with good drainage is preferred. A site in a valley is not a good site (see Diag. 13.2G: Site A). This site is more prone to landslides and loose foundations causing cracks in the walls, and occupants live in constant fear of fallen rocks and a landslide.

11) In hilly areas a good home site is on a hill spur (see Diag. 13.2G: Site B).

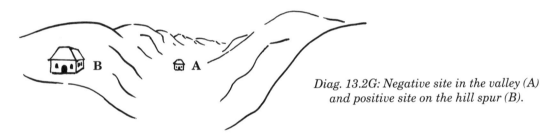

Diag. 13.2G: Negative site in the valley (A) and positive site on the hill spur (B).

12) Avoid a house site which is within 100 m (330 ft) from the end of a cul-de-sac or T-junction directly facing oncoming traffic (see Diag. 13.3A–B). People living at the end of a cul-de-sac or T-junction have a great fear that if vehicles cannot stop they could ram into the house! Furthermore, the toxic vehicle emissions and dust carried by the strong wind generated by the vehicles moving towards a house, can cause major health problems for the occupants.

The occupants living at the end of a busy cul-de-sac or T-junction tend to suffer from a higher incidence of heart and general health problems (see Diag. 13.3C).

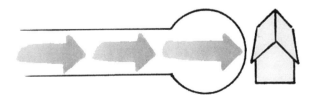

Diag. 13.3A: Cul-de-sac.

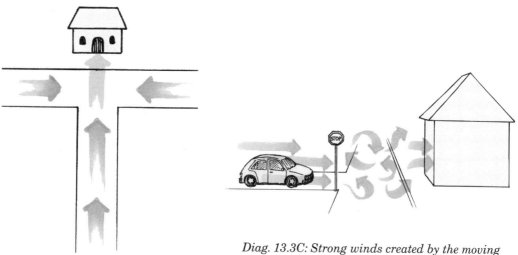

Diag. 13.3B: T-junction.

Diag. 13.3C: Strong winds created by the moving vehicle rush towards the house. Toxic fumes and dust bombard the house.

Where a cul-de-sac or T-junction is on the uphill, moving vehicles normally slow down their speed and the negative effects are less (see Diag. 13.3D and 13.3E). When these types of negative junctions are at the end of a down slope or downhill, the danger and negative effects are much greater (see Diag. 13.3F & 13.3G).

It is best to avoid these types of sites. However, for those already living at the end of these junctions, the following remedies are suggested.

Diag. 13.3D and 13.3E: Cul-de-sac uphill.

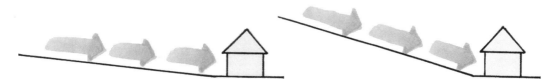

Diag. 13.3F and 13.3G: Cul-de-sac downhill.

In Asia, it is quite common to see a tall wall (as in Diag. 13.4A) erected along the whole length of a house up to 5 m (16.5 ft) high to block the attacking vehicle energy and toxic emissions from entering a house. A less costly and quick alternative remedy is to put up a thick trellis with quick-growing climbing plants like English ivy or creepers. This remedy is not the best one because some of the toxic emissions can still penetrate and enter a house (Diag. 13.4B).

13) A site on the side of a hill or cliff (as in Diag. 13.5A and 13.5B) is not a good site. These types of sites have no solid backing, which means that occupants

Diag. 13.4A: Remedy – Solid wall.	*Diag. 13.4B: Remedy – A trellis fence with plants to slow down and block some of the negative energies.*

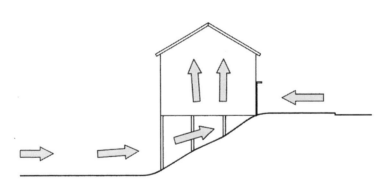

Diag. 13.5A: This house has no solid backing and is built on a weak foundation. Occupants lack prosperity. Strong earth qi blowing under the house causes health problems to its occupants.

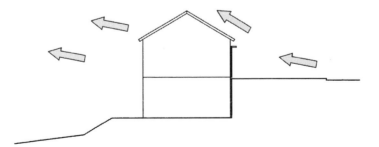

Diag. 13.5B: This house lacks solid backing and has weak qi. Occupants will have to work very hard to succeed in life.

have no backing and mentors to help them in their life. They generally lack prosperity and posterity and cannot keep steady jobs. Occupants also live in constant fear of landslides.

14) A house site directly facing fast water flow is negative because the overwhelming water energy generates too much cold yin energy that then enters the house, causing more health problems to its occupants.

The house sites are facing the direct flow of a fast flowing river. Fast flowing means water flow at a speed of at least 1 m (3.3 ft) per five seconds. Although

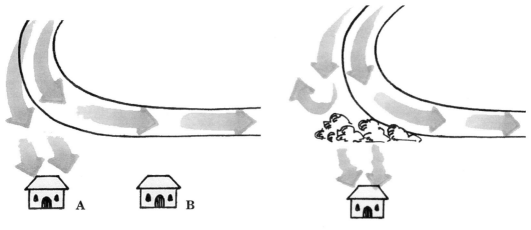

Diag. 13.6A: Houses at the turn of a river. House B has the more auspicious site.

Diag. 13.6B: A remedy is to plant thick bushes between the river and the house.

the water flows to the right in the above diagram, the energy generated by the fast river flow continues to move towards the house and generates a choking attacking energy towards the house. The occupants will tend to have more anxiety and health problems like coldness, dampness and rheumatic pains.

Although this remedy of planting thick bushy plants along the river bank in front of the house reduces at least 50% of the negative effects, the bushes do not completely block all the strong, negative cold yin energy from the river. Changing the main door to face the side would further improve the situation.

If it is a running stream 1 to 2 m (3.3–6.5 ft) wide and the house is at least 50 m (165 ft) from the bank, the stream's energy and qi will be invigorating and will bring good abundance. In this case, plant some low bushy plants along the attacking stream to further improve the auspicious conditions.

Diag. 13.7: Site facing wind tunnel.

15) A site facing a wind tunnel is a very inauspicious and dangerous place to build a house. The narrowing of the hills near the house site (see Diag. 13.7) creates a tunnel effect expediting the speed of wind to attack the house. Regular high-velocity winds can be expected daily. The occupants will tend to have a great fear that the house could be destroyed by strong winds. They will also have more depression and heart and kidney problems. It is best to avoid this type of site.

Some Very Inauspicious Sites

Some of the worst building sites are listed below. Great care should be exercised to avoid living near them. A good, safe distance away from these negative and overpowering qi is between 500–1,000 m (1,650–3,300 ft).

1) Cemeteries – Wandering spirits and the excessively yin land energy are not suitable for yang human habitation.

2) Temples, mosques, churches and other places of worship – the land energy tends to be very low and yin, and overwhelmingly negative for a residence. Wandering spirits are also common, causing strong shah qi (killing energy). Old graves may be there.

3) On sites where fights and wars took place, shia qi and shah qi are very high.

4) A prison, police station or hospital site holds plenty of sadness and negative energies.

5) An animal or human testing/experimental station or a slaughterhouse where death, fear, despair and sad energy prevails on the land is also not suitable.

6) Generally, ex-factory sites using animal parts for manufacturing are not suitable for human residence.

7) Government buildings connected with high executive authority, defence, taxes, the police, parliament, and so on generate overpowering energy on a site.

8) Check to ensure the land was not an old military training site, old battlefield or dumping ground for harmful chemicals.

9) Avoid a site within 7–10 km (4–6 miles) of a military installation or airport.

10) Ex-mining sites that have been refilled have soft, loose foundations which are not suitable for building houses. Residents will sense a sinking feeling and lack the solid foundation necessary for success and posterity.

11) Reclaimed swampy or marshy areas are not suitable for human habitation. First, the land does not have a solid foundation and buildings will tend to have cracks. Second, the toxic vegetation energy will gradually rise up, causing health problems to the occupants.

12) There should be no rubbish disposal or sewage treatment plant within 10 km (6 miles) of a house site.

13) Reclaimed rubbish dump sites are also not suitable for human habitation. It takes 10 to 20 years for the land to settle down and buildings will tend to suffer from many cracks involving high maintenance costs. The energy of toxic decomposed plants, various materials and rubbish will gradually rise up, causing health problems to people who live there.

14) No interstate high tension power lines or power substation within 150 m (500 ft). Even better is a distance of 500 m (1,650 ft), as the air, when charged with very strong electromagnetic radiation, affects people living further away.

15) Sites close to a nuclear power plant or facility. Chemical plants and chemical or radioactive storage areas are, of course, to be avoided.

16) Avoid mobile phone and TV relaying or transmitting stations. A safe distance is 3 km (2 miles) or more.

Chapter 14

LAND SHAPES

When looking for a site to build your house, select a good piece of land with a symmetrical, harmonious shape. The land is the foundation for the house, and you are therefore building the foundation for your family for the present as well as the future.

According to the Eight Trigram system, a piece of land has certain corners and areas associated with family members and our daily living situations. For example, the 'prosperity corner' determines our ability to feed our family. Unevenly-shaped land are particularly inauspicious to the family. If you only have an apartment in a house shared with several families or are in an apartment block, any possible negative effects of the land shape are reduced because all the occupants are affected and the negative effect is 'split' among all occupants.

The land is generally connected with inheritance, posterity and abundance for the family. A piece of land is divided into three sections, as shown below, for interpretation:

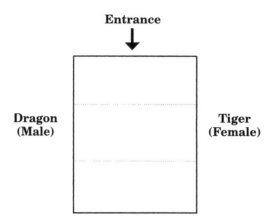

Diag. 14.1: When the land is divided into three sections from the front to the back, each area should preferably be of equal size so that each generation may have unrestricted growth and prosperity. The Formation of the Four Animals can also be applied on the land shape.

The front section represents the present – you. The second section represents your children and the third section your grandchildren. See the following diagrams for further illustrations.

Once you are living on the land, you are personally affected by its positive or negative shape. Children who move out of their parents' house are still affected by a bad or good land shape; however, the effects are less significant than if they were living on the land.

From these examples of land shapes, we can deduce in advance tendencies that can influence the future of a family. Have you ever wonder why certain prominent families or dynasties continue to prosper from generation to generation while others just dwindle or completely disintegrate in one or two generations? Among other factors, there are karmic problems, and the land shape has a significant effect on this. We often unconsciously select a piece of land that fits our karmic mission or behaviour. However, we can avoid problem land when we have an understanding of feng shui.

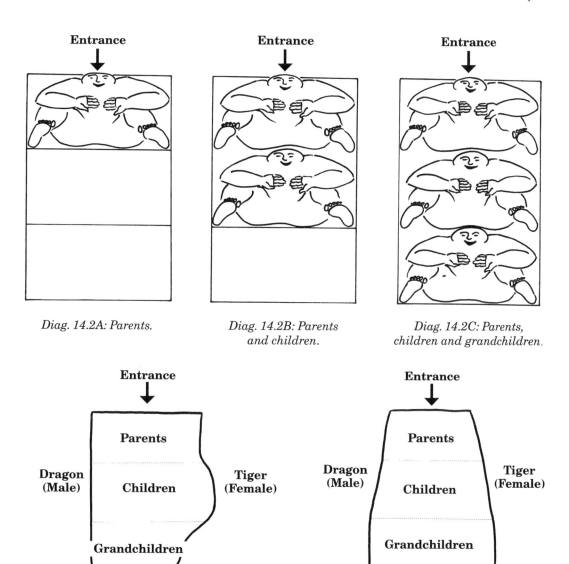

Diag. 14.2A: Parents.

Diag. 14.2B: Parents and children.

Diag. 14.2C: Parents, children and grandchildren.

Diag. 14.3: The middle (children) section is larger than the front (parents). The last section(grandchildren) is also much smaller than the other two sections. The occupants of this piece of land will do well and prosper during the first two generations. Prosperity will be at its height during the early years of their children (30–35 years) but begin to decline after the children reach 40 years. The decline will continue during their grandchildren's time. This family will also have low posterity with few descendants. The right side or female side of the land is also larger in the children's section. This means the daughters and / or daughters-in-law will be more prominent than the sons.

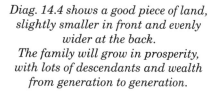

Diag. 14.4 shows a good piece of land, slightly smaller in front and evenly wider at the back.
The family will grow in prosperity, with lots of descendants and wealth from generation to generation.

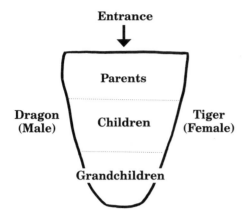

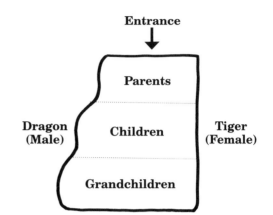

Diag. 14.5: The conditions are almost the opposite of Diag. 14.4. The back of the land becoming much smaller than the front is interpreted to mean that the children and grandchildren don't deserve to inherit plenty of wealth from their parents and grandparents. With the children and grandchildren lacking in wealth, it also means the parents and children will have to work very hard. The family will also have few descendants.

Diag. 14.6: The second section is bigger and then becomes progressively bigger during the grandchildren's time. The parents will live an ordinary life as employees or will have to work hard if they are in business. During their children's middle years, the family will become more prosperous and continue their prosperity into the grandchildren's time. The family will have many descendants. Male children and grandchildren will excel and perform well. Male occupants will also tend to have more problems, but they will live a longer life span.

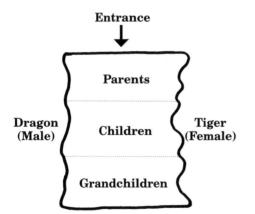

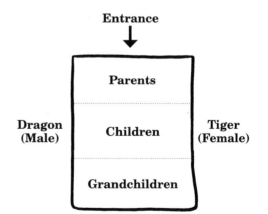

Diag 14.7: The corrugated shape shows irregular growth in the family, with lots of ups and downs in employment or in business.

Diag. 14.8: This is a very good shape for a piece of land. This land will bring good fortune and posterity to the family. The family will be generous but careful with money.
It will be a good keeper of wealth, as shown by the round edges at the end of the land.
The land looks like a cup holding everything in without any leakage.

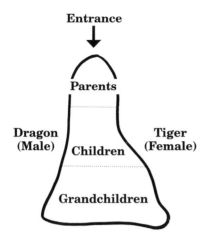

Diag. 14.9: *The parents will have to make great sacrifices and work extremely hard with little benefits. They will struggle for a living, but conditions will slowly improve during their children's time, with even more improvement during their grandchildren's time. Avoid land with this type of shape.*

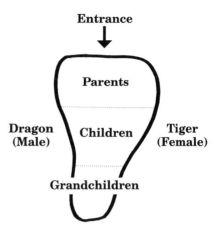

Diag. 14.10: *This is the reverse of Diag. 14.9. The parents will have to work very hard to earn a good income and some wealth, but the children and grandchildren will always get into trouble and slowly deplete the wealth and dissipate the family's posterity. The family will have lots of health and emotional problems.*

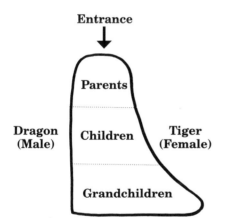

Diag. 14.11: *The parents will have to work very hard with little means. Once their children are born, their situation will improve. The grandchildren will benefit from the wealth created by their grandparents and parents. The female members of the family will have better growth and live a longer life span.*

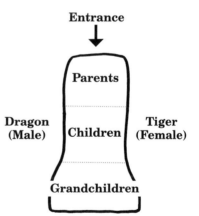

Diag. 14.12: *The grandchildren will inherit their parents' wealth and continue to grow and prosper on their own strength. The grandchildren will live a more harmonious life.*

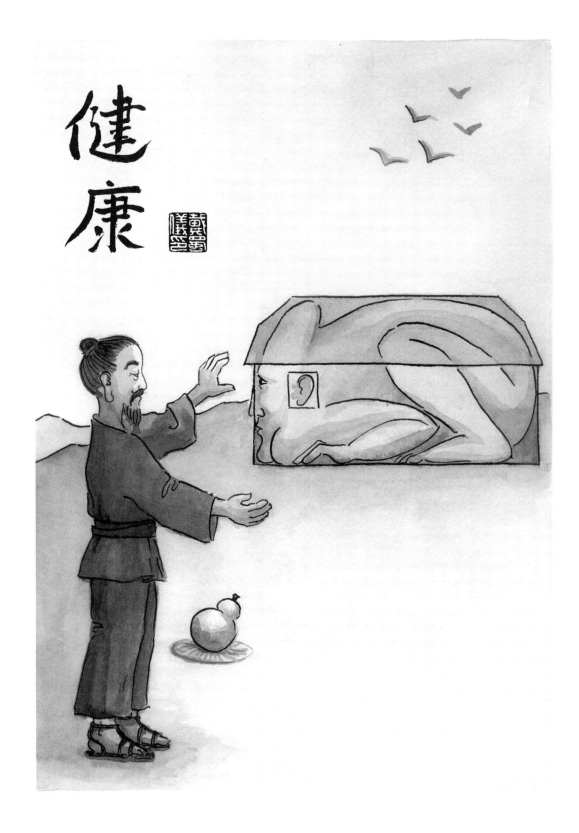

Chapter 15

SHAPES OF BUILDINGS

The best shapes for a house or a building are shown in Diag. 15.1 below.

The shape of a house should be balanced and symmetrical like a human body. Through the evolution of human living space as explained in Chapter 3, the shape of a house represents an individual occupant's body.

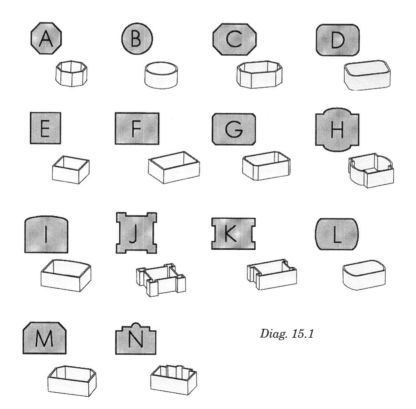

Diag. 15.1

Health Problems Connected with the Corresponding Missing Parts of a House

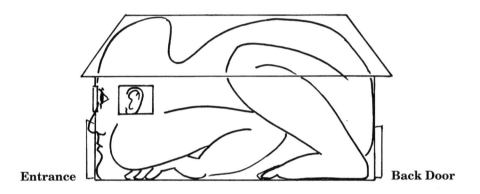

Entrance   **Back Door**

Diag. 15.2: A symbolic human body is fitted into this house. If you look at it from below, you get the 'belly perspective' of the following diagrams 15.3–15.7.

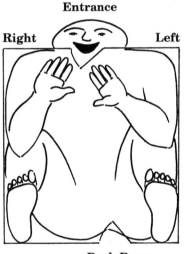

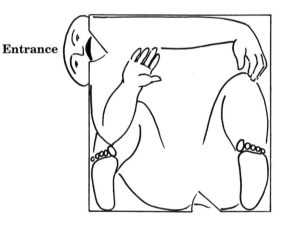

Diag. 15.3: The shape of a house as well as that of the human body should be symmetrical and in balance.

Diag. 15.4: This house has the entrance on the side, so that the head is turned sideways.

(Note: Diagrams 15.3 and 15.4 represent the view from ground up.)

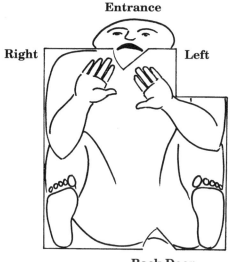

Diag. 15.5: *This house has the left shoulder missing. The occupants in this house will tend to have a higher incidence of shoulder problems or cannot carry heavy weights.*

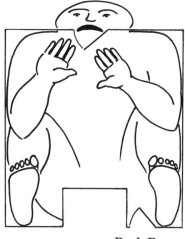

Diag. 15.6: *The backside and sex and anus areas are missing. With no backside, the occupants will lack support and confidence. They may have constipation and sex problems.*

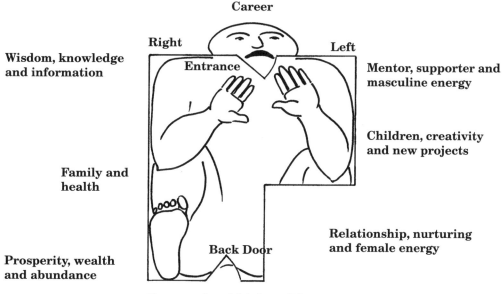

Diag. 15.7: *Scheme of the Eight Life Situations and body parts. The left leg is missing.*
(*Important note: This diagram represents a belly perspective, that is, view from bottom up.*)

The Trigrams of the Eight Life Situations

Every major section of a house also represents one of the eight daily living phenomena or 'The Eight Life Situations'. If an area is missing, it means that the respective Life Situation is also missing in daily life.

In Diag. 15.7, the 'relationship corner' is missing – the occupants in this house will tend to have more relationship problems and will have difficulty finding a partner. The missing corner also represents the left foot, lower leg and part of the thigh, indicating health problems in these areas for the occupants.

Diag. 15.8 shows the trigrams of the Eight Life Situations which can be applied to a building or a room. They will be explained more explicitly in my upcoming book about Trigrams Feng Shui.

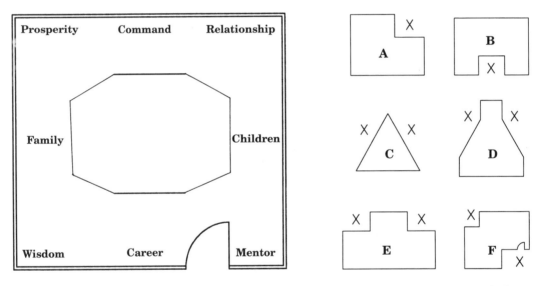

Diag. 15.8: Classic scheme of the trigrams of the Eight Life Situations – normal perspective as seen from above (as if looking at a house plan).

Diag. 15.9: Missing parts of a house.

Negative House Shapes and Remedies

Diag. 15.9 shows several incomplete and therefore negative houses shapes. Unless some remedies are carried out, many occupants living in these types of houses will suffer from health problems connected with the missing parts marked 'X'. In creating a remedy to complete the missing parts, a solid demarcation on the ground is required. The best solid demarcation is a low wall or a footpath made of the same material as that of the building to 'fill up' the missing parts.

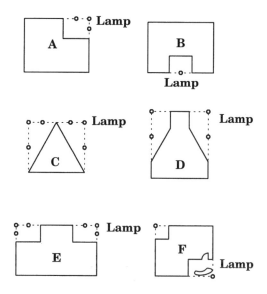

Diag. 15.10: The small circles represent lights with posts as high as the first floor or, for a single-storey house, the same level as the ceiling. The dotted lines indicate a pavement or a wall made of similar material as the building, used to demarcate the building's new boundary. They are also to separate the grass turf within the building's new built-in boundary and the grass turf outside the built-in area (garden area).

You should also install lights with posts as high as the first floor of the building in each of the missing corners to create a solid boundary post. You will also need to create 'light energy' to fill the missing parts as if they are parts of a house. Preferably, a light should be installed every 2 m (6.5 ft) along the boundary of the missing part.

To further strengthen the suggested remedies, a double eight ('88') symbol which has a balancing effect can be used. Each eight should preferably have the feng shui dimensions of width of 21 cm and height of 42 cm or other good feng shui measurements. The symbol should be placed on each side of the inner wall where the section is missing. Another double eight should also be placed on the wall facing the main door. The occupants can then see it when they enter the doorway and are immediately balanced as they enter the house.

Some students of feng shui recommend that mirrors be used inside the house on the missing walls to offset the defect. Mirrors only give the illusion of a bigger space, but they do not harmonise any imbalance that occurs.

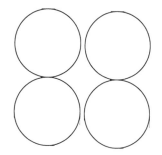

Diag. 15.11: A double eight symbol may be used in the colours of red, pink, green or blue.

屋頂

Chapter 16

SHAPES OF ROOFS

The shape of a house's roof affects the qi and the energy in the house and therefore the health and wellbeing of the occupants.

The shape of the roofs of buildings can be classified into one or several of the five elements. In Diag. 16.1 to 16.5, each roof shape belongs to one element only (fire, metal, wood, earth, water).

When the shape of a roof belongs to the water element, for example, the movement of energy in that building has the characteristics and effects of the water element, that is, wavy and cooling. However, it does not imply that a person who belongs to the fire element cannot occupy a building with a water element roof (fire is destroyed by water.)

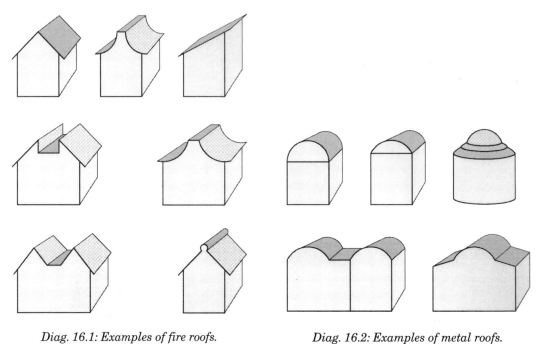

Diag. 16.1: Examples of fire roofs.

Diag. 16.2: Examples of metal roofs.

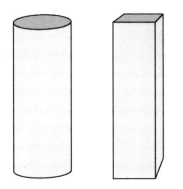

Diag. 16.3: Examples of wood roofs.

Diag. 16.4: Example of an earth roof.

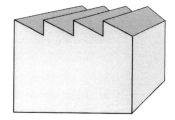 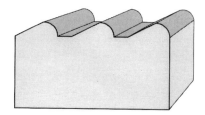

Diag. 16.5: Examples of water roofs.

Roof Structures and Designs Combining Two Or More Elements

The following roofs are a combination of two or more elements. When two or more elements are combined for a roof, they should preferably complement or be in harmony with each other, according to the productive or 'birth cycle'. Elements in conflict according to the destructive or controlling cycles should not be placed directly next to each other.

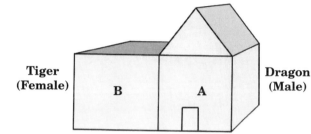

Tiger (Female)

Dragon (Male)

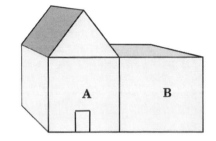

Diag. 16.6: Fire (A) and earth (B) element roofs are in good harmony as fire produces earth. The Dragon side (see the Formation of the Four Animals in Chapter 7), which is male and yang, is prominent. This house does not welcome visitors, especially males. Males rule supreme in this house and are more dominant and aggressive.

Diag. 16.7: Fire (A) and earth (B) element roofs are in harmony with each other. The Tiger side A, which is female and yin (see Chapter 7), is prominent. This house does not welcome visitors, especially females. Females control this household.

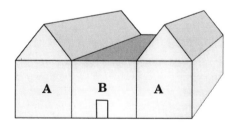

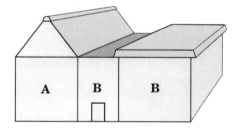

Diag. 16.8: This combination of fire (A), earth (B) and fire (A) element roofs are in good harmony. This house, with the yin and yang balanced, discourages visitors. The sharp roof gables affect and attack visitors.

Diag. 16.9: This house is friendly to visitors. (A) is a fire element roof while (B) indicates earth element roofs. Earth roof buildings should not be more than three storeys high, as the upper floors tend to have low qi because of the flat roof design.

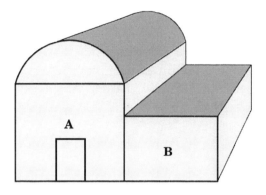

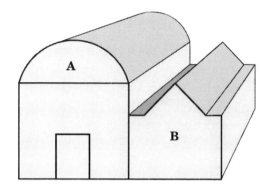

Diag. 16.10: Metal (A) and earth (B) roofs are in harmony, complementing each other. Metal and earth are like child and mother – earth produces and strengthens metal. A metal roof contains and holds qi inside, so a house with a metal element roof (see Diag. 16.18A in this chapter) tends to have higher qi and energy.

Diag. 16.11: Metal (A) and fire (B) roofs are an inauspicious combination. Fire (B) energy destroys and weakens the metal (A) element energy.

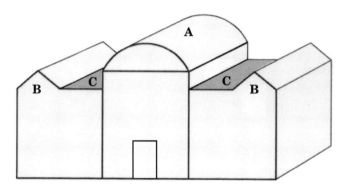

Diag. 16.12: These roofs are a combination of three elements and are arranged very harmoniously to avoid elemental conflict. Metal roof (A) is 'buffered' by earth roof (C), which strengthens it. Next to roof C is fire roof (B). Fire and earth roofs complement each other. Thus, these roofs are arranged according to the productive cycle of the five element. Fire (B) strengthens earth (C) and earth (C) further strengthens metal (A).
This building indicates high prosperity and success for its occupants.

The Fire Roof

The fire roof A in Diag. 16.13 is inauspicious. The roof is too sharp to one side, directing qi to escape upwards too quickly. The sharp apex 'X' may also attack the neighbours' houses.

Roof B has similar negative effects as roof A.

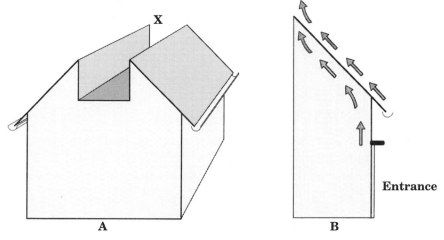

Diag. 16.13: Fire roofs.

Fire roofs are generally more suitable for countries with a hot climate. They vent hot air upwards to keep occupants cool during hot weather. It is not advisable to have a sharp pitch or fire roof buildings in temperate and cold countries. Nevertheless, most buildings in these countries have sharp fire roofs. The common explanation in Europe is that heavy snow may add exceptionally heavy weight to make a flat or low-pitched roof collapse. A sharp-pitched fire roof with a pitch of more than 15° has the following disadvantage: qi and energy are directed upwards quickly, creating an inertia inside the building that pulls more qi and energy upwards and out through the roof's apex.

Earth energy is pulled up, causing high humidity and moulds in the basement. This type of building generally has low cosmic qi of about 40%. It is unhealthy to live in a sharp fire roof house with over 25° pitch in temperate countries, especially in the attic and the basement, unless lots of feng shui remedies are carried out. People sleeping and working in such attics and basements tend to have low vitality and suffer from degenerative diseases due to dampness and a lack of qi and oxygen.

A fire roof is more positive in winter, if there is a lot of snow. Snow crystals, which have the similar blocking effect of a natural quartz crystal, reflect the rising energy back. Therefore, the qi in the house is higher in winter, creating a cosy effect.

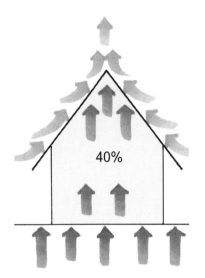

Diag. 16.14: Negative effect of fire roof. Energies and qi are directed to the apex of the roof.

Diag. 16.15A: Fire roof in winter. The snow and ice on the roof reflect the energy and qi back into the house.

Snow barriers on the roof effectively slow down the quick upsurge of energy. They improve the qi and oxygen in the fire roof house, even if there is no snow. The qi can be increased by 10–20%.

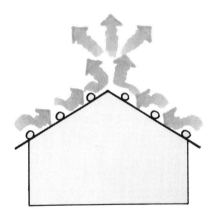

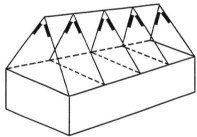

Diag. 16.15C: Remedy for a steep fire roof. Place 89 cm lengths of magnetised steel pipe 6–8 cm (2.5–3 in) in diameter as shown above. They should be about 2 m (6.5 ft) apart and the top of the pipes should not touch each other. Due to the magnetising effects of the steel pipes, an energy blockage is created at the peak of the apex. The qi and energy cannot rise and are redirected downwards.

Diag. 16.15B: Round wood used as snow barriers on the roof slows down the upward movement of energy.

You can also use bamboo flutes about 60 cm long. One piece of bamboo should be placed on each side of the slanting beam as shown in Diag. 16.15C. Make sure the 'blowing' part of each flute is on top. The flutes will 'blow' the upsurging qi down again.

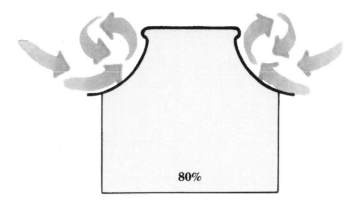

Diag. 16.16: This traditional Chinese roof is curved on both sides to redirect qi, energy and oxygen down. Cosmic qi in this type of house is usually around 80%.

Fire Roof Pitches

A low-pitched fire roof is positive. The lower the pitch, the more aerodynamic it is and the better it can keep down and contain qi and energy in a house, similar to a metal roof (see Diag. 16.18A–C). When the pitch is 15° or more, the qi will start to move upwards and escape (Diag. 16.17D), thus reducing the energy and qi in a house.

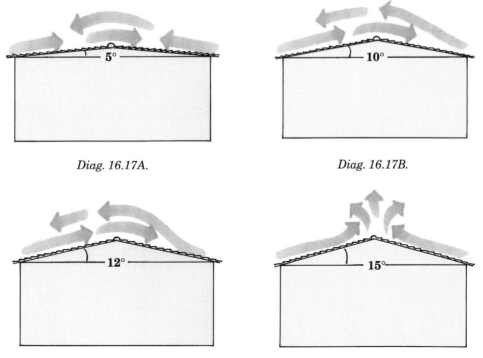

Diag. 16.17A.   *Diag. 16.17B.*

Diag. 16.17C.   *Diag. 16.17D.*

The Metal Roof

The best known examples of metal element roofs are the Eskimo's igloo and the Mongolian yurt. Round metal roof buildings require less heating in winter.

Generally, a metal element roof is a better roof for residential houses in temperate and cold countries. The curved shape is also positive when there are strong winds. Metal-shaped roof buildings generally show substantial savings in energy costs in strong wind locations. The curve of the metal element roof directs qi and energy downwards to prevent energy leakage.

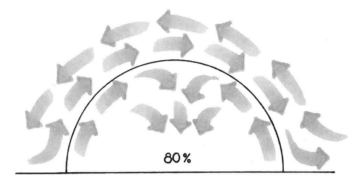

Diag. 16.18A: Houses with dome-shaped roofs generally have about 80% energy and qi.

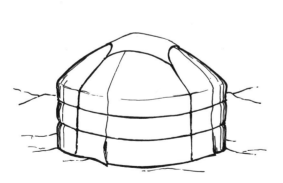

Diag. 16.18B: Energy can circulate round inside the yurt.

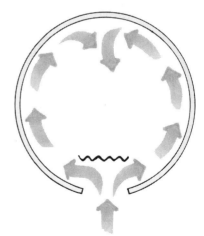

Diag. 16.18C: A Mongolian yurt with a dome-shaped roof and a circular base.

The Wood Roof

A wood-shaped roof is an auspicious shape for high-rise buildings. But care should be taken not to design a wood roof building close to or among fire roof buildings. Fire roof buildings will deplete the energy and qi of the wood roof building and adversely affect the performance and health of the occupants.

The native American teepee combines a wood circular shape with a fire roof. Because of its special spherical shape, it always has 60–70% qi inside. It is a very healthy living unit. Anyone with low vitality or in poor health should live in a teepee in their garden for several months during the warmer part of the year.

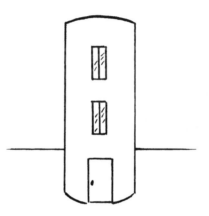

Diag. 16.19: Building with wood element roof.

Diag. 16.20: The teepee is a combination of the wood and fire elements.

The Earth Roof

Besides the metal roof and the fire roof with a pitch of less than 15°, the next best roof for a house is the earth element roof, which is flat. A flat roof, unlike the fire roof, does not pull energy and qi up to the higher floors. So an earth roof building should not be more than three storeys high, otherwise the upper floors will have very low qi and oxygen.

The only exception is when a whole building is air-conditioned, because then the air-conditioning system will direct cool air, qi and oxygen to all floors. In an air-conditioned building, the qi often stays at between 60–70% due to the recycling of some of the environmental toxins.

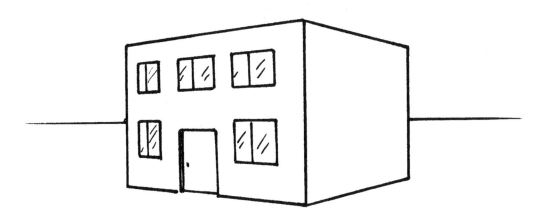

Diag. 16.21: Building with flat earth roof.

The Water Roof

The water element roof is seldom used for a single residential house. Instead, it is usually used for a cluster of houses along the side of a hill or for business or industrial buildings.

The best known water roof in the world is the Opera House in Sydney, Australia. Its structure matches its environment perfectly – it is close to the water.

When using a water roof for an industrial building, extra care should be taken to ensure that 'fire' industries that use fire or extremely high heat to produce products like plastics and steel are not set up in such buildings. The extremely 'cooling' characteristics of a water element roof will cool down machines, causing deterioration and damage, and thus slowly weaken the business.

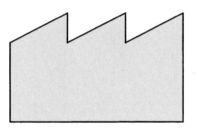

Diag. 16.22A: A cluster of water roof houses along the side of a hill.

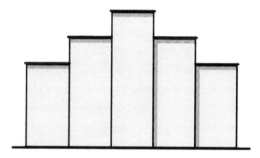

Diag. 16.22B: A graduated water roof commercial building.

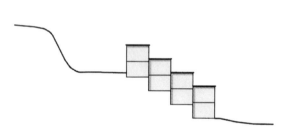

Diag. 16.22C: A water roof industrial building.

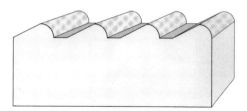

Diag. 16.22D: An industrial building with water roof.

Chapter 17

THE ENTRANCE AREA

When the occupants enter a house through the main door, their 'footprints' leave behind an electromagnetic field on the floor that attracts and directs cosmic qi into the house.

In temperate and cold countries where windows are shut most times of the year, between 70–80% of a house's qi enters through the main door. Only 20–30% comes through the windows. In warmer countries where most windows are open daily and year round, about 50–60% of qi enters through the main door; the rest of the qi comes in from the windows. It is vital to open the windows of a house more often, especially in temperate and cold countries, to allow more cosmic qi and oxygen to come in. Otherwise, feng shui remedies will have to be installed to attract more cosmic qi into the house.

The Doors of a House

In modern buildings, occupants often use a garage door, a back door or a side door in addition to the main door, to gain access. Using many entrances to access a house means a greater and faster flow of qi entering the house. This, in turn, causes a crossing of the flow of qi from different doors and locations, resulting in highly disturbed and violent qi in the house. Occupants of this type of house tend to be easily agitated and nervous. Their work performance, relationships and health also tend to suffer as a result.

Qi coming from different compass directions in a location has different qualities and speeds of flow, based on its surrounding landscape. It is important to find a direction with the best qi quality to open the main door.

Placement of Entrance Door

Different feng shui schools have different systems to determine the best location to place the main door of a house. This book explains three simplified systems to determine the best location to install a main door. These three systems represent the three best locations to place the main door:

1) For an individual, use the person's personal trigram according to their year of birth to determine the best compass direction. Tables 5 and 6 show charts for men and women, respectively, with year of birth and suggested directions where a main door should be placed.

1900*	1935	1970*
1901*	1936	1971*
1902	1937*	1972
1903	1938*	1973*
1904	1939	1974*
1905*	1940	1975*
1906	1941*	1976
1907	1942*	1977*
1908	1943	1978*
1909*	1944	1979*
1910	1945*	1980
1911	1946*	1981*
1912	1947	1982*
1913*	1948	1983*
1914	1949*	1984*
1915	1950*	1985*
1916	1951*	1986*
1917*	1952	1987*
1918*	1953*	1988*
1919	1954*	1989*
1920	1955*	1990*
1921*	1956	1991*
1922*	1957*	1992*
1923	1958*	1993*
1924	1959*	1994*
1925*	1960	1995*
1926*	1961*	1996*
1927	1962*	1997*
1928	1963*	1998*
1929*	1964	1999*
1930*	1965*	2000
1931	1966*	2001
1932	1967*	2002
1933*	1968	2003
1934*	1969*	2004

Table 4: To determine the day of commencement of spring. The Chinese lunar calendar starts on the first day of spring, which can be either 4 or 5 February. Years marked with an asterisk are years that begin on 4 February.

Example: In 1917, the Chinese lunar year starts on 4 February. Persons born between 4 February 1917 and 3 February 1918 should use 1917 to determine their main door direction – for men, it is southwest; for women, southeast. Those born on 3 February 1917 should use 1916 as the year to check their direction.

Southwest	East	Southeast	Southwest	Northwest	West	Northeast	South	North
1908	1907	1906	1905	1904	1903	1902	1901	1900
1917	1916	1915	1914	1913	1912	1911	1910	1909
1926	1925	1924	1923	1922	1921	1920	1919	1918
1935	1934	1933	1932	1931	1930	1929	1928	1927
1944	1943	1942	1941	1940	1939	1938	1937	1936
1953	1952	1951	1950	1949	1948	1947	1946	1945
1962	1961	1960	1959	1958	1957	1956	1955	1954
1971	1970	1969	1968	1967	1966	1965	1964	1963
1980	1979	1978	1977	1976	1975	1974	1973	1972
1989	1988	1987	1986	1985	1984	1983	1982	1981
1998	1997	1996	1995	1994	1993	1992	1991	1990
2007	2006	2005	2004	2003	2002	2001	2000	1999
2016	2015	2014	2013	2012	2011	2010	2009	2008
2025	2024	2023	2022	2021	2020	2019	2018	2017
2034	2033	2032	2031	2030	2029	2028	2027	2026
2043	2042	2041	2040	2039	2038	2037	2036	2035
2052	2051	2050	2049	2048	2047	2046	2045	2044

Table 5: Suggested door opening directions for men.

Southeast	East	Southwest	North	South	Northeast	West	Northwest	Northeast
1908	1907	1906	1905	1904	1903	1902	1901	1900
1917	1916	1915	1914	1913	1912	1911	1910	1909
1926	1925	1924	1923	1922	1921	1920	1919	1918
1935	1934	1933	1932	1931	1930	1929	1928	1927
1944	1943	1942	1941	1940	1939	1938	1937	1936
1953	1952	1951	1950	1949	1948	1947	1946	1945
1962	1961	1960	1959	1958	1957	1956	1955	1954
1971	1970	1969	1968	1967	1966	1965	1964	1963
1980	1979	1978	1977	1976	1975	1974	1973	1972
1989	1988	1987	1986	1985	1984	1983	1982	1981
1998	1997	1996	1995	1994	1993	1992	1991	1990
2007	2006	2005	2004	2003	2002	2001	2000	1999
2016	2015	2014	2013	2012	2011	2010	2009	2008
2025	2024	2023	2022	2021	2020	2019	2018	2017
2034	2033	2032	2031	2030	2029	2028	2027	2026
2043	2042	2041	2040	2039	2038	2037	2036	2035
2052	2051	2050	2049	2048	2047	2046	2045	2044

Table 6: Suggested door opening directions for women.

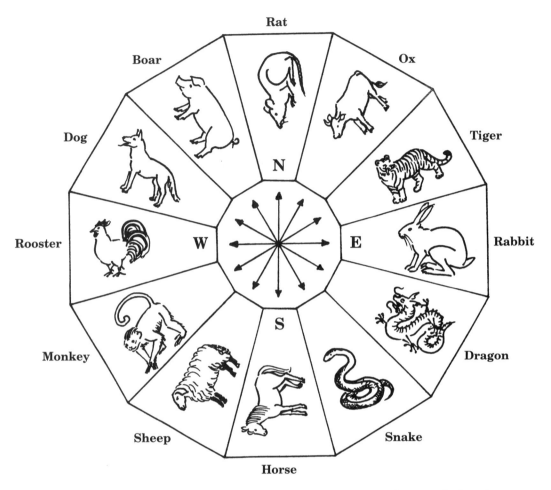

Diag. 17.1: Animal signs and compass directions to determine the direction for locating a main door. (Note: To find the animal horoscope or sign, look up Table 7.)

2) In the second method, use the person's birth year animal sign (see Diag. 17.1) to determine the compass direction. The animal sign for an individual, based on the year of birth, can be found in Table 7.

Both methods 1 and 2 give an individual the best directions to place their main door. What happens when a person is living with a partner? How do you determine the compass direction that is the most harmonious for both partners? In traditional Chinese feng shui practice, the main door should be determined by the man's horoscope or birth year. The woman is considered unimportant. But in Western countries, both partners are usually equally important. Techniques like applied kinesiology (Chapter 10) and the pendulum can help make an accurate decision in such cases.

19.02.1901	Metal	Ox	27.01.1941	Metal	Snake	05.02.1981	Metal	Rooster
08.02.1902	Water	Tiger	15.01.1942	Water	Horse	25.01.1982	Water	Dog
29.01.1903	Water	Rabbit	05.02.1943	Water	Sheep	13.02.1983	Water	Boar
16.02.1904	Wood	Dragon	25.01.1944	Wood	Monkey	02.02.1984	Wood	Rat
04.02.1905	Wood	Snake	13.02.1945	Wood	Rooster	20.02.1985	Wood	Ox
25.01.1906	Fire	Horse	02.02.1946	Fire	Dog	09.02.1986	Fire	Tiger
13.02.1907	Fire	Sheep	22.01.1947	Fire	Boar	29.01.1987	Fire	Rabbit
02.02.1908	Earth	Monkey	10.02.1948	Earth	Rat	17.02.1988	Earth	Dragon
22.01.1909	Earth	Rooster	29.01.1949	Earth	Ox	06.02.1989	Earth	Snake
10.02.1910	Metal	Dog	17.02.1950	Metal	Tiger	27.01.1990	Metal	Horse
30.01.1911	Metal	Boar	06.02.1951	Metal	Rabbit	15.02.1991	Metal	Sheep
18.02.1912	Water	Rat	27.01.1952	Water	Dragon	04.02.1992	Water	Monkey
06.02.1913	Water	Ox	14.02.1953	Water	Snake	23.01.1993	Water	Rooster
26.01.1914	Wood	Tiger	03.02.1954	Wood	Horse	10.02.1994	Wood	Dog
14.02.1915	Wood	Rabbit	24.01.1955	Wood	Sheep	31.01.1995	Wood	Boar
03.02.1916	Fire	Dragon	12.02.1956	Fire	Monkey	19.02.1996	Fire	Rat
23.01.1917	Fire	Snake	31.01.1957	Fire	Rooster	07.02.1997	Fire	Ox
11.02.1918	Earth	Horse	18.02.1958	Earth	Dog	28.01.1998	Earth	Tiger
01.02.1919	Earth	Sheep	08.02.1959	Earth	Boar	16.02.1999	Earth	Rabbit
20.02.1920	Metal	Monkey	28.01.1960	Metal	Rat	05.02.2000	Metal	Dragon
08.02.1921	Metal	Rooster	15.02.1961	Metal	Ox	24.01.2001	Metal	Snake
28.01.1922	Water	Dog	05.02.1962	Water	Tiger	12.02.2002	Water	Horse
16.02.1923	Water	Boar	25.01.1963	Water	Rabbit	01.02.2003	Water	Sheep
05.02.1924	Wood	Rat	13.02.1964	Wood	Dragon	22.01.2004	Wood	Monkey
25.01.1925	Wood	Ox	02.02.1965	Wood	Snake	09.02.2005	Wood	Rooster
13.02.1926	Fire	Tiger	21.01.1966	Fire	Horse	29.01.2006	Fire	Dog
02.02.1927	Fire	Rabbit	09.02.1967	Fire	Sheep	18.02.2007	Fire	Boar
23.01.1928	Earth	Dragon	30.01.1968	Earth	Monkey	02.02.2008	Earth	Rat
10.02.1929	Earth	Snake	17.02.1969	Earth	Rooster	26.01.2009	Earth	Ox
30.01.1930	Metal	Horse	06.02.1970	Metal	Dog	14.01.2010	Metal	Tiger
17.02.1931	Metal	Sheep	27.01.1971	Metal	Boar	03.02.2011	Metal	Rabbit
06.02.1932	Water	Monkey	15.02.1972	Water	Rat	23.01.2012	Water	Dragon
26.01.1933	Water	Rooster	03.02.1973	Water	Ox	10.02.2013	Water	Snake
14.02.1934	Wood	Dog	23.01.1974	Wood	Tiger	31.01.2014	Wood	Horse
04.02.1935	Wood	Boar	11.02.1975	Wood	Rabbit	19.02.2015	Wood	Sheep
24.01.1936	Fire	Rat	31.01.1976	Fire	Dragon	08.02.2016	Fire	Monkey
11.02.1937	Fire	Ox	18.02.1977	Fire	Snake	28.01.2017	Fire	Rooster
31.01.1938	Earth	Tiger	07.02.1978	Earth	Horse	16.02.2018	Earth	Dog
19.02.1939	Earth	Rabbit	28.01.1979	Earth	Sheep	05.02.2019	Earth	Boar
08.02.1940	Metal	Dragon	16.02.1980	Metal	Monkey	25.01.2020	Metal	Rat

Table 7: To determine a person's birth element. (Note: A person born between 19 February 1901 and 7 February 1902 is a metal person, and the Ox is their animal sign.)

3) Use the pendulum or applied kinesiology to help decide the best compass direction. When using applied kinesiology, the person being tested should face a direction, ready for the muscle test. The question to ask is: 'Is this the best compass direction to open the main door, bringing harmony, good health and prosperity to the family (or to the couple)?'

If the person tests weak, he should turn several degrees clockwise, but still remain in one spot. Ask the same question again and test the person. The person being tested should turn several degrees at a time around the compass directions until the correct direction is indicated by a very strong muscle response. The person should then remain in this position until the exact direction is checked using a compass. (Note: When taking a reading from a compass, make sure the reading is taken outside the building as steel and metal structures in the building may distort the reading. If there is an obstacle like a tree or a wall in the chosen direction in front of the house blocking the main door, we must determine the second best direction by using the muscle test.)

The technique of applied kinesiology greatly simplifies feng shui divination practice. Some of the rigid structures and traditions are taken out, making it a practical and application-oriented art and science.

Where to Place the Main Door

Qi energy comes from the universe in rays which have a different quality, strength and intensity. If the main door is placed in the right location, there will be strong qi entering the house. But due to planetary movements, these rays move. A strong qi flow from a certain direction may decrease after a period of time. In advanced feng shui practice, these energies can be calculated according to certain cycles. In this beginner's book, I would like to recommend the following simple guidelines:

Example to determine the exact location for the main door

In this example, we assume the best direction for a person's main door is south. The length of a house front can be from 5 to 20 m (16.5–65 ft), depending on the size of the house. Where along the front is the correct location to put the door?

First, we need to divide the front of the house into five sections, as illustrated in Diag. 17.2. Then, we can select the section with the most harmonious and highest qi to locate the main door.

The percentage of qi in each section can be determined using the pendulum or applied kinesiology.

Generally, it is more auspicious to open the main door in the middle of a house for better yin and yang harmony. So if the qi in the middle section 3 is not below 70%, the door should be placed here. The door may also be moved to the side, but should preferably not be located on the side near the corner.

Should the qi fall below 70%, then the next place to open the main door is in section 2, where the qi is 90% (Dragon side). We can then use feng shui remedies to increase the qi in the house to 80–100% as desired.

Exceptional care should be taken to ensure that the main door does not face negative symbols and obstructions like a tree trunk, a lamp post or some other harmful and aggressive object. If there is an obstruction in front of the selected area for the main door, then a more auspicious location has to be selected.

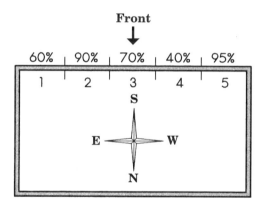

Diag. 17.2: Example of the different energies at the front of a house. The figures indicate the percentage of quality qi coming in at each of the five sections.

Diag. 17.3: The entrance represents the mouth of its occupants. This is where most of the qi comes in.

Rules for Placement of a Main Door

- A main door should face an open space, without any obstructions like trees with exposed trunks, lamp posts, water hydrants or bus signs. Any negative obstruction should be at least 75–100 m (245–330 ft) away from the house and 2 m (6.5 ft) on either side of the doorway to allow ample space for the free flow of cosmic qi to enter the house. A neighbour's sharp roof gable should not face opposite the main door.

- The main door area should be well lit to attract qi and to provide a welcoming atmosphere. A poorly-lit main entrance tends to be yin and attracts negative qi.

- A main door should preferably face calm flowing or moving water like a lake, pond, sea, stream, river, fountain or waterfall. These waters should be at least 3 m (10 ft) from the main door. When a main door cannot face natural flowing water, man-made water systems like a fountain, waterfall or running water can be created to enhance the flow of cosmic qi into the house.

- Care should be taken to ensure that the main door is diagonally opposite the back door of the house (see Diag. 17.4A and 17.4B). Avoid a main door that is in a direct line with the back door (see Diag. 17.5A). In such a house, the qi will escape immediately through the back door before it can circulate to the other rooms. Its occupants will lack vitality, success and prosperity. They will become even more severely stressed when their heart and lungs are negatively affected.

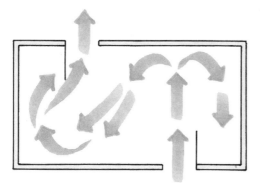

Diag. 17.4A: Positive – A main door and a back door placed diagonally to allow the qi to circulate evenly in the house.

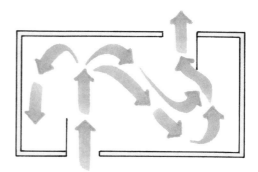

Diag. 17.4B: Positive – A main door and a back door are placed diagonally.

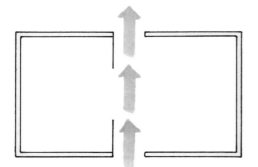

Diag. 17.5A: Negative – Placement of the main door and back door in a straight line. Qi and oxygen will escape very quickly. Result: the occupants will have low vitality, and tend to have more health and money problems.

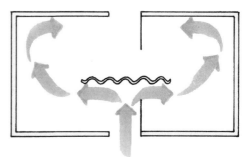

Diag. 17.5B: Remedy – A solid divider or a solid door-height bookcase or cupboard to block the qi and oxygen from going straight through the back door.

The Front and Back Door

A traditional house has a front door and a back door. Each house must have a back door so that stale energy can escape. If there is no back door, occupants will tend to have constipation and sluggish energy.

You may use a balcony or a terrace door as a back door. A window may also be declared as the back door if you put marker strips around the window to make it look like a back door.

Another possibility is to create a symbolic back door by marking coloured strips on a wall. In just a few minutes, you will notice the air in the house becoming fresher as stale energy escapes through the symbolic back door. Make sure the wall on which this symbolic back door is situated, is facing an open space. Otherwise, the stale energy of your house might escape into a neighbour's flat. In Hong Kong, Taiwan or Singapore, you can buy posters showing a symbolic back door.

A back door should normally open to the inside. If it opens to the outside, energy will escape more quickly. To remedy this, hang a small windchime with 10 cm (4 in) long solid metal tubes close to the ceiling. It should be 1 m (3.3 ft) away from the back door to slow down the qi flow (see also Chapter 22).

A back door should never be bigger than the front door; otherwise, there will be a substantial leakage of qi and wealth.

The Door-Window Line

The door-window line is found mainly in modern houses and causes qi leakage. In cases where the door and window are directly opposite each other, use a divider as shown in Diag. 17.5B. Alternatively, you may use a windchime or a natural quartz crystal to block qi from escaping through the window.

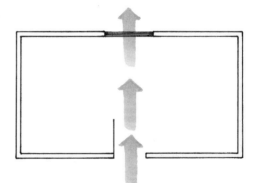

Diag. 17.6A: Negative – The door directly faces a window. A substantial amount of qi will escape before it can circulate in a room or the house.

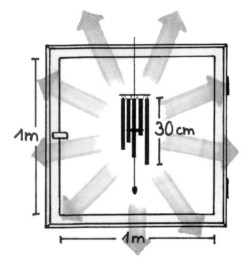

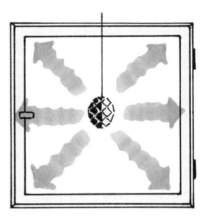

Diag. 17.6B: Remedy – Hang a windchime in the middle of the window, about 30 cm (12 in) from the window glass. Each windchime with 30 cm long hollow tubes covers 1 square m (10 square ft) of the window. A windchime with solid tubes of 15 cm (6 in) length generates more intense sound and is also sufficient to cover a 1 m square window (see also Chapter 22 on windchimes).

Diag. 17.6C: Remedy – Hang a natural quartz crystal three times the size of an adult's thumb in the middle of the window. One crystal is sufficient to cover a 1 m square window.

Stairs in the Entrance Area

A staircase should not be placed immediately in front of a main door. Otherwise, most of the cosmic qi will move upstairs or down to the basement, leaving very little qi for the other floors.

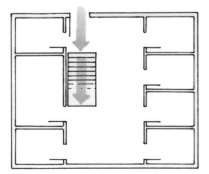

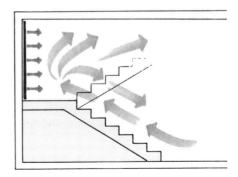

Diag. 17.7A: Negative – A main door opposite the stairs allows cosmic qi to move upstairs.

Diag. 17.7B: Remedy – Place a large mirror on the first landing area to reflect some qi back down the stairs.

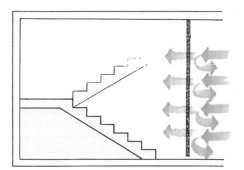

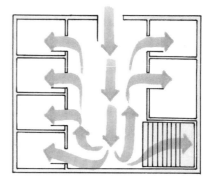

Diag. 17.7C: Remedy – Use a bead curtain to slow down the flow of incoming qi.

Diag. 17.7D: Positive – Stairs are not in direct line with the entrance. Qi can circulate to all rooms.

Sharp Corners in the Entrance Area

A main door should not be directly opposite or facing the corners of walls or furniture which attack occupants when they enter a building.

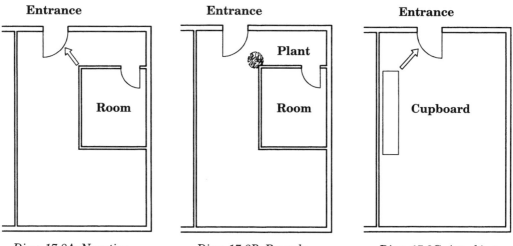

Diag. 17.8A: Negative – Attacking wall corner.

Diag. 17.8B: Remedy – Hang a ribbon or an artificial creeping plant from the ceiling to the floor to cover the corner.

Diag. 17.8C: Attacking furniture corner. Remedy – Remove the cupboard.

Mirrors in the Entrance Area

Do not place a large mirror opposite the main door. It reflects energy out again and creates turbulence at the entrance area, causing balance problems and agitation.

Mirrors on Doors

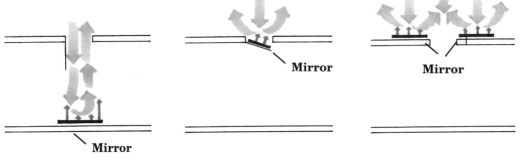

Diag. 17.9A: Negative –
A big mirror inside a
doorway reflects and
bounces the qi

Diag. 17.9B: Negative –
The mirror on the outside of
the door reflects qi away.
As a result, qi cannot enter
the house.

Diag. 17.9C: Negative –
Mirrors on both sides of the
door reflect qi away.

The Entrance and Toilet Door

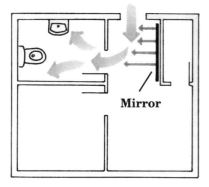

Diag. 17.10A: Negative – A big mirror
opposite a toilet and near a door
reflects qi into the toilet.

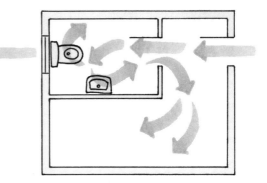

Diag. 17.10B: Negative – The qi of the entire
house goes into the toilet, and some energy
escapes through the window.

The toilet door should not face a main door. Otherwise, the whole house's benevolent cosmic qi will move to the toilet, and some qi will escape when the toilet is flushed. Unhealthy qi from the toilet also contaminates the house, causing health problems to its occupants.

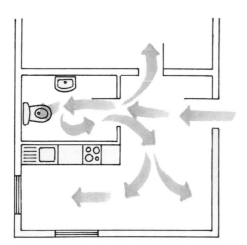

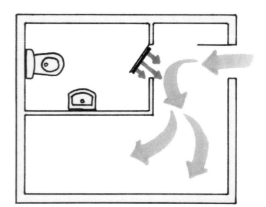

Diag. 17.10C: Negative – A toilet without windows. Qi from the main door that goes into the toilet is forced out again. Contaminated qi goes into the kitchen, dining and living areas, causing food contamination and health problems.

Diag. 17.10D: Remedy for 17.10B–C – Install a slim mirror on the outside of the toilet door to block qi from entering the toilet.

A common remedy is to place a small windchime or a small mirror (measuring 26 cm x 112 cm or another positive measurement) in front of the toilet door to reflect qi back. There is a rule for the size of mirrors to be used opposite an entrance door. Every 10 cm (4 in) width of mirror should be a 1 m (3.3 ft) distance from the entrance door to avoid qi being reflected out. Thus, for a 20 cm (8 in) mirror, a distance of 2 m (6.5 ft) should be allowed between the toilet and the main door.

Entrance in Direct Line with Room Door

The main door should preferably not face the door of a room. Otherwise, all the cosmic qi will move into one room, and the remaining rooms on the side or at the back will lack qi.

The remedy for the situation shown in Diag. 17.11 is to hang a 15 cm (6 in) long windchime with solid tubes (for a hollow-tube windchime, the tubes should be double that length) between the two doors, high up near the ceiling, to disperse the incoming qi to the other rooms. Make sure the windchime is hung at least 1 m (3.3 ft) from any door.

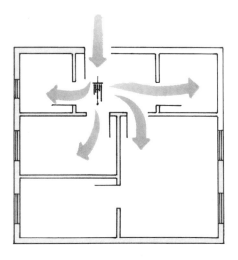

Diag. 17.11: The energy is dispersed by a windchime.

Ideally, a main door should open into the living room (representing the lungs and chest area of a human) for the cosmic qi to spread to the other parts of the house.

Overhead Beams in Entrance Area

There should be no horizontal beams or columns on the ceiling behind a main door. Beams create a curtain-like barrier, which blocks qi from moving into the house and directs qi down, attacking occupants entering and standing in the entrance area. There should be no exposed beam within 3 m (10 ft) of a door opening. The same principle applies to all rooms.

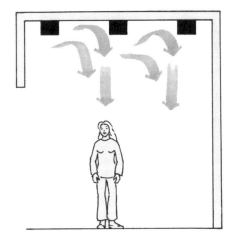

Diag. 17.12: Negative – A downward draft attacking occupants when they enter a house.

Walls Opposite the Entrance

When a main door opens into a facing wall within only 1–1.5 m (3.3–5 ft) away, cosmic qi is bounced out immediately, causing turbulence at the main door that attacks and disturbs occupants coming into the house. Such a wall should be at least 2 m (6.5 ft) away from the entrance.

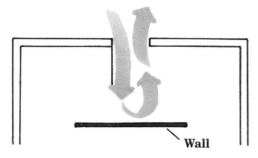

Diag. 17.13A: Negative – Main door facing a wall. The door is too close if within 1 to 1.5 m (3.3–6.5 ft) of a wall. Qi and energy are bounced out again.

Diag. 17.13B: Remedy – Place a water fountain or a picture of a waterfall behind the wall or further away from the wall to attract and pull qi quickly into the house.

Sewage Grilles

There should be no exposed sewage grilles in front of the main door of a house. An open sewage grille emits nasty smells and bad energy that will be blown into the house, contaminating food and causing health problems.

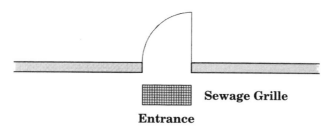

Diag. 17.14: Drain or sewage grilles in front of a door. Remedy – Cover up the grilles.

Strong Winds

A main door facing frequent and violent winds is also very unhealthy for the occupants. Fierce winds bring choking qi into a house, causing balance problems. The occupants will tend to suffer from high anxiety, nervousness, hormone imbalance and depression.

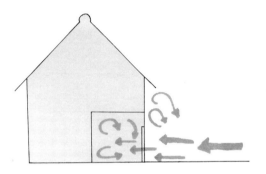

Diag. 17.15A: Violent winds blowing towards a main door cause turbulence and choking qi to enter a house.

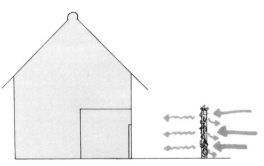

Diag. 17.15B: Remedy – Install a trellis fence at least 5–10 m (16.5–33 ft) away from the main door to block or soften the violent, attacking winds.

Effects of Direction of Door Opening

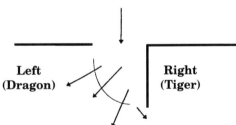

Diag. 17.16A: Door hinged on the right side (Tiger side). The left side of the room has more qi and energy. It is best to sit or sleep on the left side. The effect is reversed when the door is hinged on the left side.

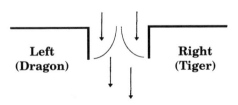

Diag. 17.16B: Door with hinges on left and right and opening in the middle. Energy tends to move into the centre; the left and right sides will tend to have less energy. Furniture or a wall can be used to direct qi to other parts of the room or house.

Arrangement of Doors

The doors of opposite rooms should not be exactly opposite each other; otherwise, there will be conflict between the occupants in opposite rooms. Occupants from opposite rooms could knock into each other when they come out quickly from their doorways.

Remedy – Hang a 6–10 cm (2.5–4 in) long windchime high on the ceiling between the two doors to create a barrier and to disperse the negative energy, thereby reducing conflicts.

 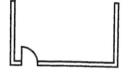 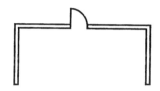

Diag. 17.18A: Door opening outwards blocks qi from coming in.

 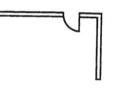 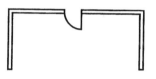

Diag. 17.17A: Negative – Doors exactly opposite each other.

Diag. 17.17B: Positive – Doors are diagonal to each other.

Diag. 17.18B: Door should open inward to allow a faster flow of cosmic qi.

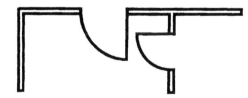 

Diag. 17.19A: Negative – Door should not open into another door. This blocks the flow of soft qi and creates unnecessary turbulence in the entrance area.

Diag. 17.19B: Positive – Door opening directions have been changed. The right door is now smaller.

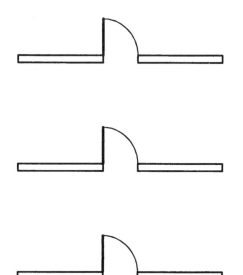

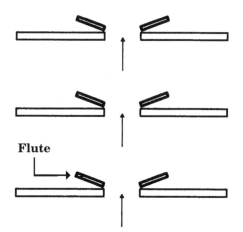

Flute

Diag. 17.20B: Remedy – Place a pair of flutes behind the top of each door to suck in more cosmic qi.

Diag. 17.20A: Putting three doors or more in a row is not auspicious. Each door frame blocks the energy from going into the next room. By the time the energy flows to the third door, it would have been depleted. The occupants at the end of the corridor will tend to be less healthy and less successful.

Diag. 17.20C: Arrangement of flutes behind the doors.

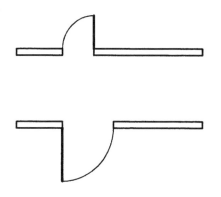

Diag. 17.21A: When one door opposite another door is larger, the larger door will overpower the room with the smaller door, causing intimidation and fear to the occupants of the room with the smaller door.

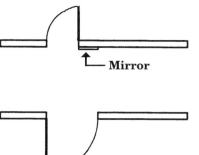

Mirror

Diag. 17.21B: Remedy – Place a mirror to reflect the big door and to give the illusion of enlarging the smaller door.

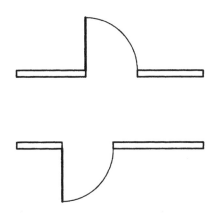

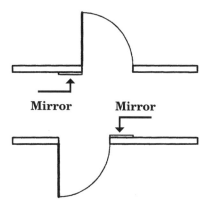

Diag. 17.22A: When two opposite doors are placed at a right angle to each other, they cause an imbalance of energy flowing into each room, creating a cutting effect.

Diag. 17.22B: A common remedy is to place mirrors on either side to balance the doors and to redirect energy into the rooms. The best remedy is, of course, to change the alignment of one of the doors so that the two doors do not face each other.

Width and Height of Door

Ideally, there should be at least a 30 cm (12 in) space between the head of an average occupant and the height of the door. The width of the door should also have at least 30 cm of space on each side of a person's body when they pass through a door. A door with less than a 30 cm head space and body width causes a disturbance to a person's electromagnetic field (aura) when they enter a room. When the height is low and the width is narrow, it is just like somebody giving us a slap.

All doors should conform to good feng shui measurements. The main door should be bigger than the other doors of the house. But it is also negative when the main door is disproportionately big. This indicates that the mouth of the house is too big.

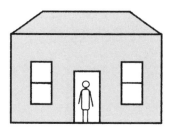

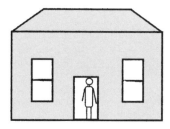

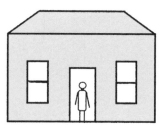

Diag. 17.23A: Normal sized door.

Diag. 17.23B: Negative – The door is too low.

Diag. 17.23C: Negative – The door is too high and out of proportion with the house.

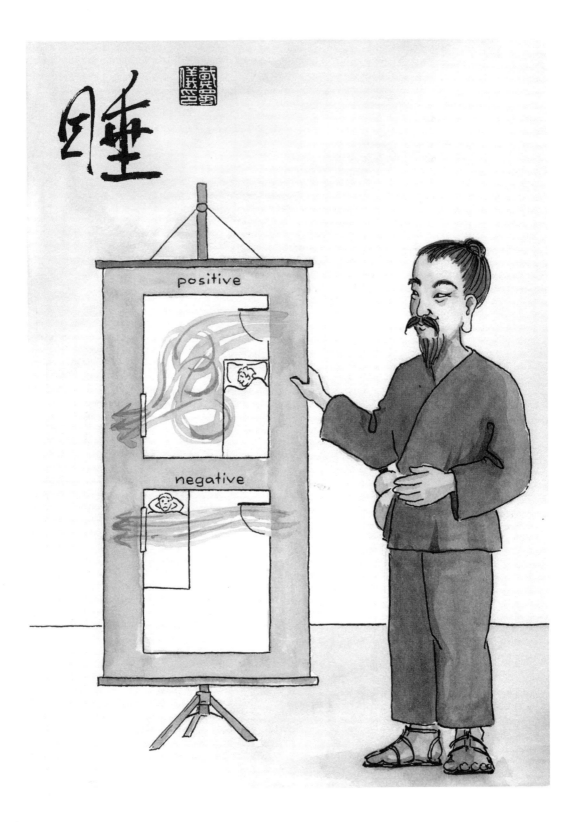

Chapter 18

BEDROOMS AND SLEEPING POSITIONS

The body and mind need to recuperate and regenerate after a long day's work. Complete rest and a sound sleep give body cells time to renew, repair and grow. The body's accumulated wastes are gradually moved out of the body for disposal in urine, sweat and faecal waste.

Sleeping is regarded as low activity – yin. Therefore, a bedroom should be placed in a low activity, yin area at the back of a house or on the first floor.

A bedroom should be painted in colours that are in harmony with the occupants according to their birth year element. It should be decorated and furnished in a cosy, calm, relaxed and happy environment to facilitate rest and recovery in preparation for the challenges of the next day.

Like all rooms, a bedroom must have a back door to allow stale air and qi to escape. A window or balcony door can be designated as a back door for stale qi to move out. Windchimes or natural quartz crystals should not be placed to block this back door.

When a bedroom does not have windows, a symbolic window has to be created by painting a look-alike window on one wall facing an open space. This has similar effects as a back door. You should try to avoid a bedroom without windows.

A bedroom should not be placed:

- Above a garage or store where stagnant energy and dirty air accumulate and move upwards, causing health problems to occupants living or working there. Remedy: Put two plants, less than 1 m (3.3 ft) high and with lots of leaves, in your room to filter the toxic air. But place the plants 2 m (6.5 ft) away from your body, especially your head.

- Immediately opposite, next to, above or below a toilet where contaminated energy is circulating.
  Remedy: For a bedroom that is situated opposite a toilet, put a mirror inside the toilet door to reflect dirty energy back to the toilet and out of the toilet window.

- Next to, opposite, below or above a kitchen. Sleeping next to a kitchen is not auspicious because radiation and electromagnetic fields from the kitchen power supply and equipment can affect the health of the occupants. Moreover, occupants near a kitchen will tend to be attracted by the smell of food and may overeat, causing obesity.
  Remedy: Change your room with someone who is underweight! Do not place your bed next to a kitchen wall – allow for a clear distance of at least 1.5 m (5 ft) from the wall.

Diag. 18.1: Negative – A bedroom next to the kitchen.

- Next to the living room or children's play room, where there is much noise and disturbance. Although the rooms may be quiet at night, the energy of the loud noises created during the day still moves in the room. It disturbs the calm bedroom energy, causing agitation and a disturbed sleep.
  Remedy: If possible, move your bedroom.

- Within 70 m (230 ft) of a tram line or railway line, which can cause severe vibrations and disturbances. If the trams or trains are powered by electricity, electromagnetic and electrical radiation is also generated. Remedy – Move out of your house as this strong vibrational energy cannot be neutralised and can cause balance problems to house occupants.

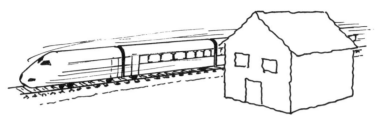

Diag. 18.2: Avoid a house next to a railway line.

- Above a butcher's shop – although the carcasses of animals seem harmless, the energy of fear and death still emit from the meat and circulate upwards. Remedy: Change your bedroom to another location. Better still, move out!

- Above a funeral parlour – a funeral parlour is always crowded with ghosts and spirits; some spirits may go upstairs, creating fear which results in depression, kidney problems as well as general health problems.
  Remedy: Hang up a pa'kua (see Diag. 23.25). It is best to move out of your house.

- Above a cafe that allows smoking – the smell of food and cigarette smoke moving upwards will affect the occupants upstairs.
  Remedy: Change your bedroom to another location or move out of your house.

- Above a bar or discotheque, where loud music is played. Although no loud music may be played after midnight, the loud, distracting energy still stays in the room and slowly moves upwards during the night, causing disturbed sleep. Prolonged loud noise causes severe heart and mental balance problems. It is best to move out of the house.

- Next to or near a street or road because of the distracting noises. Remedy: Move the bedroom to a quieter area.

- Next to or near a rubbish collection area. The bad odour and decaying rubbish present a health hazard to room occupants.

- At the end of a long corridor, where the qi and energy are rushing in too vigorously. Too much qi can cause a disturbed sleep, and occupants tend to be hyperactive and nervous. Remedy: Hang a small windchime with solid tubes about 15 cm (6 in) long from the ceiling in the middle of the corridor to slow down the energy.

Mirrors in the Bedroom

- A bed should not be placed facing a mirror or with a mirror at the back. If this is the case, the mirror needs to be covered up or removed.

A mirror behind the bed reflects and disturbs the human aura. When the person is sleeping, the soul leaves the body. When it returns, it perceives the body in the bed and in the mirror and does not know where to go. When this happens, the person wakes up with a shock. If there is a mirror in front of the bed, the person will see their image on waking, frightening themselves.

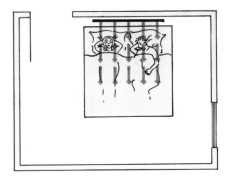

Diag. 18.3A: Negative – Mirror behind a bed.

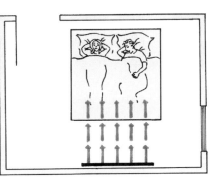

Diag. 18.3B: Negative –
Mirror in front of a bed.

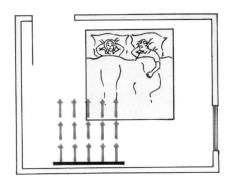

Diag. 18.3C: Negative –
Mirror reflecting on the bed.

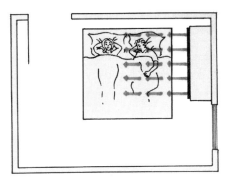

Diag. 18.3D: Negative – The reflection of the mirror is 'pushing' the sleeper to the side. Unconsciously, the sleeper will try to 'escape' by moving to the middle of the bed, thus disturbing their partner.

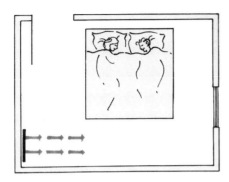

Diag. 18.3E: Positive – Sleepers are not disturbed by the mirror.

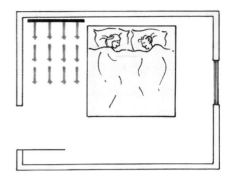

Diag. 18.3F: Positive – The mirror, if placed like this, will not cause a problem.

Where should a bed be placed in a bedroom?

The following are some general guidelines:

*   There should be no underground water lines, earth stress or other negative radiation in the bed area.

*   A bed head should preferably face magnetic north or magnetic south for those living in the northern and southern hemispheres respectively.

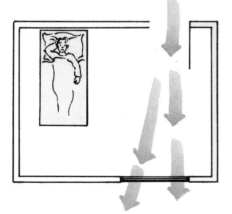

Diag. 18.4: The right way to place your bed. However, this room has a major defect in that the door is directly opposite the room's window, which leaks good qi. As a result, the occupant has low qi and low vitality.

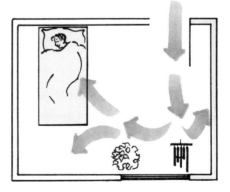

Diag. 18.5: Remedies – Place a plant and a windchime of appropriate size in front of the window to bounce the qi back to circulate in the room. Alternatively, you can hang a large-faceted natural quartz crystal (three times the size of an adult thumb) to block the window.

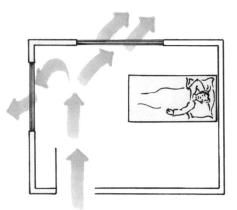

Diag. 18.6: Negative – The sleeper's feet are facing the window and the door.

The following principle is very important: When awake, we are on the alert and want to face the door to observe things happening. But when sleeping, we want a complete absence of noise, if possible. We don't want to know what is happening outside of our bedroom door. Therefore, we should not see the door from our bed.

The person in Diag. 18.6 is sleeping with his feet facing the window and the door. The worst situation is when a person's feet are directly opposite the door. Apart from not getting a sound sleep, he will also have a 'phantom fear'.

Among the Chinese, Maori (New Zealand natives) and some South American cultures, only a dead person is placed with their feet facing the door and carried out of their room with their legs first. Interestingly, hospitals in the British Commonwealth follow this rule: When a person is alive, they must be carried or moved out of their room with their head first. I have discovered from my investigations that this prevents a weakening of the immune system.

A person sleeping with their legs facing the door could shorten their life span. Readers can use a pendulum or applied kinesiology to check on this. A person who must see their bedroom door or else cannot sleep could have suffered some trauma in childhood or in a previous life, possibly sexual abuse or an attack while they were sleeping. From my experience, psychotherapy can solve this problem.

- A bed should preferably be placed between two solid walls to support the headboard and legboard and to give good support and protection. If this is not possible, you should at least have a high headboard to give you good backing and support. In olden days, all beds were designed this way.

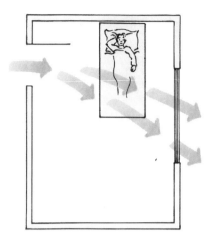

Diag. 18.7: Negative – The bed is placed in the door line and energy path.

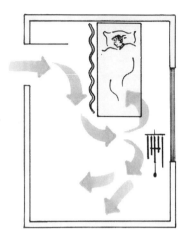

Diag. 18.8: Remedy – Place a screen or divider between your bed and the door to block and redirect the qi.

- A bed should not be placed along the energy path of the door as cosmic qi and oxygen coming in will attack the occupant, causing health problems such as heart disease and nervousness.

- A bed should preferably not be placed on the floor unless good insulation like a thick straw mat is placed underneath. The cold energy (from the concrete floor, for example) and electrical cables inside the floor may adversely affect the sleeper, causing a disturbed sleep and heart problems. Dust from the floor could also cause allergy problems.

- A bed should be placed at least 1 m (3.3 ft) away from a normal window with a 1 m (3.3 ft) concrete base below the window. For a window that is completely glass down to the floor, the bed should be at least 2 m (6.5 ft) away. Glass windows act as a conduit for qi to move out. If a bed is too close, the outgoing qi also pulls the occupant out of the window, causing much anxiety and nervousness. People who sleep within 1 m (3.3 ft) of a completely glass window in a high-rise building tend to suffer from health problems related to height syndrome.
  Remedy: Put a 1.5 m (5 ft) high piece of solid wooden board between your bed and the window to act as a barrier.

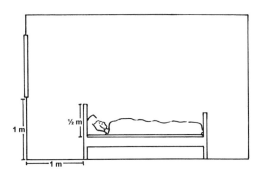

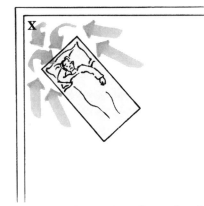

Diag. 18.9: Height of headboard and
distance from window.

Diag. 18.10: Energy is redirected at the
corner, attacking the sleeper.

Avoid placing your bed diagonally as in Diag. 18.10. Energy moves to the corner 'X' and is directed outward, attacking the sleeper. Although a headboard can somewhat soften the negative attacking energy, some subtle energy will still penetrate, causing disturbed sleep. The sharp corner at 'X' can be neutralised by a cupboard or other feng shui remedy. The sleeper's legs should not face the door.

• Avoid placing a bed next to a bathroom where a water pipe runs along the intermediate wall. Water energy is yin and cold water in a pipe radiates cold yin energy up to a distance of 1 m (3.3 ft) from a wall, affecting any person who sleeps immediately next to it. Health problems may include rheumatic body pains and weakness of the immune system, resulting in chest colds and lung problems.

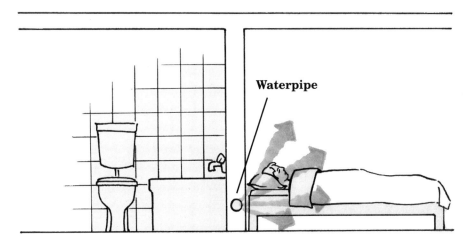

Diag. 18.11: The bed is next to a wall with a water pipe.

Remedy: Move the bed about 1.5 m (5 ft) away from the wall or put a mirror facing the wall in the area of the water pipe. (Important: The reflective side should face the wall, reflecting the water energy.) Alternatively, some mirror foil can be used. The foil or mirror should be three times the width of the pipe.

- For cleansing the air, each bedroom should have a plant less than 1 m (3.3 ft) tall placed 2–3 m (6.5–10 ft) a way from the bed (see chapter 22).

These guidelines should be sufficient for you to get started. As each bedroom is different, this book can only provide some basic rules. You can learn more by attending a good feng shui course where practical examples are discussed. You can also benefit from an individual consultation.

Chapter 19

THE KITCHEN

In olden days, women spent most of the day in the kitchen, preparing food for the family. The widespread use of modern kitchen equipment and the availability of pre-cooked, ready-to-eat food today, however, means that less time is being spent in the kitchen. Most families only cook once a day. So the importance of the kitchen has diminished.

In China, most ovens and cooking places are made of clay or earth. Traditionally, the oven or cooking place is positioned facing east to receive the eastern sun's heat and thus reduce energy costs. The east direction belongs to the wood element, which also helps to enhance the power of fire, increasing energy and therefore enhancing the abundance of the family.

In feng shui, each compass direction is attributed to an element. It is advisable to avoid placing the kitchen in areas of the house where there is an elemental conflict with the kitchen's fire element. The elements according to the East-West system will be discussed in my future book on trigram feng shui.

For this introductory book, I suggest that you avoid placing your kitchen in the north (water element) as the north, which represents cold and water, is in conflict with the kitchen's fire energy. Food prepared may not be as nourishing or health-giving. You should also avoid placing your kitchen or oven in the west (metal element) and northwest (metal element and mentor area). Kitchen fire destroys metal, resulting in unnecessary energy conflicts and unhealthy prepared food.

Guidelines for the Kitchen

1) The oven/stove (fire element) should be at least 1–1.5 m (3.3–5 ft) from the sink, dishwasher and refrigerator (water element) to avoid elemental conflict.

   Conflict between the fire and water elements will cause too much turbulence, which will then affect the quality of the food cooked and the psyche of the person doing the cooking. In this situation, the stove will require a higher temperature to cook the food, thus increasing energy costs.

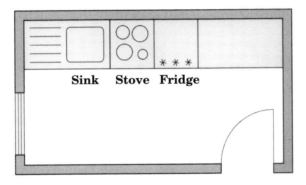

Diag. 19.1: Negative – The stove is sandwiched between the sink and the refrigerator.

Diag. 19.2: A good kitchen arrangement separating the water and fire elements.
A mirror can be placed 30 cm (12 in) above the stove so that the person doing the cooking can see people coming into the kitchen (see also Diag. 19.4).

2) A stove should not be placed below an overhead beam. The downward draft of attacking energy directed by the straight beam will disturb the stove fire, resulting in cooked food of poor quality and health problems for the occupants. The person doing the cooking will also tend to suffer from heartburn and sore throat.

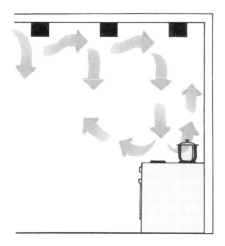

Diag. 19.3: Overhead beams above the stove.

3) There should be no window behind or near a stove. The subtle energy of the wind from outside (especially cold winds) will come in through the window (even if it is closed) and disturb the stove's heat. Winds blowing towards the stove will also cause heat problems to the person doing the cooking, that may result in dry cough, heartburn or lung problems.

4) The stove should preferably be placed where the person doing the cooking can see the door. If the cook cannot see the door, it may cause nervousness or sudden fright when somebody comes in. The remedy is to place a large mirror so that the person doing the cooking can see people coming into the kitchen (see Diag. 19.2, 19.4 and 19.5). The mirror should be raised at least 30 cm (12 in) above the stove to avoid the mirror reflecting heat to the person doing the cooking. The mirror can be as long as the wall or shorter.

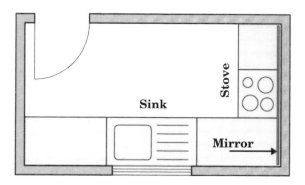

Diag. 19.4: A mirror 30 cm (12 in) above the stove.

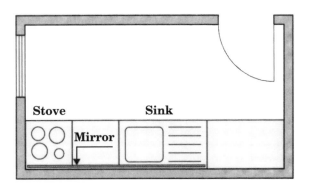

Diag. 19.5: A mirror above the stove.

5)   The kitchen stove should not be placed facing the kitchen door. The draft and qi that move in will disturb the heat of the stove and affect the health of the person doing the cooking. The energy of the food will also be distorted and may cause indigestion and health problems to the occupants (see Diag. 19.6).

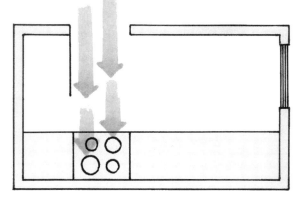

Diag. 19.6: Stove in the door line.

6)   A kitchen should not be placed above, next to, below or facing a toilet. A toilet's dirty energy will contaminate food in the kitchen, causing heath problems.

7)   A kitchen should be well lit and well ventilated to keep the person doing the cooking comfortable and happy and to drive 'yin qi' out of the kitchen, thereby avoiding accidents.

8)   Avoid the colour blue in the kitchen as it represents the water element, which will create conflict with the fire element of the kitchen.

9) Traditional Chinese families will usually put up an altar to honour the kitchen god and earth god as a symbol of respect for the kitchen spirits to induce good and harmonious qi. In the kitchen, many sharp instruments are used. So by respecting the kitchen gods in this way, unforeseen accidents can be avoided. If you have similar symbols in your religious tradition, you may also use them in the kitchen. The altars should not be placed in the door line.

10) Lastly, to ensure that you have good, tasty and healing food, you should preferably use a wood or charcoal fire, or as a third preference, a gas fire, to cook your food. Avoid using electrical hot plates because the radiation from the hot plate permeates the water and, in turn, the food, making it more difficult to digest and be absorbed by your body. My experiments to germinate seeds using water heated on an electric hot plate (and then cooled) found that it was either difficult or impossible to germinate seeds in such water.

   On the other hand, seeds germinate very quickly when charcoal- or firewood-boiled water is used. Gas fire-boiled water will also germinate seeds but more slowly.

11) Never, ever use a microwave oven to cook your food. Microwave cooking destroys the subtle nutrient energies (aura) of the food. Microwave-cooked foods are also more difficult to digest and absorb into the body. People who eat microwave-cooked food every day tend to eat more often because of the lack of essential nutrients and become obese.

   To avoid toxic radiation in the kitchen, do not install a microwave oven. People who stand within 1 m (3.3 ft) of the front of a microwave oven regularly, cooking food, tend to have a higher incidence of blood disorders and general health problems.

Chapter 20

THE LIVING ROOM, TOILET AND GARAGE

The living room is generally regarded as the activity room of the family and has a yang quality. It can be compared with the lungs of a human. The living room is the central area where cosmic qi comes in from the main door and disperses to other areas, like the lungs dispersing oxygen and air nutrients to other parts of the body.

The living room should ideally be bigger, usually double the size of other rooms, and be close to the entrance (Diag. 20.1).

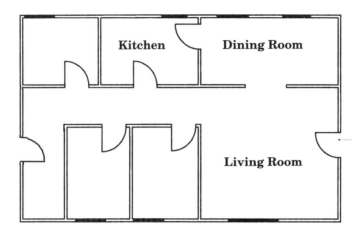

Diag. 20.1: The entrance door opening into the living room corresponds to the principle of the human nose and lungs.

A living room should have bright-coloured furnishings and furniture, harmoniously arranged to welcome occupants and guests. A living room should be spacious and square- or rectangular-shaped. Avoid the L-shape or long, narrow shape. Long, narrow shapes along the length of a house indicate that the house has weak 'lungs'. Its occupants will tend to have lower vitality.

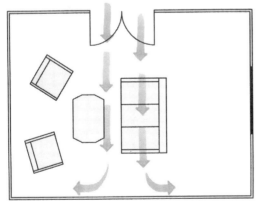

Diag. 20.2A: An inauspicious arrangement of furniture. The main sofa is placed in the door line and is attacked by the energy coming in.

Diag. 20.2B: Remedy – A screen blocks the strong incoming qi and redirects it sideways.

Avoid placing the most important seats in direct line with the door. They should be placed where you can see the door easily, so that you don't become nervous when people come in. The main sofa should be placed diagonally to the door (see Diag. 20.3B–20.4B).

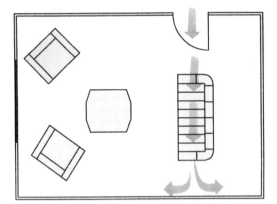

Diag. 20.3A: An inauspicious arrangement of furniture. The main sofa is placed in the door line.

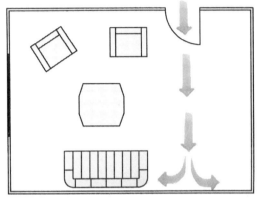

Diag. 20.3B: An auspicious layout is created by simply rearranging the furniture. A person sitting on the main sofa can easily see everyone coming in. This is a command sitting position.

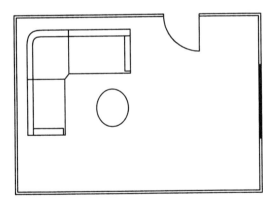

Diag. 20.4A: An inauspicious arrangement of furniture.

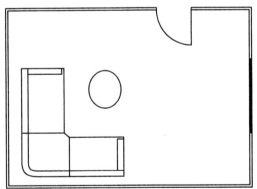

Diag. 20.4B: An auspicious arrangement of furniture. The door can easily be seen by all three people sitting on the sofa.

The Children's Room

A room in the central area of the house is best for children. If children occupy a room at the back of the house that should have been used by the parents, it may be more difficult to control them. Children occupying rooms at the back of a house tend to be more domineering and disobedient. For decoration and furniture, use colours that are in harmony with the birth year element of the child. A light, multicoloured scheme is best.

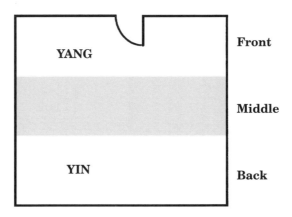

Diag. 20.5: The central area is best for the children's room.

The Study

Many different opinions have been advanced on where a study should be located in a house. The study is a place for concentration, study and learning. Logic has it that it should be in a quiet place. It should not be near a kitchen where food is prepared as this would stimulate the appetite, diverting attention away from study. A study should not be facing the main door as the occupants would then tend to become workaholics or bookworms.

Ideally, a study for children should be where parents can conveniently supervise their study, and near the front of the house, under the 'knowledge area' according to the trigrams of the Eight Life Situations (see Diag. 20.6). For adults who prefer an exceptionally quiet area to be able to concentrate, the study could be located in an area at the back of the house.

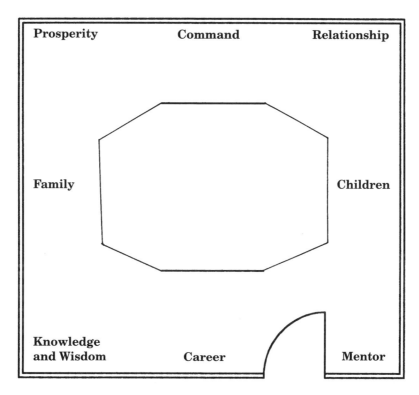

Diag. 20.6: The 'knowledge and wisdom area' of the house is an auspicious place for the study. The knowledge area is always on the left side of the door, with the mentor area on the right side.

The Toilet

The toilet, being a yin qi area, belongs to the water element. It has a draining and flushing action and is the area that handles human wastes. Where it is placed can affect the health of the occupants.

The best place for a toilet is at the back of the house. Avoid placing a toilet above or below the dining room or the kitchen.

It is inauspicious to have the toilet in the following areas:

1) A toilet should not be placed on the upper floor above a stove. In feng shui, the stove symbolises health and family wealth, and its element is fire. A toilet above the stove is not only unhealthy, but also endangers the family health and prosperity because the water qi emptied by the toilet will put out the fire qi of the stove below. The negative toilet qi could also contaminate the food. The remedy is to relocate the stove and the dining table at least 3 m (10 ft) away from the waste pipe of the toilet and the toilet itself.

217

2) Avoid placing a toilet over a bedroom. The negative and contaminated qi from the toilet will permeate into the bedroom, affecting the health of the occupants. The remedy is to relocate the bedroom should this occur. If this situation cannot be avoided, then place two healthy plants in the bedroom to filter and cleanse the air.

3) Sometimes, an occupant suffers from insomnia because a toilet flush tank is placed behind the bed on the other side of the wall. The cool water energy penetrates the wall and disturbs the head area. The remedy is to relocate the bed to another area in the room.

4) Avoid placing a main door directly opposite a toilet door. The whole house's benevolent qi will move into the toilet and be either flushed away, or the remaining contaminated qi will begin to circulate throughout the house, causing health problems to occupants. The remedy is to place a slim mirror on the toilet door (see also Chapter 17).

5) In some houses, the toilet is immediately above the main door. Contaminated energy from the toilet waste pipe radiates down and enters the house, causing health problems; the occupants also lack vitality and prosperity. The remedy is to relocate the toilet or to use it less often if you have a second one in the house.

The Garage

Today, most families own at least one car. Therefore, the garage has become a major section of a house. In feng shui, a garage is like a storeroom (yin).

A garage is not considered part of the living space unless the first floor covers more than two thirds of a garage.

A few important points to remember with regard to a garage are listed below:

1) A garage should not block or obscure the main door.

2) A garage should be built on the Dragon side of the house as car movements bring in more qi.

3) A garage driveway should not directly face the entrance door of the house. Otherwise, car exhaust and dust will be forced into the house, affecting the health of its occupants. Some occupants may also feel nervous subconsciously that cars will ram the house.

4) Vehicles should move front first into a garage so that their exhaust pipes will still be close to the garage door. This will reduce the amount of toxic exhaust fumes staying in the garage. Additional windows at the back of the garage will allow any remaining toxic exhaust to escape more quickly.

5) A door in the garage that gives access to the house should be placed near the garage door to reduce the amount of vehicle fumes going into the house.

6) The kitchen and bedroom should not be built over a garage as the subtle toxic air from car exhausts will move up and cause health problems. If a garage has an open door, ventilation is better, making it less of a health hazard.

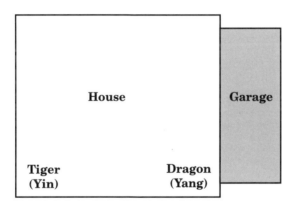

Diag. 20.7: The garage is on the Dragon side to enhance qi for the house.

Chapter 21

CONSTRUCTION AND MOVING-IN RITUALS

When you buy a piece of land, you have physical ownership of this land, with its title deed recognised by the law of your country. However, you are not the first person to use the land; therefore, 'spiritually', you do not have first claim to its use. Your land could have been used by earlier human settlements for burial or ritual purposes. Lands on top of a hill or mountain, or along the gentle slope of a hill with a good view into a valley or distant mountain range, were often used in ancient times for group ceremonies or rituals. Many areas were famous ancient battle grounds. Plenty of ghosts and spirits are often found in such sad landscapes. These choice ancient lands are also the most sought after for building houses today.

I believe that a land usage or construction ritual is a must to appease any ghosts and spirits on the land before any construction work commences, irrespective of one's religious beliefs. The ritual is also a sign of respect to those who dwelled on and used the land before you, and to the nature energies and spirits that rule the land. During their lifetime, humans created rankings; this ranking consciousness has passed on into the spiritual realms. The only difference between humans and spirits in the spiritual realm is that spirits have energy of higher frequency than us, making them invisible to most. We have a similar energy field but with a physical body.

Human Spiritual Ranking

Even though you may have inherited a piece of land, say, from your mother or father, and they may have lived on the land without any problems, it does not mean that the spirits on the land will accord you the same honour and peace. It all depends on your spiritual rank and the spiritual ranks of your children. When a person has a spiritual rank of 8/10 (for easier understanding, I have used a scale of 1–10, 1 being the lowest, and 10 the highest) or above, they are like a one-star general in the army receiving respect from all ranks. Those with a lower spiritual rank, say, 5/10, 6/10 or 7/10, would be more likely to face problems if there are encumbrant spirits on the land. Therefore, rituals are very important to appease the spirits. More than 70% of the world's population adhere to land and construction rituals.

Construction Ritual

In the West, it is a common practice to carry out a ground breaking ceremony before the commencement of construction work. As a religious person says prayers, he indirectly asks permission before hoards of people move onto the ground to celebrate. This act chases encumbrant ghosts and spirits from the land. This is not a good practice unless permission is asked well before the people descend on the land.

Before you use the land for planting food, building a house or other purpose, select a suitable day and time to carry out the ritual that is harmonious with you and better still, harmonious with your family. The Chinese have an almanac called 'Tung Shu', which helps individuals to find auspicious times to carry out rituals.

But if you are not Chinese, there are other ways you can find a suitable time to carry out your ritual. You can use the pendulum if you know how to use one or ask someone who is proficient in its use to check for you. Alternatively, you can use the applied kinesiology technique described in Chapter 10.

When you are ready to do the applied kinesiology test with your friend or your partner, select a time and date, say, 10 am on 28 November. Just ask permission from all levels of consciousness to do the applied kinesiology test. Next ask, 'Is this date and time harmonious for me and my family to carry out a beginning of construction ritual or land usage ritual on the land?' If the person tests strong, then the time and date is suitable. If the person tests weak, then select another time and date until you obtain a suitable time and date.

How to Conduct the Construction Ritual

At the auspicious time and date, go to the site with some fruits or cooked food, whichever you feel comfortable with, and place the offerings, together with some candles or incense, in a corner of the land you will not use often. Then proceed with the ritual (see Diag. 21.1). You must make it clear that you want to use the land in a peaceful way. This is what you could say:

'I am communicating with all levels of consciousness of all the spirits and nature's energies that dwell or have jurisdiction on this land that I bought (or inherited). My family and all our spiritual guides/angels come in peace and respect your energies and presence. We have decided to commence building a house on this land on ... (state date and time) to create good living energies in this environment and advance universal peace, happiness and universal love consciousness. We send love and harmony to you all.'

Or...

'We ask special permission from all spirits who dwell and have jurisdiction on this land, to give way so that we can commence construction work today at ... (state time). On behalf of our spiritual guides, we apologise to all spirits who are affected and send all the universal love and happiness to heal where and when necessary.

We also ask all spirits that have jurisdiction over this land, to offer good advice and protection at all times, to ourselves, our children, our descendants, our staff and our friends. Now we invite all spirits according to your ranking to feast on our offerings.'

Diag. 21.1: A land usage or construction ritual.

Leave immediately after completing the ritual. Your offerings of food should be left behind. When the ritual is completed and the spirits have 'eaten the aura of the food', the food will not taste good afterwards.

At the appointed time, make the symbolic commencement of construction work by using a spade to dig some earth.

Diag. 21.2: The topping-out ceremony.

In Asia, Asians hang gourd, pumpkin or root plants on the first floor beam to make offerings to the spirits in return for the peace and safety of workers during the construction of the upper floors.

Chinese and other Asian families also make offerings to spirits on or around the land on New Year's Day, Souls Day and when they have major celebrations. It is also good to make offerings to the hungry ghosts and spirits once a year on a special day.

In many cultures in Europe and Asia, there is a topping-out ceremony when the roof's support beams have been set up. Trees and flowers are put on top of the roof and a celebration is carried out (see Diag. 21.2).

House Moving-in Ritual

Again an auspicious time to officially move into your dream house has to be decided. The day you move in your belongings and cook your first meal is usually the official time and day you move into your house, even though some of your belongings may take another two weeks to come or be moved in.

The time, the day and the year you move into your house is important in calculating the life fortune of your house and how your home will affect you now and in the future.

If the day and time you move into your house is not in harmony with you, it may affect your balance and harmony for months!

Fire Cleansing

Several days before you move in, you should clean and cleanse your house. Small animal spirits and wandering spirits could have come into your vacant house during construction. It is necessary to clear them out. Decide on a time and day to do the salt cleansing (see the following section).

The Chinese traditionally put a burning fire from a stove into a container on the day they first move their belongings into their house. They then ask each member of the family to walk over the burning fire to rid the lower body of negative qi or attached spirits before they go into the cleansed house so that it remains clear.

On the day and time you first move in, it is best to boil a kettle of water to create living energy and qi. This is also to symbolise that you have officially moved into your house.

Salt Cleansing

Select an auspicious date for the salt cleansing ritual. The night before the cleansing, you should sleep early to get a good rest; eat light food so that you have more energy and are more intuitive to carry out the cleansing ritual the next day. Also, ask your own spiritual guides to help in the ritual the night before. Your spiritual guides may give you advice in your dreams or in flashes of intuition.

On the appointed day and time, bring 2 to 3 kg (4.5–6.5 lbs) of raw sea salt (not factory-manufactured table salt) to the house. Before you carry out the cleansing ritual, drink plenty of water to balance yourself. Tell the spirits and all the energies inside the house what you intend to do in the next half hour and request that they leave during this half hour.

At the end of the half hour, sprinkle the sea salt along the edges of the inside wall of the house, inside dark cupboards and in all areas of the house that look dark without lighting. The sea salt will absorb negative energies and destroy harmful bacteria, fungi and viruses in the house. Leave the sea salt until the next day. Then vacuum or sweep the floor, and immediately throw away all the contaminated sea salt and dirt from the house.

In the dark places, especially the basement, it is advisable to place bowls of sea salt and replace them monthly to absorb negative energies.

You also need to do sea salt cleansing when you move into an existing old house, to get rid of old negative energies.

Aroma Oil Cleansing

Every day for a fortnight after you move into your house, you should burn cleansing oils like sage, juniper berry or frankincense to eliminate negative energies.

Thereafter, burn lavender, jasmine, rose or orange oil to freshen the air in the rooms of your house.

If you are moving into an old house where people have lived for several years, it is even more important for you to burn aroma cleansing oil to cleanse your house of negative energies. The energies of the previous occupants are still moving and are "stored' on the walls and in the furniture of the house. If the last occupants were very negative people or members of the family were sick, you will also be affected by the bad energies that are retained in the house. You should burn aroma cleansing oil daily for one to two weeks before you move into an old house to cleanse it properly and thoroughly.

Shut all the windows in the house before you burn the cleansing aroma oil so that the intense energies of the oil will slowly neutralise and eliminate all the negative qi and energies attached to the walls, furnishings and fittings in every room.

Diag. 21.3: Negative energies on the walls of a room. Burning aroma cleansing oil generates soft cleansing energy that will eliminate the negative energies in the room.

After burning aroma cleansing oil in each room for several hours, open all the windows to allow the stale air and negative energies mixed with the cleansing energy to leave. Open completely the windows of all the rooms for several hours every day to allow clean fresh air to flow in and cleanse each room. You may need to carry out this cleansing ritual for several weeks in an old house until you do not feel or smell bad energies in any part of the house.

If you have already moved in and do not feel good about the air or energies in your room or house (for example, the air may feel tense, sticky or have a musty or unpleasant smell), you will need to carry out house cleansing. Close all the windows and doors of each room and burn aroma cleansing oil as explained earlier.

Caution: Make sure all naked burning flames of the aroma oil lamps are placed safely to prevent domestic animals or young children from knocking them over.

Water Spraying Cleansing

Another method to cleanse the air and clear negative or stale energy in the rooms of your house is to spray fine mists of water. You can use the spray mister you use when ironing. Put some essential oil into the water and spray this mist generously over the whole room to settle the dust and refresh and cleanse the stagnant stale air. Like the air after rain, it will feel refreshing and clean. You can use water spraying in addition to aroma oil cleansing. Spraying water mists daily will cleanse your room and give you better quality air.

How do you know if your room and house are cleansed? The colours of your room and house will look brighter, just like after heavy rain. The air will be lighter and fresher and will feel more comfortable to breathe.

Drums and Bells Cleansing

Some cultures use loud drums and bells to dispel negative energies and also to increase energies in a building.

Usually, the drums or bells are activated loudly to create sharp sounds that are then slowly toned down into softer and more harmonic sounds. This balances and softens the air, and helps maintain a serene atmosphere in the room or house.

A recording of rhythmic drum music played loudly has a similar effect.

花草樹

Chapter 22

PLANTS AND TREES

Plants and trees have a cold yin quality ('cold blood'), whereas humans have a warm yang quality. Plants are able to communicate with humans and animals. They have the ability to respond to a person's negative and positive thoughts and words. Plants can attack humans and animals on a physical as well as a psychic level. A yucca plant, for example, attacks everybody who looks at its sharp-pointed, knife-like leaves. By mentally talking to a plant and saying that we are friendly and not going to hurt it, a plant will respond immediately in a friendly way. To prove that plants and trees have 'feelings' and are able to respond, go to a plant and pull off a leaf. When you put this leaf into your mouth, your body will immediately become weak. Applied kinesiology muscle tests will confirm this response. The leaf becomes toxic, even though it is a nontoxic plant. Those who can see the aura will immediately perceive the plant's auric field becoming red or darker in colour.

However, if before taking a leaf, you communicate with the plant and say thank you, the plant will not 'fight back' when you take a leaf. It is vital for herbalists to talk to plants before they take leaves or parts of plants for health remedies. Otherwise, the good effects of the plants may be lost when the defensive reaction creates toxicity.

Plants and trees generally filter and cleanse the air in a room and provide a plentiful supply of oxygen during the day. However, at night, plants take in oxygen and give out carbon dioxide, which is toxic to us in large quantities. It is, therefore, not advisable to have too many plants in a bedroom. I recommend one plant in a room to filter and cleanse toxic air coming from toxic carpets, paints or the interactions of these materials in a room. A plant also stimulates qi and energy in a room when no human is present. Plants in a bedroom should not be more than 1 m (3.3 ft) high and should be at least 2 m (6.5 ft) away from the bed.

It is good to have plants and trees around the house. They attract qi and retain the energy around the building. In the hot weather, trees give valuable shade as cooling shelters. Trees can also be planted at the back of the house to create and simulate a solid backing barrier like the 'tortoise' according to the formation of the Four Animals.

Plants can also be used as a barrier to block or redirect strong winds blowing against a house.

The following table shows how much qi is attracted by plants:

Why do look-alike artificial flowers also attract cosmic qi and oxygen? The reason is cosmic qi is the lowest living intelligence and has special magnetic fields that are either attracted to magnetic fields of real plants or their symbolic shapes.

Plant	Qi and oxygen in %
Green plants and trees	50–100
Single-colour flower	150–200
Multi-colour flowers	200–300
Artificial look-alike coloured flowers	100–150
Photos of flowers	100–150
Paintings of flowers	20–50

Table 8

Auspicious Types of Plants in the Garden

As a general rule, plants and trees in the garden should be healthy and vibrant with luxurious growth of leaves and branches. Plants with weak leaves and branches become diseased easily and are not recommended. Diseased or dead branches should be cut off. When they are left on trees, they cause body and immunity problems to occupants.

Select trees and plants that have leaves and branches growing upward. Trees like weeping willows with drooping branches, although very pleasant to look at in public parks, are not recommended around a home garden. Weeping willow trees look like a person without any vitality, lacking energy; such a tree in the garden would deplete the vitality of the occupants, as well as make them feel depressed.

A garden should have some plants that can withstand the winter cold and maintain their evergreen leaves. It is very depressing to see withered trees and leafless branches in the garden during the winter months. Trees belonging to the pine family are good for maintaining year-round greenness, but only those with widespread branches are recommended.

Avoid sharp-pointed trees with thin needle leaves in your garden (Diag. 22.1C).

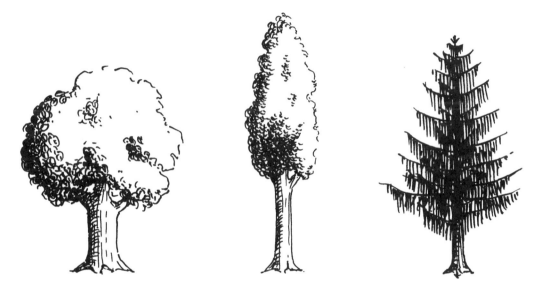

Diag. 22.1A: A good tree shape.   *Diag. 22.1B: A good tree shape.*   *Diag. 22.1C: An inauspicious tree shape.*

Multicoloured plants or plants with plenty of flowers, preferably blooms lasting for several weeks or months, are preferred to give energy, stimulate a happy mood and provide good qi and oxygen for the benefit of occupants.

Nontoxic plants are preferred in the garden. Fruit trees have two positive effects – they give abundant good energy and supply plenty of fruit to the occupants.

In the front of the house, plants and trees should not be more than 1 m (3.3 ft) high to avoid blocking good qi and oxygen from coming into the house. There should be no plants and trees in front of the main door. Tall trees can be grown to the side, especially to the back of the house.

Suitably strong and fast growing trees can be planted as a feng shui remedy to block strong winds from blowing against a house or part of a house. Ivy has very powerful yang energy and is a good plant for a trellis or a fence. However, it grows very slowly.

Remember that the branches and leaves of trees growing outside windows may be harmless, but during the wintering period their trunks may be exposed and thus attack occupants inside (see Diag. 22.2–23.4). These types of trees should not be planted immediately outside a window or a door.

Tree in Front of the Window

A straight, exposed tree trunk immediately opposite a window or glass wall attacks the occupants of the room where the window is situated and also indirectly affects all the occupants of the house. The window represents the eyes of the occupants. When such an attack takes place, the occupants will be more prone to eye problems.

Distance of Plants from House

The roots of trees spread as far as the branches. Roots should not be too near the wall of a house. Otherwise, they may cause cracks on the walls, thereby attacking and weakening the house foundation and its occupants.

Large trees should be at least 6 m (20 ft) away from the house, their branches at least 3 m (10 ft) away. This is to avoid dead leaves, flowers, pollen and branches falling into the gutter and insects and worms dropping into the house when strong winds blow. Trees planted too close to a house block the sunlight. This prevents the outer walls from drying out, thereby retaining a high level of moisture that

Diag. 22.2A: Severe attack from a straight tree trunk.

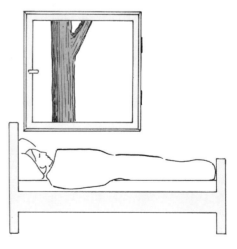

Diag. 22.2B: Severe attack from a straight tree trunk.

Diag. 22.3A: A less severe attack from a branch.

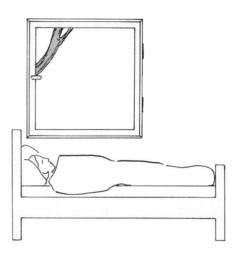

Diag. 22.3B: A less severe attack from a branch.

Diag. 22.4A: Positive – No attack as the trunk is not visible.

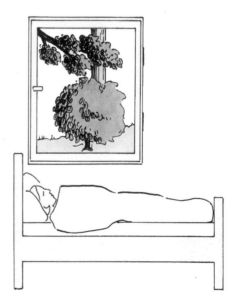

Diag. 22.4B: Positive – The straight trunk is covered by leaves. But during winter, the trunk may be exposed.

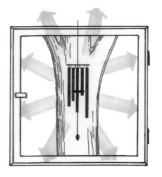

Diag. 22.5A: To neutralise an exposed attacking tree trunk, put a windchime in the middle of the window in line with the trunk. The windchime should be at least 30 cm (12 in) away from the glass.

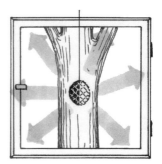

Diag. 22.5B: Hang a faceted natural quartz crystal in front of the window about 30 cm (12 in) from the glass. Glass or lead crystals are not effective.

will result in faster deterioration of the paint and wall materials. It also causes the house to become too yin and unhealthy.

Plants should not be grown on the walls of a house as their roots may break up the wall. The walls of a house represent the occupants' skin. The roots of the plants will suck up valuable nutrients and water from this 'skin'. This could cause the occupants to suffer from skin diseases.

A house should have high yang energy. When the walls of a house are closely surrounded by too many large trees or plants, the house becomes too yin. It could even attract spirits and become a haunted house. A house that is too yin is cold, chilly and unhealthy to live in. Levels of fungi are also high.

Indoor Plants

Indoor plants have a calming and relaxing effect. They attract and circulate qi in the rooms.

Plants should be planted in soil, and the soil changed once every six months to remove some of the toxic materials that bacteria cannot break down. Soil is preferred over other plant rooting media like clay because bacteria can live in and break down the toxic materials faster in soil.

Plants with rounded leaves like the money plant, chrysanthemum, philodendron, dragon tree, water lily and plants belonging to the kalanchoe family are good plants for the house.

Avoid all plants with long, straight, sharp-pointed leaves like the yucca because they attack moving people as a defence for self-preservation. Visitors who are attacked in such a subtle way may not feel comfortable to come back again.

Avoid putting the ficus benjamini and those belonging to its family in a bedroom or near a person who has asthma or bronchitis. The ficus benjamini becomes hot and emits toxic fumes if it is near a source of heat, triggering asthmatic and bronchial attacks. However, it is all right to put it in a cool living area.

The juice of the dieffenbachia plant is also toxic. This plant should be avoided in the home.

Ferns also often cause asthma and bronchitis and are best kept in the winter garden or out on the balcony.

Bamboo plants are hardy and grow very fast. Bamboo is a symbol of longevity, strength and flexibility. It is good to grow bamboo in the garden, especially bamboo with golden- or dark yellow-coloured skin, which can be likened to gold. To enhance prosperity, bamboo should be grown behind the house to provide a good backing and support for the family.

Bamboo plants have been known to absorb a lot of qi and nutrients from the air, so avoid having these plants near your dining area. Indoor bamboo plants should be well fertilised; otherwise, they tend to absorb lots of qi energy, causing health problems to people who sit too close to them.

Table 9 lists some plants that can effectively absorb and neutralise different types of toxins and chemicals. They were identified in experiments conducted by the American space agency, NASA.

Toxin	Found in	Health Problems	Plants
Formaldehyde	Wood Carpets Furniture Paper Detergents	Headache Sore eyes Lung problems Asthma Fatigue	Aloe vera Philodendron Ivy Chrysanthemum Schefflera Rubber tree
Benzol	Cigarette fumes Gasoline Synthetic fabrics Plastics Inks and oils Detergents	Skin and eye irritation Lack of appetite Fatigue	Ivy Marginata Chrysanthemum Gerbera Peace lily Dragon plant
Trichloethylene	Dry cleaning Inks and colours Polish Varnishing Glues	Cancer of the liver Leukemia and blood disorders	Gerbera Chrysanthemum Peace lily Marginata Dragon plant

Table 9: Examples of plants that absorb toxins.

Chapter 23

FENG SHUI REMEDIES

Over the last 20 years, I have seen thousands of houses and house plans around the world. Those in developed countries in the West tend to have more feng shui problems because of a lack of knowledge of feng shui principles. This may be a major reason why people in these countries tend to have more health problems than Asians. In societies where the Chinese culture has a strong influence, like Japan, South Korea, Taiwan, Hong Kong, Singapore, Malaysia and Thailand, major feng shui problems tend to be fewer.

For most feng shui problems, there are solutions. Remedies at different levels of application and consciousness can be applied to reduce or to eliminate harmful effects. It is not possible in the limited scope of this book to explain every remedy elaborately because every house's interior design and furnishings are different. Readers can attend seminars to gain a better perspective of case studies (details on courses are listed at the back of this book).

Listed in this chapter are some general remedies like 'First Aid in Feng Shui' to help readers overcome some of the common feng shui problems in and around their homes.

I classify feng shui remedies into five levels of practice or consciousness for application.

1) Physical Feng Shui Remedies

Examples are man-made waterfalls, water fountains, fish aquariums and flowers. These remedies are 100% effective in increasing cosmic qi in living spaces.

2) Physical Symbolic Feng Shui Remedies

Examples are a pair of flutes, a windchime or a fan. These remedies are effective, even though the flutes are not played and the windchime or fan do not move. These remedies are usually between 50–60% effective in enhancing and stimulating cosmic qi.

3) Photos

The use of photos of feng shui remedial features like a poster of a waterfall or running stream are quite effective. The effectiveness of photos as a remedy has been estimated at between 50–60%.

4) Paintings or Sculptures

Paintings or sculptures of feng shui features like a waterfall or wavy water in a lake can also be used. Remedies in this category are 20–30% effective, depending on how well they represent the actual features.

5) Non-Visible Feng Shui Remedies

Certain symbols can be spiritually and mentally projected, using an ancient Taoist technique, to stimulate cosmic qi or to disperse negative qi in a certain location or space in a house. This is the highest level of feng shui practice where physical symbols are not necessary.

This technique applies principles similar to those used by Uri Geller, an Israeli who became world renowned when he spiritually and mentally bent spoons from a distance. Feng shui changes can thus be made from a distance. This technique is only taught at very advanced courses to feng shui consultants.

Practical feng shui techniques and remedial features commonly used by feng shui consultants and practitioners have their specific functions and usefulness. It is, therefore, important to know how to apply them and what their effects will be in particular situations.

In feng shui practice, I often found excessive cosmic qi being generated in a house under the mistaken belief that more was better. But a room overstimulated with qi becomes a highly suffocating yang room.

Summary of Common Feng Shui Remedies

There are more than 50 groups of feng shui remedies we can use in feng shui practice. We list below 18 groups of feng shui features that can be used throughout the world.

Group 1

Moving Water

Lakes, Ponds, Waterfalls, Water Fountains, Fish Aquariums, Streams, Rivers, Waterwheels, Pictures Showing Waterfalls

Moving water causes friction that generates electromagnetic rays and attracts cosmic qi. Qi has female characteristics and attracts oxygen, which has male characteristics.

The greater the friction, the whiter the water and the greater the negative ionization, generating an abundance of qi and oxygen in the environment.

In ancient China, patients who had a weak body constitution or were suffering from terminal diseases were asked by their doctors to live near a lake or waterfall in the mountains. Clients who followed my recommendation to take up this remedy have seen their body health and vitality improve greatly.

We feel relaxed and energised when sitting near moving water in the open air. Water is the most important feng shui remedy. To the Chinese, water is like money, wealth and abundance.

It is best to place water remedies near the entrance to attract qi into a house.

Generally, a good position to place a water remedy is in the sitting room or dining area, or in the centre of the house. Avoid placing water remedies near windows as the benevolent qi attracted may be forced out through the windows.

Outside a house, water remedies like a fountain, waterfall or running water should preferably be placed in front of the house or towards the left Dragon side of the house to attract more qi. When installing running water remedies, the water ('wealth') should run slowly towards the front door of the house.

Water moving away from the house attracts and pulls qi away, and can be likened your wealth and prosperity flowing away.

Diag. 23.1: Positive – Water flowing slowly towards the front of the house.

Water remedies placed at the back of a house are negative because the water energy attracts cosmic qi and oxygen to the back of the house, thus depriving the front of the house of good qi.

Diag. 23.2A: Negative –
A river behind the house.

Diag. 23.2B: Negative –
A pond behind the house.

Waterfall Pictures

Apart from using actual water remedies, the likeness or even the symbol of moving water is also suitable to enhance qi and oxygen in a room or house. A photograph of a waterfall with water shown pouring out of the picture with plenty of white water, can be 50–60% as effective as an actual waterfall.

Pictures of waterfalls for the bedroom or places that are used for creative work should be calm and smooth flowing. Pictures of Niagara Falls and powerful and torrential waterfalls should only be used for high-activity rooms or the sitting room, where there is a need to stimulate extra energy and activities.

Fish Aquarium

The bubbling water and the colourful fish in an aquarium attract more qi and increase room energy.

Goldfish, representing ancient Chinese gold tokens, symbolise wealth, prosperity, happiness and fun. Southern Chinese pronounce fish as 'yi', which is very similar to the word 'plenty' or abundance.

A fish aquarium with an air pump generates plenty of water bubbles and vapour, which create very strong magnetism that attracts benevolent qi into a house. Make sure the water is clean and clear as stagnant water in an aquarium has no benevolent feng shui effect and often causes health problems.

The gold colour of the goldfish reflected and radiated by the light on the water creates rays of beautiful golden light around the room where the aquarium is situated, thereby radiating prosperity and a consciousness of abundance in the house. These transparent golden rays can only be seen by some people who are very relaxed or in a meditative state.

Red, yellow and orange-coloured fish can be selected for the aquarium, but avoid black-coloured fish or fish with more than 30% black stripes on their body. The black colour or black-coloured stripes symbolise mourning, and these types of fish are only put into an aquarium when a family is in mourning. In ancient China, it was the custom for wealthy families to mourn the death of a parent or a family elder for three years or more. The black fish seen in their aquariums caused people to wrongly interpret that black goldfish enhanced prosperity (see also Chapter 6).

The mere act of looking at black goldfish in an aquarium weakens our immune system. Readers who are familiar with applied kinesiology or dowsing can check the negative effects for themselves.

To avoid the problem of maintaining and cleaning an aquarium with live fish, some families have decided to decorate their aquarium with water plants and plastic goldfish, and use a pump to create plenty of bubbles. The positive feng shui effect is just as good because of the moving water and the symbol of the fish.

Most people feel very tranquil and comfortable with an aquarium. A fire element person, however, should be more careful as the water element can overpower and destroy the fire element if they are too close to each other. On the other hand, feng shui consultants recommend that a strong fire element person who is quick- or hot-tempered, install a small aquarium to cool down their emotions. Check individually by using the kinesiology test to see how an aquarium affects a fire person.

Placing an aquarium near a fireplace or under a staircase makes it less effective. Also, avoid placing an aquarium next to a toilet as it will attract unhealthy air and qi from the toilet and contaminate the house.

The best shape for an aquarium is an octagon shape, but square or rectangular shapes are also all right, provided the four sharp corners are not pointed at any person sitting in a static position. The attacking energy of the corners is reinforced by the water energy.

Some auspicious feng shui measurements for aquariums:

20 – 26 cm	103–112 cm
38 – 48 cm	125–133 cm
59.5 – 69 cm	146–155 cm
81 – 91 cm	

These measurements can be used for the width or height.

Group 2
Flowering Plants

Freshly-Cut Flowers, Potted Plants, Artificial Flowers

Flowering plants generate radiant rays and electromagnetic fields that symbolise their natural, attractive characteristics. They magnetically attract cosmic qi and insects like bees, which help in the pollination process for seed production and for perpetuating the species.

Multicoloured flowering plants placed together attract up to 300% cosmic qi around them. Single-coloured flowering plants attract 150–200% cosmic qi.

A garden with plenty of colourful flowers in full bloom all year round or most of the year attracts lots of qi and oxygen to a house.

It is very energising to have a vase of freshly-cut, multicoloured flowers on your table. These flowers attract plenty of qi and oxygen to enhance our vitality and creativity.

Freshly-cut flowers less than three days old attract between 100–150% qi, depending on the colours. Withering flowers should be removed quickly. They remind you of deterioration and symbolise the opposite of freshness and happiness.

It is, however, not advisable to have cut flowers in a bedroom during the night because that is when they take in oxygen, which the occupants of the room need most.

Multicoloured artificial flowers that look real are also a good feng shui remedy. The shapes and symbols of artificial flowers attract 100%–150% qi. I have found that photographs of beautiful, multicoloured flowers also attract 80–100% cosmic qi. A good painting of multicoloured flowers attracts 20–50% qi. Generally, flowers generate a feeling of love, joy and happiness, thus enhancing our immune system intensely. It is good to have flowers around us.

Group 3
Moving Objects

Windchimes and Mobiles

Windchimes attract or disperse qi by the sound they create when wind blows against them. A metallic or glass tube windchime should have a harmonic, rhythmic and soothing sound. Those with a dull, hollow sound are depressing and are not effective in attracting cosmic qi. However, they can be used to block or divert the flow of qi in a room or hallway.

Although a windchime that hangs indoors may not move, its sound still radiates symbolically and spiritually, as if it is moving. At night, sensitive people can often hear the sound of a non-moving, indoor windchime when they enter a relaxed state or are asleep.

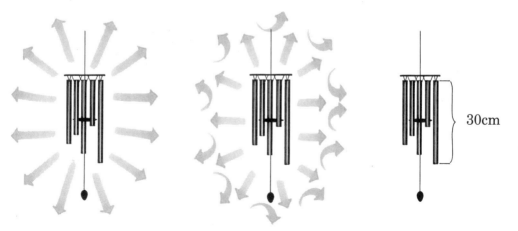

Diag. 23.3A: A five-metal-rod windchime. Subtle energies and sounds move outwards.

Diag. 23.3B: Qi and energy are bounced back.

Diag. 23.3C: The size of a windchime is calculated by measuring the length of the longest tube. This diagram shows a 30 cm (12 in) windchime.

Windchimes are used to block and divert the fast flow of qi that would otherwise go straight through, particularly in situations where a door and window are directly facing each other, or where a main door and back door are in line with each other.

A hollow metallic windchime usually has to be double in length to match the strength and effectiveness of a solid metal windchime. Solid tubes have a stronger effect because of their intense sound.

For example, to block qi leaking out of a window that is directly opposite a door, a 1 m (3.3 ft) wide window requires a 30 cm (12 in) long hollow windchime or a 15 cm (6 in) long solid tube windchime to block leaking qi effectively.

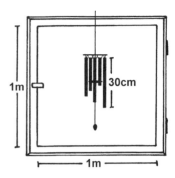

Diag. 23.3D: A 30 cm (12 in) long windchime placed in the middle covers a 1 m (10 ft) square window.

Because a windchime generally attracts qi, many people hang a windchime next to or in front of their main door, hoping to attract more qi into their house. This is incorrect. Yes, qi is attracted to the door, but the windchime also blocks qi from going through the door into the house. The general rule is, a windchime should not be hung within 2 m (6.5 ft) of a door opening to avoid causing qi turbulence or blocking benevolent qi from going into the house.

Windchimes can be painted gold, yellow, brown, orange, multi colours or rainbow colours to match the colour scheme in a room, but not completely red (fire) or green (wood), which are in elemental conflict with the metal tubes (metal).

Never hang a four-piece metal or glass tube windchime; the number 'four' has a negative meaning (see Chapter 9).

Care should be exercised to ensure that a person who belongs to the wood element does not stay continuously near a windchime (metal element). A windchime should be at least 3 m (10 ft) away from a wood person as the metal element attacks the wood.

Mobiles

A mobile is also often used as an indoor decoration. They can be made of paper, glass, ceramic or metal, in the shape of flowers and animals. Fish are suitable as a mobile as they represent prosperity and happiness.

Many people like to hang mobiles near large windows or long corridors to slow down the qi flow.

Diag. 23.4: An eight-fish mobile. In Chinese, fish is pronounced 'yi', meaning plenty, to symbolise abundance and prosperity.

A mobile does not generate a harmonious sound. Generally, a mobile is 20–30% effective in slowing down or blocking qi flow. A mobile does not attract qi unless it is painted in rainbow colours.

Group 4
Blowing Musical Instruments

Flutes, Alpine Horns, Australian Didgeridoos and Other Blowing Musical Instruments

Flutes have been used in China for over 5,000 years as a symbol that creates good music and harmonic, rhythmic sounds to enhance the flow of qi into a house.

The long Chinese bamboo flute was also a constant travelling companion of Chinese scholars, who used it both as a musical instrument and also as a lethal fighting weapon.

We have found that all blowing flutes from different countries work equally well as a feng shui remedy. The easier to blow and the louder a flute's sound, the more qi it attracts when it is used as a feng shui remedy. Ideally, the flute should have auspicious feng shui measurements.

A pair of flutes with a diameter of 2 cm and a length of 46 cm can increase the qi of a 3 m x 4 m (10 x 13 ft) room from an average room qi of 40–50% to 100%. The larger the diameter of a flute and the longer it is, the more powerful it is to enhance qi in a room.

You normally cannot have qi saturation of more than 100% in a bedroom. Otherwise, you become too energised and are unable to have a sound, restful sleep. Before we install the flutes, we can use a pendulum or applied kinesiology to check the amount of qi that flutes of different sizes will generate in a room.

When smaller or shorter flutes (shorter than 46 cm) are used, they should be placed very close to a bed or a sitting area.

Flutes should normally be installed on a wall as a pair, using double-sided stickers to secure them. They should not hang free and should not be pierced. They should be hung up, slanted opposite each other, to form a trigram (see Diag. 23.5C). The mouthpiece or the blowing part should be on top and closest to the other. The best distance between the mouthpieces is 5 cm or 21 cm. You can also use other auspicious feng shui measurements. Remember, the mouthpieces of the flutes MUST be on top to blow cosmic qi downward if they are to benefit the room's occupants. If the flutes are placed with the mouthpieces down, then benevolent cosmic qi will be blown upwards to the next floor and wasted, or will mix with the hot, stale energy near the ceiling, causing negative effects.

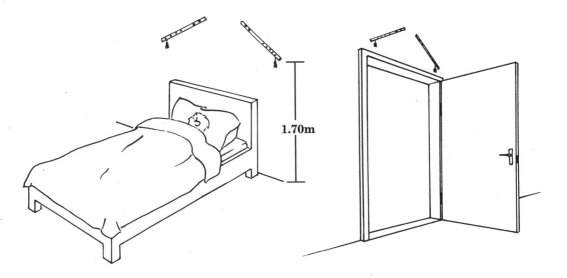

1.70m

Diag. 23.5A: Flutes should be hung up 1.70 m from the floor so that the qi blown down does not disturb the aura of the person. The flutes should be hung opposite each other and should not point directly at the person, who would be disturbed by the movement of energy.

Diag. 23.5B: A pair of flutes inside a room and above the door.

Never place flutes on windows or within 1 m (3.3 m) of a window because they pull cosmic qi from a room and disperse it out of the windows.

Only on rare occasions can flutes be placed with the mouthpiece or blowing part facing downwards. One such occasion is when we want to blow and move cosmic qi to an upper floor. In this case, the flutes should be placed on the wall of a staircase or stairwell in an inverted trigram form like a V-shape blowing cosmic qi upwards (See Diag. 23.5D).

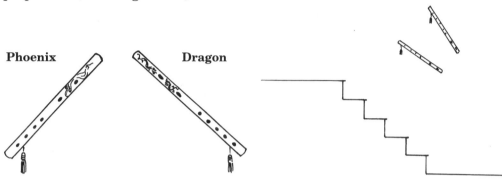

Phoenix   **Dragon**

Diag. 23.5C: A pair of flutes with mouthpieces or blowing parts on top. When a pair of flutes have Dragon and Phoenix drawings, the Dragon flute should be placed on the right side of the wall and the Phoenix (female) on the left side of the wall (when you look at the wall).

Diag. 23.5D: Flutes are hung up with the mouthpiece down if energy is to be directed to the first floor.

We found that other blowing musical instruments work equally well in feng shui practice. The Australian aboriginal blowing instrument called the didgeridoo, which is made from a hollow piece of wood and needs substantial lung power to blow, is a very powerful feng shui apparatus to enhance cosmic qi in a house. A 1 m (3.3 ft) long by 6 cm (2.5 in) diameter didgeridoo can increase the cosmic qi of a 4 m x 4 m (13 ft x 13 ft) room by 100%. Adding the original cosmic qi already present, the total qi in a small room can go up to 140–180%, which is too much for a small room.

The didgeridoo and other powerful blowing musical instruments like the Swiss alpine horn should only be used in a big hall or conference room to benefit more people. Using such powerful blowing instruments in a small, confined space would cause an overwhelming suffocating and choking energy. The cosmic qi of a room or house should be similar to outside in the open air – about 80–100%. We found that when cosmic qi in a room is raised to more than 120%, there is too much yang energy, causing restlessness and insomnia.

Group 5
Heavy Objects
Heavy Rocks, Boulders, Statues and Sculptures

Heavy objects or rock formations are used in feng shui for different purposes.

Rock formations that look like a hill or mountain are placed at the end of a hall or in the garden behind a house, as a solid anchor to give a stronger foundation and backing to a house and to enhance success and prosperity for the occupants.

Various types of statues or sculptures are also placed either inside or outside a building, as feng shui remedies or to strengthen certain feng shui weaknesses.

Diag. 23.6: A rock formation looking like a solid hill or mountain.

Diag. 23.7: Round, solid concrete blocks to strengthen the foundation of a building. Five round, solid concrete blocks are placed around a glass-walled building to give it strong support.

Group 6
Wind and Air Movement Instruments
Ceiling Fans, Air Conditioning, Hand Fans

Ceiling and wall electrical fans can stimulate and move stagnant qi and energy in a room. An exhaust fan is very useful in both hot countries and cold countries, where windows are closed most of the year. Exhaust fans draw out stagnant and dirty air so that fresher and more vibrant qi can come into the house.

Air conditioning helps to maintain a qi level of about 60% in rooms and buildings.

Hand fans are widely used all over the world as wall decorations. Their beneficial effects often go unnoticed by those who do not recognise them as feng shui symbols that move and stimulate qi in a room. Although hand fans placed on a wall are a static image, symbolically and spiritually, they still move qi and energy. It is annoying to sit or sleep with a large hand fan facing you within 1–2 m (3.3–6.5 ft). You can experiment using applied kinesiology to check your response to its effect.

A hand fan should not be placed in the following positions.

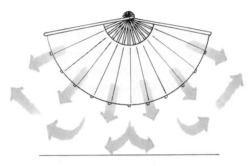

Diag. 23.8A: Negative – A person sleeping on a bed with a large hand fan pointing downwards will have a disturbed and stressful sleep.

Diag. 23.8B: A hand fan pointing downwards causes wind drafts on the floor, moving light dust into the air. Occupants in such a room may suffer from lung and allergy problems.

Diag. 23.8C: Negative – A hand fan pointing upwards moves more qi and energy up, forcing hot, stale air near the ceiling to come down. The unhealthy, mixed air will circulate in the room, giving occupants low vitality and general body weaknesses.

Diag. 23.8D: Correct position for a hand fan. A hand fan should preferably be painted in multicolours or have paintings of green scenery. Chinese hand fans are often painted red to symbolise good luck.

Group 7

Colours

Colours and Combinations of Colours

Each colour of the rainbow has a specific meaning and quality, and activates one of the seven main chakras (energy centres) of the body. A specially selected colour scheme for a room can help to invigorate and enhance energy and change moods. It can lift depression, especially during the dark and gloomy winter months. A good, harmonious colour scheme can also enhance work performance and contribute to overall good health.

Most Chinese restaurants in Hong Kong, Singapore, Europe and North America use a lot of red colour to stimulate the appetite. From my experience, restaurants are most successful when they use bright and happy colour schemes to create a harmonious environment for their guests.

Colour schemes should be based on colours that harmonise with the birth year elements of the occupants of the room (see the Five Elemental Principle in Chapter 8).

Colours Supporting the Elements – The Productive Cycle

- The colour green (wood element) supports and strengthens a fire element person as well as the colours red, pink, violet and purple.

- The colours red, pink, violet and purple (fire element) support and strengthen an earth element person and the colours brown, beige, yellow and orange.

- The colours brown, beige, yellow and orange (earth element) support and strengthen a metal element person and the colours gold and silver.

- The colours gold and silver (metal element) support and strengthen a water element person and the colour blue.

- The colour blue (water element) supports and strengthens a wood element person and the colour green.

Colours Weakening the Elements – The Destructive Cycle

- The colour green (wood element) weakens and destroys the energy of an earth element person and the colours brown, beige, yellow and orange.

- The colours pink, red, violet and purple (fire element) weaken and destroy the energy of a metal element person and the colours gold and silver.

- The colours brown, beige, yellow and orange (earth element) weaken and destroy the energy of a water element person and the colour blue.

- The colours gold and silver (metal element) weaken and destroy the energy of a wood element person and the colour green.

- The colour blue (water element) weakens and destroys the energy of a fire element person and the colour red.

Group 8
Lights
Artificial Lights, Candle Light

In practical feng shui, the use of artificial lights to simulate normal daylight is common. In old houses and houses that do not have enough windows to let in natural light, commonly used areas in a house should be well lit throughout the day to raise the yang qi.

Dim and dark areas in a house allow bacteria and fungi to grow, slowly creating yin areas which often attract unwanted spirits and ghosts. Yin qi affects the health of occupants negatively.

In general living conditions, artificial lights should be bright like daylight and yet not too bright to become glaring. Spotlights can be used in the house to focus on special objects, but cannot be used to replace normal lights because they are too bright and hot. They dry up the moisture in a room and destroy cosmic qi and oxygen.

The best light is a full spectrum light (living light) consisting of all the seven colours of the rainbow. This type of light is commonly used in Scandinavian countries. People exposed to full spectrum lights tend to have fewer health problems. Monkeys and chickens living in cages lit by full spectrum light live twice as long.

The next best lighting comes from the familiar and traditional clear light bulb, widely used around the world. Halogen lights have a very bright and glaring light. Use them only for indirect lighting. They must be covered with protective glass because they emit strong UV light. The newly-invented energy-saving lights are not recommended because their radiation and light spectrum are similar to fluorescent lights. The most unhealthy light is the fluorescent light. Its constant flickering causes nervousness, eye problems, rapid emotional changes and other health problems.

Harmful microwave radiation is produced at both ends of the fluorescent tube create a toxic environment in a room. Researchers in Canada and the United States have found that children in classrooms with fluorescent lights consistently performed badly in class work compared to children in classrooms without fluorescent lights.

Fluorescent lights in low-ceiling buildings have been found to affect human hormonal balance and to cause baldness, especially in men.

It is a good feng shui practice to light up the entrance and walkway leading to the front door of a house to attract cosmic qi. A dark front entrance attracts less qi to the house.

Lights on poles are often used in feng shui to light up a missing section of a house to 'fill up' the missing part. For example, an L-shaped house may have the 'prosperity corner' missing (see Diag. 23.9). This can be remedied by installing a bright light at the corner. The light only has to be lit at night.

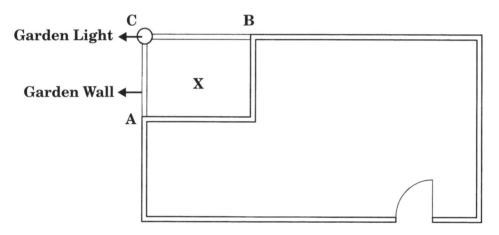

Diag. 23.9: A 3 m (10 ft) high garden light. A light alone is not sufficient to 'fill up' the missing part X. The missing lines should be demarcated by solid pathways or by a fence made of similar material as the house.

Group 9
Reflective Objects
Mirrors and Cut Natural Quartz Crystals

In feng shui practice, mirrors are commonly used as a reflective remedy. In ancient China, polished brass was used for similar purposes.

Like everything on this planet, mirrors have both negative (yin), positive (yang) and neutral effects, depending on how and where you use them. Generally, mirrors are used in feng shui to divert attacking and overpowering qi. They are used to ward off negative qi and spirits, to direct qi, to make a room look bigger and to correct a badly-shaped room or area.

Pa'kua Mirrors

In most parts of Chinese Asia and southern China, the octagon-shaped eight trigrams, or pa'kua, with a convex mirror can be commonly seen above the front door frame of main entrances or on windows. The pa'kua with convex mirror (which has a reducing and distorting effect) should not be placed inside a house as it will affect the psyche of the occupants. Hang it outside, above the entrance door.

However, the pa'kua, with the yin and yang or Tai Chi symbol in the middle, can be placed inside a house. The pa'kua is the highest spiritual symbol and commands respect. It wards off ghosts and spirits and can disperse negative shia and shah qi that cause bad luck and health problems. If your house is haunted, hang a pa'kua mirror outside, above your door (see Diag. 23.10B). This symbol also helps if you live less than 200 m (650 ft) from a place of worship, a cemetery or a crematorium.

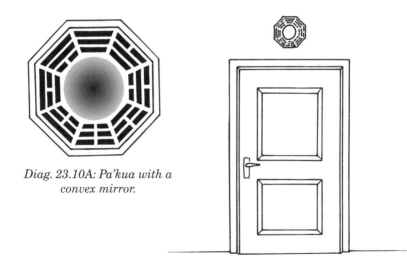

Diag. 23.10A: Pa'kua with a convex mirror.

Diag. 23.10B: The pa'kua with a convex mirror should always be placed outside buildings to deflect harmful shia and shah qi caused by the spiritual realm. Concave mirrors (the type of mirror where you can see your face enlarged) are used to distort and disperse attacking negative qi like the sharp-pointing apex or corner of a neighbour's roof (see Chapter 12). To disperse negative qi and to prevent an overwhelming attack from a neighbour's house, care must be taken to ensure that a mirror does not point directly at your neighbour's house. Otherwise, you reflect the negative energy back and become the aggressor, attacking your neighbour's house and its occupants. Bear in mind that this is like attacking your neighbour's body.

Concave mirrors are also used to disperse and neutralise the attacking negative energy of a lamp post, bus-stop sign post, power line pole or tree trunk in front of a house entrance, as explained in Chapter 17. Place the concave mirror above your front door or on the side if this is more convenient, so that it is pointing at the foot of the attacking post or tree trunk. Do not point the mirror directly at an attacking tree or the feng shui mirror may kill the tree. A mirror that is placed outdoors should be cleaned regularly to retain its reflective effect.

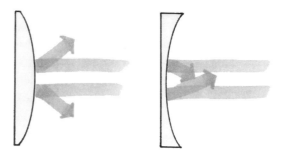

Diag. 23.10C: Convex (left) and concave mirror (right).

Normal mirror

All mirrors reflect qi and incoming light. If a large mirror is placed too close to a main door, it reflects benevolent cosmic qi out of the door and also causes lots of turbulence at the entrance area. The house concerned will have very low cosmic qi.

In some places, it is common to see a large mirror immediately in front or by the side of the main door in houses. Example: A family in Hamburg built a large seven-room house that supposedly followed feng shui principles. But there were lots of health problems and disharmony in the family. On investigation, I found that most of the benevolent cosmic qi for the house was reflected out by a large antique mirror, measuring 2 m x 2.5 m (6.5 ft x 8 ft), placed 2 m away, facing their main door. The family's relationship and health improved considerably after the mirror was removed.

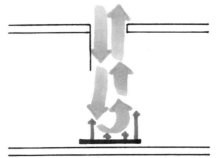

Diag. 23.11: A large mirror within 2 m (6.5 ft) of the main door creates lots of turbulence at the entrance area and reflects qi out.

Safe Distances for Mirrors

The larger the mirror, the further away it should be placed, to avoid reflecting good cosmic qi out and causing unnecessary turbulence at the entrance. Generally, I do not advise placing a large mirror immediately opposite a main door or door of a room, as it can cause shock when a person sees their image in the mirror. When a mirror is placed on the side of a main door, make sure it is not placed immediately opposite a toilet or another door. The mirror may reflect most of the cosmic qi directly into the toilet or into another room, leaving other areas and rooms in a house with little cosmic qi.

A guideline distance for installing a mirror at the front entrance is as follows: For every 15 cm in width by 89 cm in length, keep the mirror a distance of 1.5 m from the entrance door. For a 30 cm mirror, for example, the distance is double, that is, 3 m.

Large mirrors are often placed along the walls of the sitting and dining area to give the area more width and to make it look bigger. But care should be taken because, depending on where the mirror is placed, the good cosmic qi may be reflected out of the room.

Wall mirrors are sometimes installed facing windows to bring a beautiful landscape into a room. In such a situation, make sure that the mirror used for this purpose is not too large or it will reflect good cosmic qi out of the windows.

Natural Quartz Crystals

Natural quartz crystals radiate harmonic rays. They can be used as an alternative to windchimes to block cosmic qi from escaping through the windows.

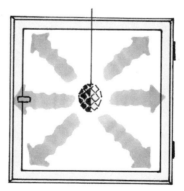

Diag. 23.12: A natural quartz crystal hanging in the middle of a window to block qi from escaping.

Guideline: A faceted natural quartz crystal three times the size of an adult thumb is effective to block cosmic qi from escaping from a 1 m (3.3 ft) square glass window. The crystal has to be hung in the middle of a window to be more effective.

Cut and faceted natural quartz crystals hung in front of a window emit beautiful rainbow-coloured rays day and night, projecting living light into a room. This is very uplifting, especially during the darker winter months.

The larger the cut facets in the crystals, the more rainbow lights are reflected. However, spherical or pear-shaped quartz crystals with small, smooth facets producing less reflection, are preferred for wearing in front of the body to absorb negative energies. They radiate soft energies to give protection against harmful radiation such as electromagnetic fields and computer radiation.

As all natural quartz crystals both radiate and absorb energies from the environment, they have to be cleansed at least once a month to maintain their clarity and effectiveness. To cleanse natural quartz crystals, just put them in a jar of clear water, preferably clear spring water, for 24 hours. Sea water may also be used, but this is less suitable because of its corrosive qualities.

Many feng shui consultants also recommend the use of glass prisms and man-made lead crystals to produce rainbow rays to attract cosmic qi. But these are less effective and cannot block cosmic qi from escaping through the windows.

Spherical natural quartz crystals produce less rainbow rays. They are therefore not as suitable for hanging in front of windows.

Group 10
Indoor Dividers and Screens
Dividers, Window Screens, Bead Curtains, Cloth Drapes

Dividers

We can use a solid divider or screen to block and divert qi. If we have an entrance and back door in one line, we can put up a strong, solid screen to interrupt this line and disperse qi to other areas.

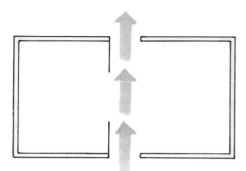

Diag. 23.13A: A house with front and back door directly opposite each other, leaking large amounts of benevolent qi. The house has low qi and its occupants have low vitality.

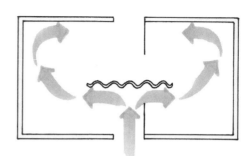

Diag. 23.13B: A solid wooden screen or 2 m (6.5 ft) high cupboard is used to block the direct line and redirect qi.

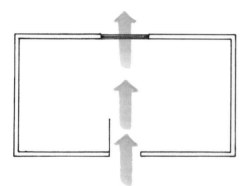

Diag. 23.14: Door and window are directly opposite, and qi escapes too fast. Window screens made from aluminium or wood will help to slow down the qi flow and block some of the qi from escaping.

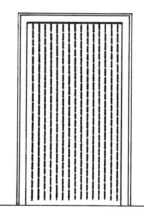

Diag. 23.15: A bead screen can also be used to slow down and redirect qi.

Bead Screens

In many tropical countries, bead screens are hung from doors to stop flies and insects from going into kitchens or dining rooms. In feng shui practice, a bead screen made from sea shells or rolled coloured paper and beads can be installed to slow down and direct the flow of qi into other rooms, particularly when a main door is directly facing the door of a room.

Cloth Drapes

Low overhead beams divert qi and energy, creating downward drafts with 'cutting' effects. This creates turbulence and pressure, causing anxiety to persons sleeping or sitting immediately under it. The beams also slow down and reduce the qi flow to the back of the room. Remedy: Hang soft cloth drapes over the beams to smoothen the flow of qi. Alternatively, the corners of the beams can be rounded to achieve a similar effect.

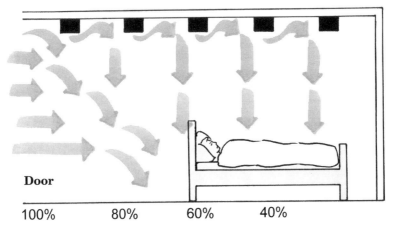

Diag. 23.16A: When there are overhead beams that are arranged horizontally to the door, the end of the room tends to have lower qi as the qi flow is slowed down by the beams. Qi is also directed downward by the beams, affecting the occupants.

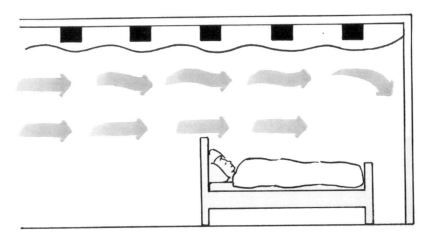

Diag. 23.16B: Remedy – A cloth is draped over the beams to smoothen the qi flow. This neutralises the negative effects of the overhead beams.

Group 11
Outdoor Dividers

In feng shui, common types of outdoor dividers include boulders, trees and bush fences, which are used to re-demarcate an inauspicious piece of land (see also Chapter 14 on land shapes).

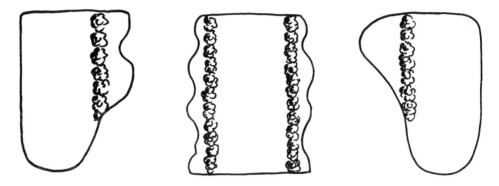

Diag. 23.17: Bush and tree fences used as demarcation lines to remedy inauspicious land shapes.

A trellis can be used to soften and slow down strong winds that tend to blow during certain periods. In Europe, for example, fierce cold winds from Siberia can cause lung and throat problems.

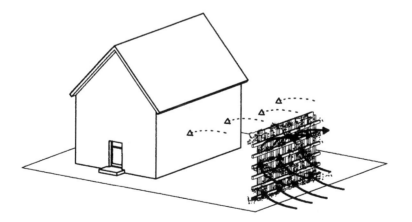

Diag. 23.18: A trellis gives protection from strong winds.

A trellis also provides protection from attacking building energies.

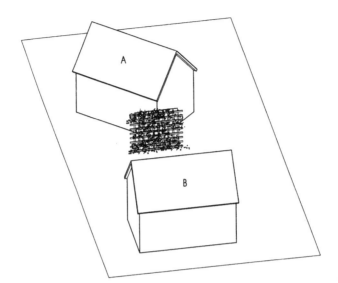

Diag. 23.19: The sharp corner of house A is attacking the middle of house B. Occupants of house B will have a higher incidence of health problems connected with their back. Remedy – Position a trellis with creeping plants to protect house B from the attacking corner.

Group 12
Pyramids and Pyramid-Shaped Objects

Pyramids were designed and used in ancient times to preserve food and to act as tombs to preserve the corpses of royal and noble family members.

Basically, the design of a pyramid is such that it causes an upward thrust of energy from all sides to its sharp apex, lifting low-lying qi and energy inside the pyramid to the top.

The upward thrust of air and energy causes an upward inertia inside the pyramid. The resulting lack of qi inside the pyramid inhibits bacterial growth, making the pyramid an excellent place to preserve meat and store other foods. The ancient Egyptians used pyramids to preserve the corpses of their royal families, while the ancient Chinese and the Incas and Aztecs in Central and South America used pyramids to store food.

A little-known phenomenon of pyramids is that a pyramid is an attacking symbol. When we look at a pyramid, our immune system becomes weak.

Why? It is believed that many ancient cultures in South America used pyramid platforms for occult rituals and sacrifices. Such platforms can still be seen in countries like Mexico and Peru. We may have 'stored' those experiences from past lives, such that looking at a pyramid today still causes fear and anxiety. The ancients intuitively used pyramids to store food and to house their royal dead because robbers and thieves feared going near a pyramid. This is a major reason why many Egyptian pyramids, storing the mummies of royal families, remained untouched for a long time.

The famous glass pyramid in the yard of the Louvre in Paris is, I believe, causing lots of problems to the French. I would, therefore, advise architects not to design a pyramid-shaped roof or building for human use because it slowly destroys the energy of the people living or working in it.

Avoid sleeping under a pyramid. The upward thrust of energy pulls the human electromagnetic field (aura) up too fast, causing anxiety and balance problems.

The pyramid has another little-known phenomenon. A small pyramid can be placed inside a room or a house to increase energy and qi because the upward inertia creates a 'sucking effect' that attracts more energy. All pyramids that are used to improve qi and energy and to preserve foods in a house should not be visible to the human eye. This means that a pyramid should to be placed behind a divider or a screen. And people should not live or work in the area above the tip of the pyramid.

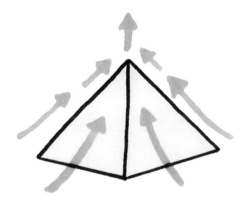

Diag. 23.20A: Energy movements in a pyramid.

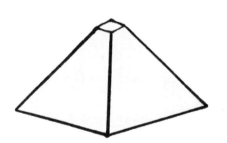

Diag. 23.20B: A pyramid with a platform.

Group 13
Rounded and Wavy Objects
The Circle, Figure Eight, Wavy Shapes and Discs

Humans, through their long evolution, feel more comfortable and protected with round objects. The round and curved shields used for battles that gave protection to warriors are a good example. You feel comfortable and safe under a curved or dome-shaped object. If you look at the human body, you will notice that all parts of the body are curved, from the head down to the toes. How we look is an outward expression and reflection of what we like or what we are, in harmony with our inner consciousness.

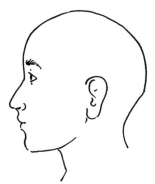

Diag. 23.21: Curved shape of a human head.

The circle represents the earth and the universe. It belongs to the earth element and is widely used to neutralise attacking sharp corners and the effect of negative numbers, such as the number 4. It is also often used for company logos.

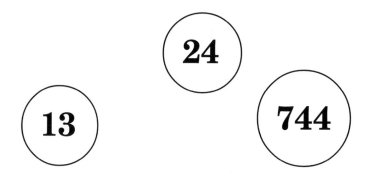

Diag. 23.22: Inauspicious numbers such as 13, 24 or 744 can be neutralised by drawing a circle around them. The figure 8 is a symbol of infinity and the sign of the coming Aquarian Age of peace, love and fun. The Aquarian Age will begin in the year 2008; 2 + 8 = 10 = 1, the first year of a new age. To the Chinese, the sound of 8, 'paat', is very close to 'fatt' (prosperity and abundance); 8 is thus a very auspicious symbol. The double eight ('88') is used by the Qi-Mag International Feng Shui and Geobiology Institute as a remedial symbol to help balance occupants when they are affected by negative symbols or an architecturally-defective house.

Sharp corners of walls, cupboards and furniture create aggressive leylines and should be rounded off for good flow of qi and also to prevent them from attacking occupants. Wavy lines like ribbons or strings are a good remedy to cover sharp corners along the whole length of a wall corner or cupboard to negate their negative effect.

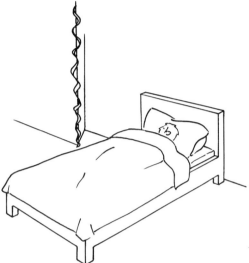

Diag. 23.23: Sharp corner attacking a person and the bed. Remedy –
Place a colourful ribbon along the whole length to neutralise its effect.

A sharp apex can be neutralised by placing a round plate or round lamp in front of it.

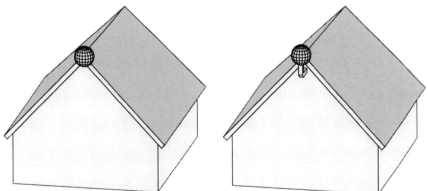

Diag. 23.24: Round plates or spherical lamps to cover the apex.

Group 14

Symbols of Protection

Swords, Rulers, Solomon's Seal and Chinese Pa'kua

In China in the old days, swords and other weapons were placed on a wall facing the main door to 'threaten' strangers who might want to cause harm to the occupants. In Europe, it is also common to see old pistols and hand weapons displayed on walls as a threat so that visitors will behave in a friendly manner. Some die-hard feng shui consultants still use weapon remedies. But in today's modern world, hand weapons are no longer as threatening and no longer reflect the modern consciousness. It is also very negative and unfriendly to display them on the wall or in cupboards.

Several schools of feng shui use the common measuring ruler as a 'justice' symbol, threatening harm to strangers and wandering spirits entering a house. Usually a ruler and a sword or a flute are placed together on a wall that is visible from the main door.

We have found that this ruler and sword remedy lacks effectiveness in today's society. When we apply feng shui remedies, we should also consider the time factor. Some remedies may have been very effective 1,000–2,000 years ago. But in modern times, they may be obsolete.

Two symbols that I found still effective for protection against spirits today are the pa'kua and Solomon's seal. They can be hung up on the wall or be worn as a pendant (see also Chapter 11, Group 16).

Diag. 23.25: Chinese pa'kua and Solomon's seal.

Group 15

Indoor Landscapes

Indoor Design with Water and Plants

A small, indoor landscaped water garden close to the foyer or entrance of a large house is an excellent feng shui remedy. This type of green water garden facilitates qi movement to lift depression and negative moods, especially during the colder, cloudy months in temperate countries. It also improves the vitality of the occupants.

A smaller house can also have an indoor miniature landscaped water garden to combine with a winter garden. Such a winter garden should preferably be placed at the front or along the side of a house to pull in as much benevolent qi and oxygen as possible.

A winter garden should not be placed at the back of a house, especially not in a direct line with the entrance door. Otherwise, qi will be pulled to the back of the house, and then escape through the glass walls without circulating through the rest of the house. Because of the many glass walls, a winter garden has low energy. A small water garden with a fountain should therefore be installed.

Group 16

Outdoor Landscapes

Gardens with Water

Specially-planned outdoor landscapes and water gardens are a common sight throughout the world. Most old palaces and government buildings in Europe, built before the First World War, have very well planned landscapes and water gardens.

A small landscape, together with a water garden where the water spurts and flows from one area, positioned towards the front of a house or even a pond with moving water, are excellent feng shui remedies to enhance qi and oxygen in and around a house.

When a water garden is added to the house garden, the water garden should preferably face the main door; or else, the water should gently move towards the main door to ensure that as the benevolent qi and oxygen are generated, they move into the house. When a water garden is at the back of a house, qi and oxygen are attracted there instead, depriving the house of good qi. Occupants will lack vitality and find it more difficult to be successful and to prosper.

When it is not possible to install a water garden, planting multicoloured flowers in front of your house also improves qi.

Group 17

Protection from Attack

Remedies to Counter Attacking Energies

When your neighbour's house is purposely built with negative features that visibly attack your house, a counterattack may be the only solution to protect you and your family. But such cases are very rare, and only a senior feng shui consultant or master is competent to use this technique.

Counterattacking techniques often cause bad karmic effects on those who recommend the solutions and those who implement them. These techniques must be carried out with the greatest care. Therefore, this book will not illustrate any practical solutions.

A good example of an aggressive building is the new knife-shaped Bank of China building in Hong Kong. This building was designed and built at a time when there was strong disagreement between China and the British government in Hong Kong, over issues involving the return of Hong Kong to the Chinese on expiry of the land lease on 1 July 1997. The building attacks the governor's house and other large commercial banks and business houses nearby. When the building was completed, I believe the first casualty was the then governor who died as a result of the strong attacking qi coming from the building. In a situation like the Bank of China building, counterattacking measures may be necessary to lessen the negative effects. A commercial building nearby installed two large cannons as a counterattack to the Bank of China building, in an attempt to lessen the negative effects. But this remedy has little positive effects against the huge 'knife'.

Remedies and counterattacks are best left to feng shui masters. If they are not carried out in the right way, they may cause considerable harm to those involved.

Group 18
Animal Symbols
Power and Protection Using Animal Symbols in Different Cultures

Many cultures around the world revere at least one animal or creature they believe is powerful and protective. Statues of these animals are placed outside a village or a building as protectors to warn strangers to be more careful and peaceful.

Guarding animals at the entrance can be effective to ward off unwanted intruders if their eyes are 'spiritually open'. In Asia, a monk or a spiritual person usually carries out this task. When the eyes of guarding animals are spiritually opened, their eyes turn red or white at night.

The Chinese like to place a pair of lions outside their main door. The male lion, holding a ball, is placed on the left side, the Dragon side (when looking out from the door). The female lion, holding a cub, is placed on the right side – the Tiger side.

Lions have also been adopted in Europe as a symbol of power and protection. Lion statues can be seen outside the gates and doors of government and private buildings. But in this case, we only see male lions, symbolising male power. Apart from the lion, other animal symbols include the eagle and the bear.

The Thais revere the elephant as a national protective animal. A pair of elephant statues is usually placed outside a government building or a private house belonging to an upper class family.

Diag. 23.26: A pair of Chinese lions.

267

APPENDIX

Suggested Remedies for those Affected by Geopathic and Earth Stress Lines

(Note: Consult your doctor or health therapist before using these herbal teas and food supplements.)

When people sleep or sit over a fault line or a geopathic stress line caused by underground running water, the crystals of their body cells absorb and store a substantial amount of the stress radiation. Unless this radiation is eliminated, it will continue to emit frequencies that disturb the cells' own normal, healthy frequencies and functioning, causing unnecessary stress and imbalance. The whole body becomes stressed and cannot carry out its normal functions and self-healing. People who have high levels of stress radiation in their body tend to suffer from general fatigue and weakness of the immune system. The following are some common remedies to reduce and eliminate stress radiation and their negative effects in a human body:

BATHS

Dissolve half a kilogram (1.2 pounds) of raw sea salt (not artificial, factory-manufactured toxic salts) and half a kilogram of baking powder (sodium bicarbonate) in a bathtub of bearably hot water. Put enough hot water so that your whole body can be submerged up to the neck. Soak in the water for about 10 minutes. While the water is still warm, get out of the bathtub and rinse your body under a shower. Don't drain the water while you are still in the bath; your aura will be disturbed. After the bath, you will feel very energised and light. Repeat this bath three to five more times over one or two weeks.

For those who work with computers every day and absorb a lot of radiation into their bodies, this bath will help eliminate some of the radiation. Take this bath every month (or more often, if necessary) as a health maintenance programme.

HERBAL TEAS

The following teas are recommended:

a) Soak one large tablespoon of mistletoe tea overnight. The next morning, add enough water to make two cups of tea and boil over a gas or firewood fire (an electrical hot plate generates electrical radiation in the water and is unhealthy; it destroys some of the beneficial frequencies of the herbal tea). Drink two cups of tea daily for three weeks.

b) Mix the following herbal teas and drink two to three cups daily for three weeks. Two teaspoons of this mixed tea in boiling water makes one cup. Allow to steep for ten minutes before drinking:

10 gm	Hyssop tea
10 gm	Horsetail tea
5 gm	Burdock root
5 gm	Yarrow
7 gm	Plantain
5 gm	Wood sorrel

FOOD SUPPLEMENTS

Take food supplements daily for six months and then gradually reduce the quantity to half for another month and half again for another three months.

a) Take 30 mg co-enzyme Q10 – three capsules two times daily before 6 pm (in case of general fatigue)

b) Take 50–75 mcg selenium

c) Take 1,000 mg Vitamin E with soya oil base

d) Take 1,000 mg Vitamin A or 250 ml of fresh carrot juice daily

e) Take 2,000 mg Vitamin C

f) Take five grapefruit seeds and chew

g) Soak 10–15 whole almonds with skin on overnight and eat daily

h) Take kelp or seaweed with meal

i) Take five tablespoons of aloe vera juice with water or fresh fruit juice.

A person affected by radiation also tends to have high levels of worms, parasites and fungi in their body. It is necessary to de-worm and get rid of all parasites, worms and fungi. Walnut husk tincture and pumpkin kernels are good remedies for this.

Courses Offered by the Qi-Mag Feng Shui & Geobiology Institute

Australia, New Zealand, China, Hong Kong, Singapore, Sri Lanka, India, U.S.A., Austria, Germany, Switzerland and the European Union.

Qi-Mag Feng Shui l
Practical 'First Aid Feng Shui' for house and flat. Common feng shui problems and remedies which can be applied immediately.

Qi-Mag Feng Shui ll
Selecting auspicious areas in room and building which are harmonious with an individual. Selection of auspicious trigram areas for sleeping and working to enhance vitality, success and abundance. Five elemental principle, yin and yang harmony, Eight Trigrams and feng shui astrological system.

Qi-Mag Business Feng Shui
First comprehensive and practical business feng shui course for the workplace and commercial buildings to enhance success. Design of positive logos and symbols for business. Study of ancient subtle techniques to empower peak performance.

Qi-Mag Feng Shui Consultant Course I & II
Intensive, including the following topics: landscape feng shui, auspicious designs for house and flat, Eight Trigrams East-West system using the lo'pan, astrological aspects and interpretations, for example, the Lo-Shu system of flying stars.

Qi-Mag Feng Shui Consultant Course III
Water Dragon and landscape feng shui courses in Austria, Germany and Europe.

Completion of Consultant I, II and III Qualification: International Feng Shui Consultant Diploma (FSC) for worldwide practice.

Qi-Mag Feng Shui Consultant Courses IV-VIII

Architect design courses:

Qi-Mag Feng Shui Architects Consultant Course for Architectural Design Level IV
Design of healthy houses and buildings with high energy for high vitality living.

Level V – Designs for harmonic balance and successful commercial buildings, including interior business design.

Completion of IV and V International Diploma: Feng Shui Architecture & Consultant for Home and Commercial Buildings (FSARCH).

Level VI – Successful and harmonic business feng shui in the 21st century for business feng shui consultants.

Level VII – Advanced environmental and geomantic designs for landscapes, town planning and traffic, including techniques to enhance the success and prosperity of towns and cities.

Level VIII – Advanced feng shui master techniques.

N.B. *Advanced Courses can only be attended by those with Diploma in FSARCH or FSC. On completion of Consultant I–VIII and Practical, participants will receive an International Degree in Feng Shui and Geobiology. All Consultant, Advanced Architecture and Master Courses are taught by Professor Dr. Lim and his team. Dr. Lim's courses are in English and Chinese and can be translated into German or other local languages.*

Qi-Mag Geomancy and Geobiology I & II
Identification and study of harmful earth and environmental energies. The harnessing, manipulation and application of positive energies for daily use; health and healing, and building design; designing an eco-friendly environment, increasing plant yields without artificial fertilizers.

Feng Shui Correspondence Courses are also available.

Contacts for Professor Lim's courses are listed on the following pages:

Worldwide Contacts

For groups of over 100 persons, internet information, seminars, feng shui supplies, and for individuals interested in feng shui courses in English, German and other languages, and feng shui consultancy. Internet: www.feng-shui.com, www.qi-mag.com

Qi-Mag Healthy Building Design Centre
Prof. Dr. Jes Lim
Fax: +49 700 5677 8899
Fax: 0049 8376 920828

Tel: 0049 700 5677 8899
Internet: www.qi-mag.com
E-mail: office@qi-mag.com
For building designs, seminars and international consultations.

Germany

Vielharmonie
Postfach 11 11, D-87466 Oy-Mittelberg
Tel: +49 700 1188 8999
Fax: 0049 700 3888 9999
Internet: www.vielharmonie.com
E-mail: qi@vielharmonie.com
Feng shui supplies, video tapes and seminars.

Gerhard Waldner
Unterschwarzenberg 18, D-87466
Oy-Mittelberg, Germany
Tel: +49 (0) 83 66 / 9 86 87, Fax: 9 86 86
E-mail fslife@aol.com
Seminars, consultant.

Dr. Meyer Anderson & Partner
Stolberger Str 8, D-28205 Bremen
Tel: +49 (0) 4 21 / 4 98 98 38,
Fax: 4 98 98 87
Tel: +49 (0) 41 64 / 8 82 71
Seminars, supplies and consultancy.

Wasili Pantazoglou
Ringstr 40c, D-86911 Riederau, Germany
Tel: +49 (0) 8807 / 88 58, Fax: 88 73
Consultant.

Daniela E. Schenker
Happy Dragon International
P.O. Box 1218
D-82231 Wessling/Munich Germany.
Tel: +49 (0) 8153 952017 Fax: 952016
Mobile: +49 (0) 171 3516988
Internet: www.feng-shui.com
E-mail: dschenker@feng-shui.com

Dieter Kugler
Schonbichlstr. 9 0b, D-82211 Hersching
Tel: +49 (0) 8152 / 96 98 48 Fax: 96 98 47
Mobile: +49 0171 / 1810612
Geomancy and earth energies consultant, seminars.

Christian & Ute St. Paul
Almeidaweg 1, Starnberg
Mobile: +49 (0) 172 816 1118
Fax: +49 (0) 8151 277769
Consultation, videos and correspondence courses.

Rudolf & Ulrike Bleicher
Tel: 0049 8267 96 0898
Fax: 0049 8267 96 0868
Seminars and consultations.

Austria

Dr. Doris Hirschberg,
Mollardgasse 85A/11/2/80,
A-1060, Austria
Tel: +43 1 / 597 46 71, Fax: 597 09 31
Consultant.

Andreas A. Hager
Postfach 1 58, A-8010 Graz, Austria
Tel / Fax: +43 (0) 3133 3152
Mobile: +43 0664 3288888
Internet: www.fengshui.at
E-mail: office@fengshui.at
Seminars, video tapes, supplies,
consultant.

U.S.A.

Stephen Quong
Box 578, San Ramon, CA
Tel: 001 925 244 9141
Fax: 001 925 327 1346
Email: quong@jyotisha.com
Seminars and Vedi astrology.

James A. Moser
Feng Shui Warehouse Inc.,
P.O. Box 6689, San Diego
CA 92166
Tel: 001 619 523 2158
Fax: 001 619 523 2165
Email: Fengshuiwh@aol.com
Seminars, supplies.

Canada

Ms Marcia Small
179 Lakeshore Road East,
Oakville, On.,
Canada L6J1H5
Tel/Fax: 001 905 338 6868
Email: fengshui@cgocable.net
Seminars, supplies.

Great Britain

Master Chan Kun Wah
29 Barnton Park View,
Edinburgh EH46HH
Scotland, U.K.
Tel / Fax: 0044 131 336 1801
Tel: 0044 1506 634 257
Consultation and courses.

Australia

Kevin Masman
Tel: +61 3 5472 2833
Fax: +61 3 5472 1291
E-mail: Masmans@castlemaine.net.au
Feng shui and geomancy consultancy and
seminars.

BIBLIOGRAPHY

Art & Divination Section (18 writings on Geomancy), 1726 edition, Section XVII of the Imperial Palace, British Museum

Bachler, Kathe, *Earth Radiation*, Wordmasters Ltd, Manchester, 1976

Bao Li Ming, *Chinese Feng Shui Study*, Taipei , 1995

Bring, Mitchell and Wayembergh, Josse, *Japanese Garden Design and Meaning*, New York, 1981

Chan Shih Shu, *Ten Books of Yang Dwelling Classic*, China

Chao Chiu-feng, *Ti-li Wu Chieh (Five Explanations of Geomancy)*, China

Che Ying (Ching Dynasty monk), *Ti Li Zhi Zi Yuan Zhen: Truth for Landscape Feng Shui*

Chen Zian Li, *Nine Stars and 24 Mountains* (2 vol.), Zin Yuan, Taipei

Chien Lung (Ching Dynasty Imperial Palace), *Wan Bao Qian Shu: Manuals for Daily Life and Feng Shui* (6 books)

Chung, Lily, *The Path to Good Fortune*, Lewellyn Publications, U.S.A.

Coat, Callum, *Living Energies*, Gateway Books, Bath, U.K.

Corsan, David & Girdlestone, Rodney, *Safe as Houses – Ill Health and Electro-stress in the House*, Gateway Books, Bath, U.K.

De Barry, Chan Wing Tsit, Watson, B., *Sources of Chinese Tradition*, London, 1960

Dowsett, Eric, *A Guide to Feng Shui for Your Home* (video tape), Broadcast Media Television Productions, Sydney, 1994

Encyclopaedia (The Ku Chin T'u Shu Chi Ch'eng), British Museum

Feuchtwang, Stephen D.R., *An Anthropological Analysis of Chinese Geomancy*, Southern Materials Centre Inc., Taipei, 1974

Gordon, Rolf, *Are You Sleeping in a Safe Place*, Dulwich Health Society, London, 1993

Graham, David, *Folk Religion in Southwest China*, Washington, 1961

Graves, Tom, *The Diviner's Handbook*, The Aquarian Press, Wellingborough, U.K.

Groves, Derham, *Feng Shui and Western Building Ceremonies*, Graham Brash (Pte) Ltd, Singapore, 1991

Gu Jing Tu Shu Ji Cheng: Collection of Ancient and Current Books on Feng Shui, Ching Dynasty Imperial Palace

Harwood, Barbara Bannon, *The Healing House*, Hay House Inc., California, U.S.A.

Heselton, Philip, *The Elements of Earth Mysteries*, Element Books Ltd., U.K., 1991

Hor Chan Kuang, 5 feng shui books, Juxian Guan Ltd, Hong Kong

Hsiao Zhi, *Wu Hsin Ta Yi*, China, 600 A.D.

Huang Wei De (Ching Dynasty), *Pu Shi Zhen Zong: Eight Trigrams for Houses and Life* (6 books)

Huang Zhong Xiu (Ming Dynasty), ed., *Landscape, Land, Humans and Heaven Classic* (12 books)

Hubbard, Murray and Lim, Dr. Jes T. Y., *Doctor Comes to the Aid of 'Sick' Homes*, Gold Coast Sun, Gold Coast, Australia, November 1992

Jiang Ping Jie, *Di Li Zheng Shu*, Taiwan, 1980

Jing Sa Dao (Song Dynasty monk), *Lu Di Yan Qian Shu: Complete Classics for Grave Sites*

Kann, C.Y., *Feng Shui, its Implication on Chinese Architecture* (thesis), Hong Kong University

Krunic, Alexander and Lim, Dr. Jes T. Y., *Feng Shui Remedies for Business*, Perspektiven Magazine, Innsbrucks, Austria, December 1994

Kuo P'o, *The Burial Classic, Imperial Encyclopaedia*, 4th Century, British Museum

Kwok Man-ho and O'Brien, Joanne, *The Elements of Feng Shui*, Element Books Ltd, U.K., 1991

Lim, Dr. Jes T. Y., *Bad Feng Shui – Results in Cancer & Degenerative Diseases*, Auckland, New Zealand

Lim, Dr. Jes T. Y., *Bankruptcy & Company's Turnaround – Feng Shui Remedies Essential*, Kota Kinabalu, Malaysia, 1980

Lim, Dr. Jes T. Y., *Company's Success – Commercial Knowledge of Feng Shui*, Sydney, 1993

Lim, Dr. Jes T. Y., *Feng Shui and Negative Earth Rays – Cause Cancer & Terminal Diseases*, Second World Healers Conference, Hamilton, New Zealand, 1990

Lim, Dr. Jes T. Y., *Feng Shui Remedies for Abundance*, Auckland University, 1991

Lim, Dr. Jes T. Y., *Improve Company's Profitability – Feng Shui Remedies*, Singapore, 1973

Lim, Dr. Jes T. Y., *Marital Problems – A Feng Shui Cause*, Stockholm, 1991

Lip Mong Har, *Feng Shui, Chinese Colours and Symbolism*, Journal of the Singapore Institute of Architects, Singapore, 1978

Lip, Evelyn, *Chinese Geomancy*, Times Books International, Singapore, 1979

Lip, Evelyn, *Personalise Your Feng Shui*, Times Books International, Singapore, 1997

Liu Pei Zin, *Feng Shui, Chinese Views to Environment*, Son Tian Bookshop, Shanghai, China

Lo, Raymond, *Feng Shui – The Pillars of Destiny*, Times Books International, Singapore, 1994

Lonegren, Sig., *Spiritual Dowsing*, Gothic Image, Glastonbury, U.K.

Lu Bing Zhong Ping Sha Yu Chi Jing Cheng Ji, *Classic on Moulds* (3 books), Yuan Dynasty

Marfori, Mark D., *Feng Shui – Discover Money, Health and Love*, Dragon Publishing, Santa Monica, U.S.A., 1993

Muller, Karen and Lim, Dr. Jes T. Y., *Feng Shui – Die Fernostliche Philosophie vom Einrichten*, Wienerin Magazine, Vienna, September 1994

Needham, Joseph, *Science and Civilisation in China*, London, 1943

Nielson, Greg and Polansky, Joseph, *Pendulum Power*, Aquarian Press, Wellingborough, U.K., 1991

Pai Hoh Ming, 21 feng shui books, Juxian Guan Ltd, Hong Kong

Rossbach, Sarah, *Interior Design with Feng Shui*, E.P. Dutton Inc., New York, 1987

Shui-lung Ching (Water Dragon Classic), China

Si Mah Qian, *The Records*, China 1916

Skinner, Stephen, *The Living Earth Manual of Feng Shui – Chinese Geomancy*, Graham Brash (Pte) Ltd., Singapore, 1982

Taoist Luo Guan (Ching Dynasty), *Ba Zai Ming Jing: Explicit Explanations on Eight Trigram Houses*

The Dwellings Manual, Imperial Encyclopaedia, British Museum

Too, Lillian, *Applied (Pa-kua and Lo Shu) Feng Shui*, Konsep Lagenda Sdn Bhd, Kuala Lumpur, 1993

Too, Lillian, *Chinese Numerology in Feng Shui – The Time Dimension*, Konsep Lagenda Sdn Bhd, Kuala Lumpur, 1994

Victorio Hua Wong Seng Tian, *Authentic Feng Shui – Practical Geomantic Analysis for Modern Living*, Eastern Dragon Books, Kuala Lumpur, 1994

von Pohl, Freiherr, *Earth Currents – Causative Factor of Cancer & Other Diseases*, Ilse Pope, Romford, Essex, U.K.

von Pohl, Gustav, *Earth Rays as Pathogenic Agents for Illness and the Development of Cancer*, Progress for Everyone, Feucht, Germany, 1978

Walters, Derek, *Chinese Geomancy*, Element Books Ltd., U.K., 1989

Walters, Derek, *Feng Shui – Perfect Placing for Your Happiness and Prosperity*, Asiapac Books, Singapore, 1988

Walters, Derek, *Ming Shu – The Art and Practice of Chinese Astrology*, Asiapac Books, Singapore

Wang Wie, *The Yellow Emperor's Dwellings Manual, Imperial Encyclopaedia*, 5th Century, British Museum

Wu Yi Jian, *Ti Li Bu Qiu Ren: Landscape of Land Determines Fate* (compilation from 88 ancient books from Yuan to Ching Dynasties)

Yang Yun-sung, *Manual of the Moving Dragon and Method of the Twelve Staves*, 9th Century, China

Yang-chai Shih Shu (10 Writings on Yang Dwellings), China

Zhang Jie Zheng (Ching Dynasty), *Yang Dwellings for Common People* (2 books)

Zhang Zi Nan, *San Yen Di Li Tu Wen Jian Gie*, Taipei, 1965

Zhang Zi Wei (Song Dynasty), *Ti Li Yu Sui Jing: Best Landscape and Land Classics*

Zhao Jou Feng (Ching Dynasty), *Three Factors for Yang Dwellings*

German Books

Kettenring, Maria, *Raumdüfte*, Joy Verlag, 1995

Lam Kam Chuen, *Feng Shui Handbuch*, Joy Verlag, 1996

Rossbach, Sarah, *Feng Shui – Chinesische Kunst des gesunden Wohnens*, Knaur

Walters, Derek, *Feng Shui – die Kunst des Wohnens*, Scherz Verlag, 1996

ABOUT
THE AUTHOR

In the early 1980s, Dr. Jes T. Y. Lim founded the Qi-Mag Health and Longlife Centre to combine feng shui with natural science and help people suffering from severe diseases.

In 1990 he founded the Qi-Mag International Feng Shui & Geobiology Institute and the Qi-Mag East-West Medicina Alternativa Academy.

These two institutes offer courses in 15 countries in Europe, North America and Asia. More than 20,000 people have attended the courses in the 1980s and 1990s.

Dr. Lim teaches feng shui from beginners' level to consultant courses leading to an international diploma and a degree.

He is a Professor at the Medicina Alternativa Institute, which was originally founded by the United Nations in 1962 in Alma-Ata, as well as a Professor at the Open International University for Complementary Medicine, Sri Lanka.

His qualifications include: Bachelor of Natural Science (Natural Medicine), Australia, Doctor of Acupuncture and Diploma in Sports Medicine, Sri Lanka, Singapore and China, and Diploma in Hypnotherapy, Psychotherapy and Past-Life Therapy, New Zealand.

In 1996 he was conferred the title 'Sir Jes Lim' by Medicina Alternativa for his contributions to world healthcare,.

Dr. Lim is well-known through TV appearances and international publications.